Academic Li
Student Div

NEW PERSPECTIVES ON LANGUAGE AND EDUCATION

Series Editor: Professor Viv Edwards, *University of Reading, Reading, Great Britain*

Two decades of research and development in language and literacy education have yielded a broad, multidisciplinary focus. Yet education systems face constant economic and technological change, with attendant issues of identity and power, community and culture. This series will feature critical and interpretive, disciplinary and multidisciplinary perspectives on teaching and learning, language and literacy in new times.

Full details of all the books in this series and of all our other publications can be found on http://www.multilingual-matters.com, or by writing to Multilingual Matters, St Nicholas House, 31–34 High Street, Bristol BS1 2AW, UK.

NEW PERSPECTIVES ON LANGUAGE AND EDUCATION: 42

Academic Literacy and Student Diversity

The Case for Inclusive Practice

Ursula Wingate

MULTILINGUAL MATTERS
Bristol • Buffalo • Toronto

Library of Congress Cataloging in Publication Data
Wingate, Ursula.
Academic Literacy and Student Diversity: The Case for Inclusive Practice/Ursula Wingate.
New Perspectives on Language and Education: 42
Includes bibliographical references and index.
1. Literacy—Study and teaching (Higher) 2. Language and languages—Study and teaching (Higher)—Foreign speakers. 3. Language and languages—Variation. 4. Literacy programs. 5. Language acquisition. I. Title.
P53.475.W56 2015
418.0071'1–dc232014044712

British Library Cataloguing in Publication Data
A catalogue entry for this book is available from the British Library.

ISBN-13: 978-1-78309-348-9 (hbk)
ISBN-13: 978-1-78309-347-2 (pbk)

Multilingual Matters
UK: St Nicholas House, 31-34 High Street, Bristol BS1 2AW, UK.
USA: UTP, 2250 Military Road, Tonawanda, NY 14150, USA.
Canada: UTP, 5201 Dufferin Street, North York, Ontario M3H 5T8, Canada.

Website: www.multilingual-matters.com
Twitter: Multi_Ling_Mat
Facebook: https://www.facebook.com/multilingualmatters
Blog: www.channelviewpublications.wordpress.com

Copyright © 2015 Ursula Wingate.

All rights reserved. No part of this work may be reproduced in any form or by any means without permission in writing from the publisher.

The policy of Multilingual Matters/Channel View Publications is to use papers that are natural, renewable and recyclable products, made from wood grown in sustainable forests. In the manufacturing process of our books, and to further support our policy, preference is given to printers that have FSC and PEFC Chain of Custody certification. The FSC and/or PEFC logos will appear on those books where full certification has been granted to the printer concerned.

Typeset by Techset Composition India (P) Ltd., Bangalore and Chennai, India.
Printed and bound in Great Britain by Short Run Press Ltd.

Contents

	Acknowledgements	vii
1	Academic Literacy and Student Diversity: What is the Problem?	1
	Aim and Purposes	1
	Student Diversity	3
	Academic Literacy	6
	The Problem	9
	Outline of the Book	13
2	Approaches to Academic Literacy Instruction	15
	Introduction	15
	Part 1: Overview of Approaches	16
	Part 2: Genre Approaches to Teaching Academic Literacy	24
	Summary	34
3	Current Practice in Academic Literacy Instruction	37
	Introduction	37
	Part 1: Limitations of Current Academic Literacy Instruction	37
	Part 2: Calls for Transformation of Academic Literacy Policies and Instructional Practices	49
	Summary	54
4	Discipline-Specific Approaches to Academic Literacy Instruction	56
	Introduction	56
	Collaboration and Integration	56
	Genre-Based Literacy Instruction	67
	Corpus-Informed Literacy Instruction	72
5	Reading and Writing	78
	Introduction	78

	The Reading Process	80
	The Reading-to-Write Process	87
	Reading-to-Write Interventions	95
	Summary	101
6	Academic Literacy Development and the Student Experience	102
	Introduction	102
	Part 1: Overview of Research into Academic Discourse Socialisation and the Student Experience	103
	Part 2: Undergraduate 'Home' Students' Academic Literacy Development	114
7	Towards an Inclusive Model of Academic Literacy Instruction	126
	Introduction	126
	Proposing an Inclusive Model of Academic Literacy Instruction	127
	The Content of the Instructional Approach	131
	The Methodology of the Instructional Approach	140
	The Evaluation of the Instructional Approach	144
	Summary	148
8	Towards the Implementation of an Inclusive Model of Academic Literacy Instruction	150
	Introduction	150
	Institutional Changes	152
	Pedagogical Design	155
	Conclusion	161
	Appendices	164
	References	172
	Index	190

Acknowledgements

This book is the outcome of several years of close cooperation with my colleague, Chris Tribble, who was the driving force behind the compilation of the multidisciplinary King's Apprentice Corpus and the development of academic literacy learning resources based on the corpus. Our work and our discussions together influenced my thinking and brought about the idea for this book. Chris has been my constant advisor on this book, from the initial idea and proposal right through to scrutinising each chapter and making numerous comments and valuable suggestions. I am heavily indebted to him.

I am also grateful to my colleagues at King's who stood in for me during my sabbatical term and were wholly supportive throughout the time I was writing the book. Many thanks also to all the students who were involved in the various writing interventions and willingly participated in interviews, discussions and surveys.

1 Academic Literacy and Student Diversity: What is the Problem?

Aim and Purposes

Over the past two decades, there have been regular reports in the media about declining academic standards due to university entrants' low levels of literacy and numeracy. Students' 'appalling' writing skills (Newman, 2007) have been making headlines in the UK press, and similarly, there is a long history of complaints about the quality of student writing in the US (Horner, 2014) as well as in Australia (e.g. Dann, 2008: 'A sad loss of literacy down under'). These complaints have paralleled the expansion of higher education systems, and have some rather typical elements. For instance, they tend to be reported from the perspective of university lecturers who bemoan the loss of previously better standards and blame students for their inability to spell or use accurate grammar. They also tend to blame secondary schools for sending students with such deficiencies, and lament that universities have to make up for this lack of preparation through extra language or writing classes.

This discourse of deficiency and remediation is disturbing for several reasons. One is that widening access to higher education has obviously not been accompanied by a sufficient understanding that student populations are now more diverse and less prepared for academic study and therefore need more support when settling into university than the highly selected student intakes in previous elite systems. Another reason is that the difficulties students encounter at university tend to be trivialised as language problems at the level of grammar and spelling, when in fact numerous studies have revealed that students struggle with understanding the epistemology and ways of communication of their discipline (e.g. Lillis, 2001; Kapp & Bangeni, 2009). Lea and Street (1998), for instance, noticed that lecturers commented on surface errors in syntax or structure when they were unable to pinpoint underlying epistemological problems. This failure to appreciate the nature of the challenges students face leads in turn to inadequate measures of remediation which only cater for subsets of the student populations. As I will show in Chapter 3, language support is often only on offer for non-native speakers of English, whilst some limited and skills-oriented provision is available for the rest. This means that while higher education has become more inclusive, the support provision remains exclusive. A further negative aspect of this remedial approach is that it is entirely focused on student writing, neglecting the fact that writing is only the end product of a far more comprehensive and complex process that entails dealing with specific information within the broader context of the discipline's epistemology and literacy conventions. In other words, a weak performance in the output, that is, writing, cannot just be treated by remedying language issues; as will be argued in later chapters, academic literacy support needs to include reading, evaluating sources, and ways of presenting and debating knowledge in the relevant discipline. It is of particular concern that the remedial support offered to students largely neglects academic reading, although this aspect of academic literacy is equally important as, and fundamental to, academic writing. Academic reading is different from all other types of reading and therefore needs to be taught to students (Sengupta, 2002). While reading for leisure typically requires only a receptive approach to the information from the text, academic reading requires a purposeful approach and active engagement with texts. Information cannot just be received, but must be questioned, compared with information from other sources, used in new conceptual contexts and transformed into different types of presentation (e.g. writing). Most students new to university also struggle with the extensive reading required at university, which involves multiple and lengthy texts with an unfamiliar style and terminology. Although the need to help students to develop adequate reading strategies and processes has been recognised in a number of publications (e.g. Abbott, 2013; Jolliffe & Harl, 2008; MacMillan, 2014), reading remains largely invisible in higher education pedagogy (see the discussion in van Pletzen, 2006).

The aim of this book is to promote a clearer understanding of the concept of academic literacy, and to show that this understanding necessitates approaches to literacy instruction that are fundamentally different from those currently in place. Such approaches need to recognise student diversity as well as the discipline-specific nature of academic literacy. The book has the following purposes:

(1) To address common misunderstandings regarding students' academic literacy needs, most notably the perception that it is writing only that constitutes the problem, that it is mainly language proficiency that causes deficiencies in writing, and that this problem only affects certain student groups.
(2) To examine existing models of literacy/writing pedagogy and consider their suitability for the literacy development of diverse student populations.
(3) To propose a model of inclusive academic literacy instruction and present an intervention study in which aspects of this model were applied.

Before focusing on the 'problem' that I see in the academic literacy support currently available in higher education, I must lay the ground by providing some background information on student diversity and by explaining the concept of academic literacy.

Student Diversity

Two main developments have led to the diversification of student populations in Anglophone and other higher education systems: that of widening participation and internationalisation.

Driven by government policy and a range of inclusion initiatives, there has been, over the past decades, a massive expansion in the number of students participating in higher education. In the UK, participation increased from a mere 5% of the age group of 18 to 25-year-olds in the 1960s to 43% by 2010, with the sharpest rise in numbers starting in the 1990s (Chowdry *et al.*, 2010). A report on effective approaches to widening participation, commissioned by the Higher Education Funding Council for England (HEFCE) and Office for Fair Access (OFFA), shows that that there have been similar substantial increases in student numbers in the USA, Australia and South Africa (HEFCE, 2013). Although this growth in numbers demonstrates the inclusion of previously underrepresented groups, inequalities persist in all four countries. In the UK, for instance, only 14% of pupils who are eligible for free school meals (i.e. coming from lower socio-economic groups) participate in higher education, and only 2% from this group gain access to a 'top' university. Recent research by HEFCE (2014) shows that ethnicity and disadvantage are significant factors influencing the chances of students in the UK to get a first or upper-second class degree.

In the USA, where there has been a substantial rise in participation by black and Hispanic students, only 18% of black people and 13% of Hispanic people held a BA in 2009, as compared to 29% of the white population. South Africa saw a massive increase in enrolments by African and coloured students between 2001 and 2010; however, the retention rate of both groups is low, and African students have the lowest graduation rate. The case study on South Africa, which is part of the report commissioned by HEFCE and OFFA, showed that of the 2004 student intake, by 2009 63.5% of the white student had graduated, as compared to only 38.3% of the African students and 42.1% of the coloured students (HEFCE, 2013). These figures suggest that student diversity, achieved through the inclusion of students from lower socio-economic and educational backgrounds, poses substantial challenges to higher education systems, and that adequate responses have not yet been found.

Internationalisation is, as Montgomery (2008: 19) states, a 'socio-political force' caused by increased student mobility and globalisation. According to the Organization for Economic Co-operation and Development (OECD), the number of students enrolled at universities outside their country of citizenship has increased from 0.8 million in 1975 to 4.3 million in 2011 (OECD, 2013). The greatest movement of foreign students has been into universities in English-speaking countries. The latest statistics on international student mobility released by the OECD (2013) show that 40% of the overall international student enrolment worldwide between 2000 and 2011 can be explained by increases of enrolments in Australia, Canada, Ireland, the UK and the US. In these countries, Australia has the highest percentage of international students with 19.8%, followed by the UK with 15.6% and New Zealand with 15.6% (OECD, 2013: 317). In the UK, for example, according to the statistics provided by the UK Council for International Student Affairs (UKCISA, 2014), in the academic year 2012–13, 49% of all full-time research postgraduate and 71% of all full-time taught postgraduate students were from international backgrounds. In some fields of study, for instance the Social Sciences, Business and Law, international student numbers are particularly high. Many students coming to study in Anglophone countries are non-native speakers of English from the outer or expanding Kachruvian circles (Kachru, 1985)[1] who aim to obtain – at great expense – a degree in the 'inner circle of the Anglo-American sphere' (Horner & Lu, 2012: 59). Gaining a degree from within that 'powerful inner sphere' (Horner & Lu, 2012: 59) is prestigious and helpful in terms of career prospects. Several countries with developing economies, for instance Brazil and China, are currently investing heavily in sending students to universities in Anglophone countries to produce a workforce that can function through English. According to the OECD, 53% of international students come from Asia

(2013: 313). As universities depend increasingly on the income from international students, who pay higher study fees than domestic students, they have developed sophisticated marketing and recruitment strategies. More recently, there have been a growing number of universities in non-English-speaking countries which offer English-medium study programmes, particularly in Europe and Asia. This trend, according to the OECD (2013), is likely to continue and shows that more countries are trying to take their share of the lucrative international student market.

This level of student mobility has led to a substantial rise in the diversity of student populations. Whilst the coming together of people from different linguistic and cultural backgrounds is certainly beneficial as it enhances students' intercultural competence (e.g. Byram, 1997; Deardorff, 2006), serious concerns have been raised about the disadvantages experienced by international students. Some concerns relate to social adjustment and welfare, including issues such as racism, alienation and marginalisation affecting international students (Brown & Jones, 2013; Guo & Chase, 2011). Most publications, however, focus on international students' academic progress, which may be hindered by difficulties with Western learning styles and the cultural predispositions of some groups of international students, most notably those from Confucian-heritage backgrounds (e.g. Kim, 2011; Wu & Rubin, 2000). Recent research examined these international students' performance and attainment (e.g. Iannelli & Huang, 2013; Li *et al.*, 2010; Morrison *et al.*, 2005). Whilst Morrison *et al.* refer to some studies from the 1980s and 1990s that showed that international students in Australia performed better than so-called 'home' students, later research revealed that international students as a whole, and particularly Chinese students at the undergraduate level (Iannelli & Huang, 2013), persistently achieve lower attainment levels than other groups. A major determinant for lower performance for these students is English language proficiency (e.g. Li *et al.*, 2010), and this finding has been confirmed as being a problem for international students in many studies (e.g. Berman & Cheng, 2001; Holmes, 2006). Despite the fact that universities have been making major support efforts through language classes specifically targeted at international students (typically English for Academic Purposes pre-sessional and in-sessional courses, see Chapter 3 for a detailed discussion), the research evidence shows that a lack of English language competence continues to disadvantage international students.

As will be discussed in Chapter 3, a number of scholars have criticised Anglophone universities for the imposition of language conventions on students from other cultures and for the failure to embrace linguistic diversity. However, as I shall argue, relaxing linguistic standards and conventions would not address important student needs which lie at the level of academic literacy.

Academic Literacy

The term 'academic literacy' is widely used with reference to the teaching of academic reading and writing (e.g. Belcher, 1994; Spack, 1997; Gibbons, 2009), with study skills or English for academic purposes (EAP) courses often being described as 'academic literacy support' (see for instance Ivanič & Lea, 2006: 9). This use represents a narrow view of literacy, particularly as these courses tend to be limited to a focus on grammatical accuracy and rhetorical appropriateness in academic writing. By contrast, in this book academic literacy is understood as the ability to communicate competently in an academic discourse community. This concept is underpinned by Hymes' (1972) notion of communicative competence, situated learning theory, i.e. Lave and Wenger's (1991) community-of-practice (CoP) model, genre theories which explain language use by their social context (e.g. Miller, 1994; Halliday, 1978) and language socialisation theory (Ochs, 1986). Conceptualising academic literacy as communicative competence emphasises the way in which its social dimensions require more than just linguistic knowledge. According to Allen and Brown (1976: 248),

> communication competence, unlike linguistic competence, involves awareness of the transactions that occur between people. Competence in this perspective is tied to actual performance of the language in social situations.

Hymes defined communicative competence as 'the capabilities of a person' (1972: 282) consisting of language knowledge and the ability to use language appropriately in a specific context. Both language knowledge and the ability to use language relate to four parameters of communicative competence, which are formal possibility, feasibility, appropriateness, and probability of an utterance or language behaviour (Hymes, 1972: 281). From the perspective of social practice and genre theories which regard communicative function and linguistic form as integrally related (Halliday, 1975; Hymes, 1972, 1977), this means that an individual can understand and use the appropriate communicative functions of language for particular social situations and activities (Gee, 1990).

In academic contexts, the social situations and core activities are mainly concerned with knowledge construction, presentation and debate, and accomplished through genres (such as the lecture, the research proposal or the essay). These genres are in turn achieved through contextually appropriate language functions (such as reporting, reasoning, proposing, hedging). Thus, the capabilities of an academically literate, or communicatively competent, person involve, in addition to linguistic proficiency, (1) an understanding of the discipline's[2] epistemology, i.e. the ways in which subject knowledge is created and communicated, (2) an understanding of the sociocultural context, i.e. the status of the participants in the academic community and the purpose of the interactions occurring in the community, and (3) a command of the conventions and norms that regulate these interactions. As these interactions are manifested in genres, communicative competence in an academic discourse community can be understood as the ability to understand these genres and express oneself through them.

The development of academic literacy can be explained by language socialisation theory. Language socialisation refers to the process in which novices learn the language of a specific community, and become competent members of that community through the use of the language (Ochs, 1986). As Duff (2007: 311) explains, in this process 'experts or more proficient members of a group play a very important role in socializing novices and implicitly or explicitly teaching them to think, feel, and act in accordance with the values, ideologies, and traditions of the group'. Novices, on the other hand, 'teach' the more expert members of the community what their communicative needs are, making the process 'bidirectional' (Duff, 2007: 311). Language socialisation theory draws on both sociocultural theory and the community-of-practice (CoP) model. A shared understanding among the three theories is that human interaction is fundamental to learning, and that the learning of novices is supported by more competent persons (Lantolf & Thorne, 2007; Lave & Wenger, 1991). Sociocultural theory contributes to language socialisation theory the concept that learning involves semiotic tools and artefacts that are typical for a specific community, while the CoP model contributes a focus on the legitimate peripheral participation of novices in the community that gradually leads to expert membership (Duff, 2007).

Summing up this argument, to gain communicative competence in their academic contexts, students need to learn more than subject knowledge. They need to develop the levels of epistemological and sociocultural knowledge that were outlined above. The development of this necessary knowledge requires interaction and negotiation between expert and novice members of the discourse community, and occurs through 'exchanges of language in particular social situations', because 'the process of becoming a competent member of society is realised to a large extent through language, by acquiring knowledge of its functions, social distributions, and interpretations in and across socially defined situations' (Ochs & Schieffelin, 1994: 470). In more concrete terms, it is the task of the subject lecturers as experts in the community to raise students' awareness of epistemological and sociocultural issues. The 'particular social situations' for raising this awareness would be the same as those in which subject knowledge is taught and learned, i.e. lectures, seminars and tutorials. This is because subject knowledge is shaped by the epistemological and sociocultural context of the community, and expressed through genres. Thus the development of academic literacy, i.e. communicative competence, cannot be separated from the teaching of the subject. This understanding, as shall be seen, is fundamental to the argument I develop in this book.

Lastly, it should be noted that the terms 'academic discourse community' and 'discipline', which I use interchangeably in this book to describe the context in which students are studying, are both problematic. Hyland (2008a) points out the problem that 'community' might apply to disciplines, specialisms and domains, and simply defines a discourse community as 'a group who have texts and practices in common' (Hyland, 2008a: 549). Both terms have been criticised for suggesting homogeneous and static entities when in fact communities of practice are open and dynamic (Lave & Wenger, 1991). In particular, the notion of discipline has been described as 'nebulous' (Hyland, 2011: 178), as boundaries are not stable, and many study programmes are interdisciplinary. Swales (1990) proposed six characteristics of a discourse community of which three apply particularly well to 'discipline', namely that (1) it has 'a broadly agreed set of common public goals', (2) it utilises and possesses one or more genres for their communicative aims, and (3) it has 'acquired some specific lexis' (Swales, 1990: 24–27). The problem with the use of the term 'discipline' lies in the fact that this is too large a context for the literacy needs of most students. The programme in which a student is studying usually represents only a small subsection of the discipline. For students in undergraduate programmes, for instance, some genres of the discipline (such as the research article or the grant proposal) will be irrelevant. However, the discipline's overall 'agreed set of common public goals', its ways of communicating knowledge, as well as some of the 'specific lexis', are relevant in every sub-discipline and in every study programme of that discipline. I therefore will refer to discipline as the academic discourse community, bearing in mind that for instructional purposes, the concept will have to be defined more narrowly. For instance, the initial academic discourse community for undergraduate students will be the people teaching, assessing and learning in the specific study programme, and communication will be restricted to a small subset of the discipline's genres, such as textbooks and essays for 'knowledge-telling' (Bereiter & Scardamalia, 1987), i.e. presenting what they have learned. However, even at this stage, successful communication requires an understanding of the epistemology of the discipline.

I will now turn to the question of how universities deal with student diversity and academic literacy, or more precisely, the extent to which they ensure that students from all backgrounds gain the communicative competence to be successful in their study programmes. This is where the problem lies.

The Problem

The problem is the persistent failure by universities to support students adequately in their development of academic literacy, particularly at the initial stages of their study. While it can be argued that most students will eventually, through a lengthy process of tacit socialisation, manage to negotiate the required literacy conventions, the absence of sufficient provision of explicit information holds many back and is particularly detrimental to student groups who have additional disadvantages through their linguistic and educational backgrounds. In the absence of a holistic literacy instruction that includes epistemological and sociocultural knowledge, many students will not understand the meaning of the literacy conventions required of them. One example is a widespread perception by students who have not learned the epistemological rationale for academic attributions that referencing is just a technique to avoid plagiarism (e.g. Abasi & Graves, 2008).

As stated earlier, acquiring communicative competence requires interaction between experts and novices in the relevant social situations. This means that literacy instruction would need to be situated in the academic discourse community, and that the experts in the community would enable novices' gradually increasing participation, as implied by the CoP and language socialisation theory. Despite this need, instruction and support at universities is predominantly offered in special units outside the disciplines. Within the disciplines, as Turner (2011: 15) points out, language 'is taken for granted rather than recognised for its importance'. The way in which language is used in academic discourse is rarely made explicit to students. The experts in the discourse community, i.e. subject lecturers, usually feel only responsible for teaching subject content, and even if they are explicitly aware of the language use and literacy conventions of their discipline, may be unwilling to teach these. It seems to be generally assumed that students will gradually and implicitly understand what is required. When they do not, and their difficulties become apparent through weak performance in academic writing, the problem is typically diagnosed at the linguistic level and remedied through English language or skills classes offered to students from all disciplines. In these classes, some form of generic academic English is taught, with a strong focus on surface language features, and without much consideration of discipline-specific discourses. Consequently, all students are faced with the lengthy process of finding out what the discipline-specific literacy requirements of their study programmes are. Their academic writing, however, is assessed right from the beginning of their study, and, in the absence of explicit and appropriate instruction, some students are doomed to either low achievement or early failure. Although some subject lecturers might be providing support with academic literacy, this is not available to all or on a regular and systematic basis. Thus, the current instructional provision at universities, which is discussed in more detail in Chapter 3, leads to two types of exclusion: the first is that the majority of students do not receive literacy instruction at all, and the second is that those who do receive instruction remain excluded from the genres and discourses of their academic disciplines. There are two main misconceptions that underlie the current remedial approach to literacy instruction.

The first misconception is that of academic literacy being equal to linguistic competence. This perception is evident in the admission procedures of Anglophone universities, where students from second language speaker backgrounds are required to achieve certain scores in standardised tests such as IELTS (International English Language Testing System) and TOEFL (Test of English as a Foreign Language). These tests are entirely focused on language proficiency, such as grammar, structure and the use of cohesive devices, and have been shown to have little predictive value of students' ability to use language in academic contexts (e.g. Coffin & Hewings, 2004; Green, 2007). The real challenge that students face when entering university, namely learning a new use of language or 'a secondary discourse', as Gee (1990: 153) puts it, is rarely recognised. Teaching academic literacy is not part of Anglophone academic culture, and therefore lecturers are not trained to understand that students' learning needs are not at the level of grammar. Consequently, they identify weaknesses in students' assignments mainly at the surface level. This misconception of academic literacy is also obvious in the preoccupation with academic writing, and in the neglect of the complex processes, particularly academic reading, that facilitate writing. Writing is commonly seen as the only area where students need help, while in fact it is only the end product of a series of complex literacy activities. As a result, instruction is restricted to grammar-oriented writing classes. As Boughey (2002: 296) notes,

> an understanding that students are experiencing difficulties with academic literacy and not with language *per se* calls into question many of the language intervention programmes, which have been established on the assumption that what students lack is tuition in the structures and vocabulary of English. (italics in original)

The second misconception is that of diversity in relation to academic literacy. Problems with academic literacy have been traditionally attributed to students preconceived as disadvantaged or deficient. The assumption is that students from certain backgrounds, for instance those called 'non-traditional' in the UK (e.g. mature students and/or those without the usual entry qualifications) or non-native speakers of English have deficient academic literacy, while 'traditional' students can cope with the university's literacy demands. This assumption is a legacy from the old elite system, in which high-achieving students from homogenous backgrounds arrived at university well prepared by their previous education. For the limited number of students from different backgrounds, extra support was available through English or skills courses, as explained earlier. The fact that this additional, extra-curricular provision has not changed suggests that the previous perception of literacy being the problem of a few 'different' students is still widespread. Many universities offer EAP exclusively to international students, although, as I will explain in Chapter 3, the distinction between international and 'home' students is flawed. The assumption that literacy instruction and support is only needed by certain student groups is, of course, closely linked to the misconception that academic literacy is the same as language proficiency. However, once academic literacy is understood as communicative competence in an academic discourse community, the conclusion that *all* students have to gain this competence and will therefore benefit from support and instruction is obvious. While there is doubtlessly a number of students who need additional English language support, academic literacy instruction is unrelated to this and needs to be provided to all students.

The argument that all students, regardless of their linguistic and cultural backgrounds, are novices in their chosen academic disciplines and therefore need to learn the relevant discourses has been made by several scholars (e.g. Boughey, 2002; Gee, 1990). Bourdieu and Passeron, for example, pointed out that academic language is 'never anyone's mother tongue, even for the privileged classes' (1990: 115). Therefore, it is not student diversity but the diversity in academic disciplines, their specific ways of communication, genres and discourse conventions that should influence the provision of academic literacy instruction. In addition to the need to offer instruction to *all* students, there is also the need to make this instruction discipline-specific. I will take this argument further in later chapters by asking for literacy instruction to be embedded into study programmes and be part of the regular teaching and learning within disciplines. In this way, it will benefit all students, not just specific groups. English language support can then be offered to those students who need it as an additional offer. In my proposal for an inclusive literacy pedagogy, I will therefore avoid the native/non-native speaker of English dichotomy.

There is one more factor adding to the problem of inadequate academic literacy instruction in contemporary higher education that I want to discuss. This is the lack of a strong and unified voice calling for change and convincing university managers and academics of the need for change. Many researchers and practitioners have criticised the current provision of literacy instruction (e.g. Hounsell, 1987; Lea & Street, 1998 in the UK; Beaufort, 2007 in the US; Thesen & van Pletzen, 2006 in South Africa), and some have reported initiatives for providing alternative practices (e.g. Morley, 2008; Foster & Deane, 2011; Percy & Skillen, 2000; Archer, 2012). However, these voices come from different camps and tend to advocate an individual model (e.g. 'Academic Literacies', 'Writing in the Disciplines') when, by contrast, drawing on a range of models might be more productive for the development of a widely applicable instructional model. Literacy researchers and practitioners have tended to align themselves to one literacy model without considering what can be learned from others. Instead of looking for convergence, some scholars have taken rather acrimonious stances towards models other than theirs, as evidenced in the debate between proponents of process and genre approaches (e.g. Hyland, 2003b) and between genre and social practice approaches (e.g. Lillis & Scott, 2007). As a result of these 'silo' perspectives, there has been limited cross-fertilisation between models.

Similarly, projects and initiatives aimed at improving the provision of academic literacy instruction are often reported from the perspective of specific local settings and student groups, and lack the vision of, and applicability to, mainstream[3] higher education. Furthermore, while there are various influential and widely used models of teaching academic literacy (mostly writing), these also tend to be restricted to particular contexts. These models include Composition Studies offered in freshman courses in the US, EAP initiatives which are largely reserved to non-native speakers of English around the world, and the 'Academic Literacies' model in the UK which has been largely concerned with students from less privileged backgrounds. This segregation of target groups for literacy instruction is also reflected in the literature where many books and two entire journals, the *Journal of English for Academic Purposes* and the *Journal of Second Language Writing* are largely devoted to the writing of non-native speakers of English. For these reasons, academic literacy pedagogy is currently a fragmented field in which various models with their different theoretical underpinnings co-exist but do not cross-fertilise. Although the number of publications in the field has increased considerably over the last decade, a broader perspective of an inclusive pedagogy in mainstream higher education remains missing. The narrow focus of many of these publications and the fact that they are scattered around journals and books published under the banner of specific models[4] may explain why they had limited impact on those who implement change, and why universities' provision of literacy instruction has not kept pace with the needs of students in contemporary higher education. It is therefore time that literacy experts bring together useful components of the various models and draw on previous initiatives and research findings to develop pedagogical approaches which are applicable to the mainstream. In this book, I present my attempt to do so, and hope to contribute to a better understanding of students' academic literacy needs and to the much needed change in literacy pedagogy.

Outline of the Book

In the following chapter, I examine existing models of academic literacy instruction and their theoretical underpinnings, contexts and educational aims. As shall be seen, most models are concerned with academic writing only, thereby reflecting the previously mentioned narrow view of academic literacy. Chapter 3 focuses on the dominant practices in academic literacy instruction at Anglophone universities and highlights some flaws in university policies and the underlying beliefs. In Chapter 4, I discuss various types of discipline-specific approaches and consider the organisational and methodological requirements for making these approaches inclusive of all students. Several examples of innovative practice from universities in Anglophone countries are presented. Chapter 5 draws attention to the fact that academic literacy does not just consist of academic writing. It is concerned with academic reading, and reading-to-write. Although the ability to read and integrate source materials is crucial for success in academic writing, this aspect of academic literacy tends to be neglected by literacy researchers and practitioners. Chapter 5 also provides a detailed account of students' difficulties with reading-to-write, and therefore forms a thematic link between the previous chapters that focused on instructional provision, and the following Chapter 6. This is devoted to the student experience and the difficulties they encounter as novices in their academic discourse community. As the literature on this topic is largely concerned with international students, I present in the second part of Chapter 6 findings from a study into the experience of undergraduate 'home' students at a UK university which I recently conducted.

In Chapter 7, I propose a model of inclusive curriculum-integrated academic literacy instruction that draws on the 'best aspects' of existing literacy models. I then present an intervention study conducted across four disciplines in which some of the model's principles and features were applied. The interventions were particularly concerned with the development, implementation and evaluation of discipline-specific learning resources and took a constructivist teaching approach. In the final chapter, I will consider the limitations of small-scale initiatives such as the intervention study presented in Chapter 7, and discuss the feasibility of implementing the model of inclusive curriculum-integrated academic literacy instruction more widely in higher education.

Notes

(1) Kachru's model of the use of English distinguishes between the Inner Circle, that is, mother tongue countries, the Outer Circle, consisting of former colonies where English is often the second and one of the official languages, and the Expanding Circle in which English is learned as a foreign language. Although the model has been declared outdated, it is helpful to explain the aspiration of students to benefit from the linguistic, and assumed socio-economic, capital of the Inner Circle.
(2) The use of the term 'discipline' or 'academic discourse community' will be discussed further below.
(3) With 'mainstream' I mean *all* students across disciplines and universities.
(4) Most notably under labels that include 'second language' and 'writing', thus projecting exclusive target groups and partial aspects of academic literacy.

2 Approaches to Academic Literacy Instruction

Introduction

The aim of this chapter is to examine existing approaches to academic literacy instruction in higher education. The definition of academic literacy as the ability to communicate competently in an academic discourse community, proposed in Chapter 1, implies that instruction should include all aspects of literacy such as its epistemological foundations, oral discourses and particularly reading; yet the publications in the field show that most of the research and pedagogical activity is restricted to academic writing. This demonstrates on the one hand the importance of the written text as the main mode of knowledge construction and communication in higher education, but also the clear neglect, mentioned in the previous chapter, of important literacy activities that lead to writing, in particular the selection, evaluation and synthesis of sources. However, students' academic literacy performance is judged on writing only, which is the main assessment tool in higher education (Lillis, 2001). The preoccupation with students' academic writing is reflected in the instructional approaches presented in this chapter. To do justice to the concept of academic literacy, however, I will discuss the far fewer publications on academic reading instruction in Chapter 5.

In the first part of this chapter, I provide an overview of all approaches to academic writing. In the second part, I discuss in detail the three main genre approaches, because the instructional model I propose in this book is mainly based on genre theories and pedagogies. I will discuss their contexts, theoretical underpinnings and pedagogic principles, as well as the critiques they have received from movements such as Critical EAP and Academic

Literacies. The chapter finishes with a reflection on the contribution that the various approaches can make to an inclusive literacy pedagogy.

Part 1: Overview of Approaches

The existing approaches to academic literacy instruction can be broadly divided into those which are concerned with the content and methodology of writing pedagogy (presented in rows 1–4 in Table 2.1), and those which are driven by ideological concerns about the socio-political factors influencing writing (see rows 5 and 6 in Table 2.1). For a comprehensive representation of all approaches, I refer to three well-known classifications which are shown in Table 2.1. The first, by Lea and Street (1998), is research-focused, as it distinguishes three models of 'educational research into student writing in higher education' (Lea & Street, 1998: 158). Hyland's (2002a) classification includes approaches to both writing research and teaching; although it also contains three broad categories, they differ from Lea and Street's. Ivanič (2004) distinguishes six 'discourses' around writing which underpin the associated teaching approaches. Ivanič's classification is the most nuanced and comprehensive one, as she considers each discourse in relation to underlying beliefs about writing, beliefs about learning to write, approaches to the teaching of writing, and assessment criteria. For this reason, the discussion

Table 2.1 Classifications of approaches to teaching academic literacy

Lea & Street (1998)	Ivanič (2004)	Hyland (2002a)*
1. Study skills	1. Skills	1. Text-oriented: texts as objects
	2. Creativity	2. Writer-oriented: personal growth, creativity
	3. Process	2. Writer-oriented: cognitive processes
2. Academic socialisation	4. Genre	1. Text-oriented: text as discourse (genre)
3. Academic literacies	5. Social practice	2. Writer-oriented: writing as situated act
		3. Reader-oriented: writing as social interaction/construction
	6. Socio-political	3. Reader-oriented: writing as power and ideology

*Note: The numbering represents Hyland's three categories: (1) text-oriented; (2) writer-oriented; and (3) reader-oriented, and relates these categories to Ivanič's categories.

follows the order of Ivanič's classification; also, this order reflects best the historical development of writing education.

Ivanič's first category, in which writing is viewed as a set of linguistic skills – in line with Lea and Street's 'skills' category and Hyland's sub-category of 'texts as objects' – has its roots in the period of the 1950s and 1960s when language teaching aimed at the acquisition of 'linguistic competence', defined by Chomsky (1965) as the innate grammatical knowledge that a native speaker possesses. Ivanič's second and third categories, creativity and process approaches, which became popular in the late 1970s, were a reaction against the narrow view of writing as grammatical competence and linguistic correctness. These approaches were concerned with the writer as an individual, and viewed writing as solitary individual action. Subsequent approaches, from genre to socio-political (categories 4 to 6 in Ivanič's classification), were based on the understanding of language knowledge as communicative competence (Hymes, 1966), and of writing as a situated, social activity. Attention in research and teaching turned to the immediate and wider situational contexts of writing, the audience, as well as cultural and political factors that impact on writing. These shifts in focus are also reflected in Hyland's classification which moves from text-oriented to writer-oriented, and finally to reader-oriented approaches.

Lea and Street's (1998) classification is the least detailed one, and does not contain the categories 'Creativity' and 'Process'. Their three categories are not further sub-divided, and the second, 'Academic socialisation', is not clearly defined. In Table 2.1, Ivanič's classification is presented in the centre, and the other two are aligned to it according to categories. Largely absent from the three publications discussed here are references to the contexts where the approaches have actually been used. Some have in fact been more or less confined to specific contexts, such as first-year composition in the US or second language learning, and there has been limited cross-fertilisation. In the second part of this chapter, I discuss these contexts and argue that the synthesis of 'best aspects' of existing approaches is needed for an effective and inclusive literacy education.

The skills approach

This approach still underpins much of academic literacy instruction in contemporary universities, as I will show in Chapter 3. It sees academic writing as a set of 'atomised skills' (Lea & Street, 1998: 158) which include spelling, grammatical accuracy, as well as some rhetorical aspects. The linguistic rules taught in this approach are regarded as universal and transferable across writing contexts and text types (Lea & Street, 1998; Ivanič, 2004).

Skills-oriented pedagogy is based on the perception that writing is a 'unitary, context-free activity' (Ivanič, 2004: 227), and assessment of writing focuses solely on the text as product or object (Hyland, 2002a), without consideration of the situations in which the text was produced. Writing classes that follow the skills approach resemble generic grammar courses and are typically offered to students from all disciplines. The discourse surrounding this approach is one of remediation and deficiency, as newspaper articles, which regularly appear in the UK (for examples see Turner, 2011: 26, 27), attest. These articles bemoan declining writing skills among students; the fact that students 'can't spell or write English' (Shephard, 2006) is generally regarded as a sign of falling standards in university education as a whole.

Ivanič (2004: 227) rightly suspects 'that a substantial proportion of many writing curricula is founded on this belief that learning to write consists of learning a set of linguistic skills'. In many Anglophone universities around the world, this approach means that students who struggle with the literacy demands in their disciplines are referred to a central unit in their university, which provides individual advice and courses on writing. These courses have no relation to the content or literacy conventions of the students' disciplines and therefore tend to be perceived as irrelevant by students (Durkin & Main, 2002). The belief underpinning the skills approach is also evident in the language tests for entry to Higher Education such as International English Language Testing System (IELTS) or Test of English as a Foreign Language (TOEFL). These assess individual skills such as reading, listening and writing, and are decontextualised and discipline-unspecific. In the US, the compulsory first-year composition (FYC) classes , also called 'College Composition' or 'Freshman English', have traditionally been basic skills courses (Beaufort, 2007) aiming to enable students to produce acceptable writing; in the in the 'most reductive versions' (Horner, 2014: 408), composition courses teach students how to conform to the conventions of standard written English.

In the next chapter I will consider how the skills approach trivialises and marginalises academic literacy instruction in universities. However, despite the various shortcomings of the skills approach, it is important to recognise that attention must be paid to language and linguistic correctness (see Turner, 2004, for a discussion) and that help must be available for students with linguistic problems. However, the correct use of English should not be the main, or only, focus of literacy instruction.

Process approaches

Ivanič's categories 'Creativity' and 'Process' are treated in one section here, because they are two of several strands of research and pedagogy that emerged under the umbrella term 'process approach' (Racelis & Matsuda, 2013). This approach is classified as 'writer-oriented' in Hyland's (2002a) classification where he distinguishes, in line with Ivanič's two categories, between writing as personal expression and writing as a cognitive act. A third strand, mentioned by Hyland but not Ivanič, is concerned with writing as a social act, investigating the social nature of the writing process and the influence of context and writers' prior experience. The creativity strand, which transformed writing instruction in the UK and US in the 1970s, understands writing as a way of self-expression and personal growth (Elbow, 1973). Writing is regarded as an enjoyable process in its own right, and as an ability that is learned rather than taught. The role of teachers is reduced to that of facilitators who suggest stimulating topics and offer advice rather than impose rules. Style and content are regarded as more important than accuracy. As writing is about the expression of the writer's voice and his/her personal experience, a typical genre produced in this approach is the personal narrative. The creativity approach has been applied more widely in the primary and secondary school system rather than at universities, and has sometimes led to a total abandonment of grammar teaching (for a discussion of the impact of process approaches in the Australian school system see Cope & Kalantzis, 1993). The approach has been heavily criticised for lacking a theoretical foundation and disadvantaging certain social groups. Following the conceptualisation of writing as personal expression, researchers in the late 1970s became interested in the cognitive processes involved in the writing process. In their cognitive process model, Flower and Hayes (1981) identified three sub-processes of writing which are influenced by the writer's long-term memory and the task. These are planning, translating ideas from planning into writing, and reviewing.

As is obvious from Hyland's classification, process approaches focus on the writer as an individual, and this entails a number of problems. In the first place, the approaches are asocial, lacking consideration for the social context and communicative purpose of the text, as well as for the reader. Furthermore, as Hyland (2003: 19) argues, creative writing requires social and cultural capital which 'principally advantages middle class L1 students who, immersed in the values of the cultural mainstream, share the teacher's familiarity with key genres'. Students from different cultural, social, educational and linguistic backgrounds may not have access to the Western values underpinning creative writing, such as individualism, learner autonomy, personal voice or critical thinking. They will therefore experience difficulty in finding out what is expected, particularly as explicit instruction is discouraged. A further critique of process approaches is that they encourage learners to write texts that are irrelevant to their work or study, preventing them from gaining access to the educational and professional genres that are needed for success. Lastly, the assessment of writing is problematic in process approaches, which are, as Hyland (2002a) points out, clearly under-theorised and have no objective criteria of what defines good writing. It is also problematic to evaluate the extent to which effective processes have been employed in the production of text, and available assessment criteria refer to the product rather than the process of writing.

Process approaches were particularly prevalent in College Composition in US universities. They played an important role in the history of literacy instruction as they moved beyond 'narrowly-conceived product models' (Hyland, 2003: 17) to the consideration of how texts are produced by individuals. This development parallels the general trend at the time towards learner – rather than teacher-centred education. The cognitive process approach in particular has made an ongoing impact in writing education, and since the 1980s most syllabuses and teaching materials have incorporated activities concerned with planning, drafting and revising texts (Ivanič, 2004). However, the emergence of genre research and pedagogies led to fierce debates between the proponents of process and genre approaches and a polarisation between the two camps.

Genre approaches

These approaches are, according to Hyland's classification, text- rather than writer-oriented. However, unlike the skills approach, texts are not seen as context-free products, but as part of a communicative event (Ivanič, 2004). Examples of such events could be a recipe, a research article or a condolence letter, i.e. types of writing that have clear purposes and social contexts, and in which the writer interacts with a more or less specific audience. Texts can be grouped into genres according to their structural, rhetorical and linguistic features; these features are determined by the social context or event to which the genres belong. Genres fulfil a particular communicative purpose in the event, and this purpose is understood by the participants, i.e. the relevant discourse community. Genre research focuses on identifying the textual features required by the communicative event. In most genre pedagogies, these features are taught explicitly to students. As genre approaches are central to my proposal for an inclusive instructional model, I will discuss the main genre schools in more detail in the second part of this chapter.

Given the development of genre theories and genre-based pedagogies over the last two decades, Hyland's classification of genre approaches as text-oriented is somewhat one-sided, as it does not consider the attention given in genre pedagogy to audience and the discourse community. It contradicts

Johns' (2008: 237) description of genre as 'the most social constructivist of literacy concepts'; however it chimes with the accusations made by process approach proponents, which blame genre models for being text-oriented, prescriptive and teaching genres in 'simplistic and reductive ways' (Racelis & Matsuda, 2013: 388). These accusations have been echoed by members of the Academic Literacies movement which blame genre-based teaching for focusing solely on texts and for being 'normative' (Lillis & Scott, 2007: 9). However, as I will explain in more detail later, this critique is outdated, as genre approaches have, over the last two decades, provided 'a much richer account of the contexts in which they occur' (Jones, 2004: 257) than previously, and widened their focus from text to the discourse community (Swales, 1990; Flowerdew & Peacock, 2001). In view of these developments, genre approaches would need to be listed in Hyland's classification in both the text- and the reader-oriented categories. Undeniably, there are still many academic writing programmes which claim to be genre-based but which are, in fact, skills-oriented. These are often found in English for Academic Purposes (EAP) courses where text types such as the academic essay are taught generically without consideration of specific academic disciplines and their conventions, and of reader expectations (see Chapter 3 for further discussion). It is likely that criticisms of genre-based approaches refer to these teaching formats.

Social practices approaches

The research associated with this category is more concerned with 'the broader sociocultural context of writing' (Ivanič, 2004: 234) than with texts. Hyland categorises social practice approaches as 'reader-oriented' and distinguishes between writing as social interaction and writing as social construction. Social interaction happens between writers and readers, when the writer attempts to fulfil the expectations that the reader brings to the text as a result of the rhetorical and social situation. Successful writing, therefore, depends on the writer's knowledge of the audience and his/her ability to anticipate the readers' reaction and to shape the text in a way that it responds to the readers' needs. Hyland's second sub-category, writing as social construction, considers the writer as a member of a discourse community fulfilling a social act in which writers need 'to explore the regular features of texts as the preferences of particular communities' (2002a: 34). The social practice view of writing makes it very clear that literacy instruction cannot be restricted to language features or processes of writing. However, the understanding of writing as social interaction and social construction is very much part of genre models, too. As the previous section has shown, the concept of discourse community and of texts being shaped by the preferences of the community is at the centre of genre theory.

The difference between genre and social practices approaches can be best explained by their different emphasis on teaching and research. Whilst the priority of most genre approaches is the teaching of writing on the basis of texts, social practices approaches have research into the practices surrounding writing at the forefront of their activities. Ivanič (2004: 234) gives the following examples of social practices in which researchers are interested:

> patterns of participation, gender preferences, networks of support and collaboration, patterns of use of time, space, tools, technology and resources, the interaction of writing with reading and of written language with other semiotic modes, the symbolic meanings of literacy, and the broader social goals which literacy serves in the lives of people and institution.

These practices are at the heart of Academic Literacies research, which has produced various ethnographic studies of students struggling with literacy conventions (e.g. Lea & Street, 1998; Lillis, 2001), as well as studies of the multimodal nature of literacies (e.g. Kress & van Leeuwen, 2001). However, when it comes to the teaching of writing, social practices approaches have little to offer; as Ivanič (2004: 235) notes, 'the social practices discourse of writing does not encompass any pedagogic or assessment practices'. The Academic Literacies movement has never developed a coherent, widely applicable teaching approach, perhaps because their research findings do not easily translate into writing pedagogy. By contrast, Rhetorical Genre Studies, which is genre-based but strongly oriented towards social practices, has developed a pedagogic approach. Johns (1994, 1997, 2002), for instance, proposed ethnography as a method of helping students to understand the social practices which are manifested in genres. In this method, students are encouraged to act as researchers and conduct ethnographic investigations of the literacy practices of the discourse communities that are relevant to them, such as a professional or academic environment. Through exposure to the social contexts, students are expected to develop knowledge of the associated genres.

The socio-political approach

This approach broadens the spectrum of the social practices approaches by investigating the political context of writing. It is underpinned by Critical Discourse Analysis (CDA), which explores the relationship between language and social and cultural structures, such as institutional hierarchies and power relations (Fairclough, 1995). In this approach, writing is perceived as influenced by powerful social groups which restrict the choices a writer can make in terms of genre, style, and content. Research in the socio-political approach has mainly been carried out by Academic Literacies researchers who revealed the influence of power relations and social conventions on students' identity (Clark & Ivanič, 1997; Ivanič, 1998). Pedagogical recommendations related to the socio-political approach have been put forward by Critical EAP scholars (e.g. Benesch, 2001); these will be discussed later in this chapter.

According to Ivanič (2004), the socio-political approach has an explicit teaching agenda, referred to as 'Critical Literacy' or 'Critical Language Awareness' (Ivanič, 2004: 238). This teaching approach, which became more widespread in the 1990s, involved the critical analysis of writers' linguistic and semiotic choices in relation to the socio-political context. Nevertheless, the approach does not appear to have been taken up widely, as issues of power and identity seem to be rarely addressed in the writing classroom.

Summary for Part 1

Having commented on the lack of impact of the socio-political approach, I want to finish this part by briefly considering the use of the other approaches in classroom instruction. Ivanič (2004) differentiates between explicitly and implicitly taught approaches and explains that all approaches apart from 'creativity' and most of 'social practices' are, or can be, explicitly taught. In the creativity approach, as mentioned earlier, direct teaching is not encouraged. As to social practices, knowledge of the discourse community's practices can only to a certain extent be directly instilled through classroom instruction. Much of this knowledge is gained through language socialisation which occurs through students' gradually increasing participation in the community (Lave & Wenger, 1991; Ochs, 1986). However, this process can be accelerated through ethnographic activities as proposed by Johns (1997, 2002), and supported by genre-analytical work in the classroom.

Of the two approaches that put the text at the centre of instruction, the skills approach is widely used and at the same time, being decontextualised, least helpful for students who need to learn the specific discourses of their disciplines. Unfortunately, this type of instruction is often the only one available to students. By contrast, genre approaches aim at enabling students to understand the genres of their academic discipline in relation to their communicative purposes and social context. Although there is much consensus that genre is 'a robust pedagogical approach perfectly suited to the teaching of academic writing' (Hyland, 2008a: 543), genre pedagogies have been developed for, and used in, quite specific contexts, and have yet to be drawn together for an inclusive instructional approach that does not single out native or non-native speakers of English. The main genre schools and their contexts are discussed next.

Part 2: Genre Approaches to Teaching Academic Literacy

The three most widely used genre models, Rhetorical Genre Studies (RGS), the Sydney School/SFL and English for Specific Purposes (ESP), all emerged as a result of dissatisfaction with grammar-focused, general language teaching that aimed at linguistic competence and disregarded social context and interaction. Two models, the Sydney School/SFL and ESP, have their origins in Halliday, McIntosh and Strevens' (1964) seminal publication 'The linguistic sciences and language teaching', in which the authors called for the examination of the specialised needs of language users in specific contexts that required special registers. As Halliday et al. claimed,

> once this [specific use of language] has been observed, recorded and analysed, a teaching course to impart such language behaviour can at least be devised with confidence and certainty. (1964: 190)

Based on these insights, language instruction began to be underpinned by the analysis of the rhetorical functions appearing in specific registers, and the ways in which they are expressed and arranged in texts. An example of register was 'scientific language', and the rhetorical patterns and linguistic features of scientific texts were taught explicitly to students. However, this approach, as Swales (2001) explains, was, in the same way as the previous grammar-oriented language courses, based on the widely held belief in the universality of scientific language, ignoring the fact that there are many specific scientific communities or disciplines. Furthermore, the concept of 'register' proved too loose to capture the characteristics of language use in specific academic contexts. Since the early 1980s scholars gradually provided evidence for the fact that academic language and communication is highly discipline-specific and shaped by their discourse communities (e.g. Bazerman, 1981; Peck MacDonald, 1987). From the analysis of academic discourses, the concept of 'genre' emerged and replaced the concept of 'register', regarded by

Swales (2001: 47) as one of the 'emancipations' in the teaching of English for academic purposes, because,

> a focus on genre redrew the map of academic discourse by replacing rhetorical modes such as exposition or registral labels such as scientific language with text-types such as research article, term paper, final examination, MA thesis and conference abstract.

The conceptualisation of genre as a social process (Martin, 1992) or 'communicative vehicles for the achievement of goals' (Swales, 1990: 46), situated in a particular community of users, has been significant for the development of academic literacy instruction. It meant that the focus of analysis and instruction turned away from the universal register of 'scientific language' to the specific genres that students need to use to interact in their communicative contexts. Learning the features of genres in relation to their communicative purposes helps students to meet the expectations of the discourse community.

The three main genre approaches were previously categorised by Hyon (1996) into New Rhetoric, Australian Systemic Functional Linguistics (SFL), and English for Specific Purposes (ESP). The term New Rhetoric has more recently been replaced by Rhetorical Genre Studies (RGS) (Bawarshi & Reiff, 2010), which I will use in this book. Naming the Australian model is more difficult, as various labels are in use. Some scholars (e.g. Johns, 2011; Coffin & Donohue, 2012) refer to it as SFL because systemic-functional linguistics is the theoretical framework for genre analysis and pedagogy. Others call the model 'Sydney School' (e.g. Flowerdew, 2013) in reference to the major literacy interventions undertaken by researchers at the University of Sydney. As my discussion will variably refer to either the pedagogical applications or the underlying theory, I will use the term 'Sydney School/SFL' to avoid confusion. ESP is also referred to as English for Academic Purposes (EAP) which is in fact a branch of ESP and became a discipline in its own right in the early 2000s. In this book, I will use the term ESP.

Although the three models share the conceptual understanding of genre as socially situated, they differ in their analytical frameworks and pedagogic aims, due to the fact that they are underpinned by different disciplines and have different target groups of learners. According to the models' theoretical orientations, Barwarshi and Reiff (2010) distinguish between the sociological genre approach, represented by Rhetorical Genre Studies (RGS) and the linguistic genre approaches, represented by the Sydney School/SFL and English for Specific Purposes (ESP). RGS is a rather distinct approach from the more related concepts of the Sydney School/SFL and ESP. It is mainly concerned with the situational contexts of genres, whilst the linguistic approaches focus on 'the lexico-grammatical and rhetorical realisation of communicative purposes in a genre' (J. Flowerdew, 2002: 91). This distinction also relates to the models' pedagogic orientation: whilst the Sydney School/SFL and ESP have been engaged in the explicit teaching of genre, RGS scholars have expressed doubts about the extent to which genres can be taught. The origins and contexts of the three genre-based models are discussed in the next section, followed by a comparison of their pedagogical principles and aims.

Origins and contexts of the three genre models

RGS

Rhetorical Genre Studies is rooted in the North American higher education system and emerged from the academic discipline of Composition Studies. The discipline is concerned with writing research and instruction related to first-year College Composition courses. These courses were first introduced at Harvard University in the 1870s (Clark & Russell, 2014), and have since the mid-20th century become a compulsory component of first-year study at most US universities. College Composition has traditionally been situated in basic skills courses (Beaufort, 2007), aiming to enable students to produce acceptable writing in standard written English (Horner, 2014). At one stage, in the mid-20th century, composition classes had a strong focus on rhetorical modes such as exposition, persuasion, description, and narration (Herrington & Moran, 2005). This emphasis was based on the assumption that writing ability is monolithic and can be transferred to other contexts, and that therefore the types of genres and texts used in composition classes are of secondary importance. According to Russell *et al.* (2009), composition courses traditionally use literary texts, which obviously have little in common with the genres most students would encounter in their academic disciplines.

RGS followed, as Artemeva (2008: 9) points out, the 'rise and fall of product- and process-oriented approaches in composition studies', and developed from the recognition that a more principled, theory-based approach was needed for the teaching of composition. In an influential article, McCarthy (1987) revealed that generic composition courses are unhelpful in preparing students for writing in the disciplines. At around the same time, researchers began to provide evidence for the situated nature of writing and the fact that specific discourse communities have specific conventions and requirements for writing (Bazerman, 1981; Berkenkotter & Huckin, 1995). The understanding that composition courses have no 'overt linking to any intellectual discipline' (Beaufort, 2007: 10) and mislead students and writing instructors into believing that writing is a generic skill, gave ground to the 'genre turn' (Bawashi & Reiff, 2010: 6). The genre turn was also based on social constructivist perspectives that began to influence composition studies in the 1970s and 1980s (Artemeva, 2008). In these perspectives, writing is part of a social process by which knowledge is constructed in response to the needs, goals and contexts of a community. The genre turn and its theorisation of writing instruction came alongside the professionalization of teachers of first-year writing courses that started in the 1970s.

RGS has a sociological orientation and is interdisciplinary in nature, due to the fact that its scholars come from a variety of disciplines, including rhetoric, sociology, psychology, phenomenology and communication (Bawarshi & Reiff, 2010). In contrast to the linguistically-oriented genre schools, RGS examines primarily the social and rhetorical actions of which genres are textual instantiations (Artemeva & Freedman, 2008). According to Miller's seminal definition of genres as 'typified rhetorical actions based in recurrent situations' (1984: 31), the purpose of RGS is to help users to understand and perform these actions and the associated social roles. Miller calls for genre analysis to be ethno-methodological, focusing on the genre's context rather than on form and linguistic features. As Hyon (1996: 696) explains, RGS scholars conduct ethnographic research in order to offer 'thick descriptions of academic and professional contexts surrounding genres and the actions texts perform within these situations'.

As will be further discussed below, RGS uses genre as an analytical framework for investigating academic, workplace and institutional contexts, but its scholars have questioned the explicit teaching of genres in the classroom. Therefore, the extent to which RGS theory has impacted on first-year composition courses is unclear; however, it has influenced the movements 'Writing in the Disciplines/Writing across the Curriculum' (WiD/WAC) which have developed innovative approaches to teaching writing at US universities. WiD and WAC emerged in the 1970s, also as a reaction to the generic and skills-oriented writing instruction in College Composition, and promoted the teaching of writing within the disciplines (Horner, 2014). The movements had a more visible impact in US higher education than RGS, as 65 per cent of US universities now have WAC programmes (Clark & Russell, 2014). Despite some influence from RGS, WiD and WAC do not have strong theoretical foundations (Ochsner & Fowler, 2004), and no universal format. They are realised in many different versions, including writing centres or collaboration between writing and subject teachers.

The Sydney School/SFL

The term 'Sydney School' describes an instructional model developed in Australia which is also referred to as 'genre-based literacy pedagogy' (Martin, 1999). The term was, as Jones (2004) points out, originally used in relation to the Writing Project, the first large literacy intervention directed by researchers from Sydney University. As explained earlier, the model is also often referred to as Systemic Functional Linguistics (SFL) which is in fact the name of the underlying linguistic theory. SFL, developed by Halliday from the 1960s onwards, studies language in its social function of creating meaning, and identifies the links between linguistic forms and their functions in particular contexts. The related genre theory emerged from Martin and others' analysis of text types produced in primary schools, and underpinned major literacy programmes, starting in 1979 with the Writing Project, which was an initiative by Martin, Rothery and Christie to address literacy needs of primary school children in Australia (Rose & Martin, 2012). The 'second generation' (Mahboob et al., 2010: 26) of the Sydney School extended genre-based literacy pedagogy to secondary schools with large-scale literacy interventions such as the Write it Right Project. In the 'third generation', the pedagogy was applied to adult migrant English teaching, whilst the 'fourth generation' applied the principles developed in the earlier phases to academic literacy instruction in universities (e.g. Humphrey et al., 2010).

Halliday's central concept in SFL was that of register, which refers to the linguistic choices available in a particular context of situation. Context of situation is SFL's term for social situations and activities related to specific groups of people, for instance professional or interest groups. Examples of registers include school lessons, sports commentaries and, as explained earlier, scientific language (Halliday et al., 1964). Variations in context of situation are determined by the three parameters 'field' (type of activity/social action), 'tenor' (relations between the participants of the activity/social action) and 'mode' (type and role of language, e.g. written/spoken). As mentioned before, the concept of register was found to be insufficient for explaining the variations occurring within specific registers. Jim Martin and colleagues, when analysing text types produced by primary school children, noticed the limitations of Halliday's (1978) classification of 'genre' as an aspect of the parameter 'mode' within the concept of register. They found that these text types varied independently from register. For instance, descriptions, reports, recounts and narratives 'could be about almost any field, they could be spoken or written [i.e. mode], and their producers and audience could be close or distant, equal or unequal [i.e. tenor]' (Martin & Rose, 2008: 16). As a result, the notion of genre was reconceptualised by Martin (1984, 1992) beyond register at the level of context of culture, a stratum which encapsulates that of context of situation. The new stratum of context of culture enabled the analysts to use the parameters of field, tenor and mode in relation to members of a culture and their communicative purpose for producing the genre, 'rather than an unpredictable jungle of social situations' (Martin & Rose, 2008: 17). As

Flowerdew (2013: 138) explains, the concept of 'communicative purpose' is the defining characteristic of genre as opposed to register. For example, whilst register would refer to a specific situation, such as a lecture at university to a specific group of students (e.g. a mathematics professor lecturing mathematics students), genre would regard the lecture at the level of context of culture, where it is a regular communicative event that occurs across different academic disciplines, but has the same communicative purpose.

Martin (1984) subsequently defined genre as 'staged, goal-oriented social processes'. Staging, i.e. the structure and sequence of texts, is an essential feature of genre, as particular steps have to be taken to fulfil the communicative purpose of texts. For instance, the genre of the laboratory report, 'one of the most predictable [genres] in terms of its staging' (Nesi & Gardner, 2012: 28), usually follows the IMRD format of Introduction, Methods, Results, Discussion, but, as Nesi and Gardner show, there are variations to this format across disciplines. As will be seen, the Sydney School/SFL definition of genre resonates closely with that of ESP, which is unsurprising considering their shared roots in Hallidayan linguistic theory.

ESP

ESP pedagogy has traditionally been concerned with second language learners' acquisition of the specific language required in academic and professional settings. Unlike RGS and the Sydney School/SFL, ESP is therefore not linked to a specific geographical and educational context, but is applied in second language teaching around the world. Similar to the Sydney School/SFL, ESP's primary goal has been the detailed analysis of textual features that are specific to the relevant genres, in order to teach these features explicitly. Earlier ESP work consisted of the description of special registers, such as scientific language (for examples of register analyses see Swales' 'Episodes in ESP' (1985)). Register analysis produced quantitative descriptions of the distribution of lexical and grammatical features in scientific texts, without considering the function of these features in their contexts. In the 1980s, researchers began to narrow their focus from 'general' scientific language to specific types of texts (e.g. the journal article) in specific areas (e.g. astrophysics, see Tarone *et al.*, 1981). It was predominantly the work of Swales (1990) and Bathia (1993) that transformed ESP into a genre-based pedagogy. Swales, who had long been engaged in the analysis of research article introductions across disciplines (1981), came up with the seminal ESP definition of genre as

> a class of communicative events, the members of which share some set of communicative purposes. These purposes are recognised by the expert members of the parent discourse community and thereby constitute the

rationale for the genre. This rationale shapes the schematic structure of the genre and influences and constrains choice of content and style. (1990: 58)

Swales' definition is very similar to that of Martin. Martin's goal-orientation is described by Swales as the communicative purpose that is a genre's rationale. Staging is referred to by Swales as the schematic structure that is shaped by the purpose. Martin's use of 'social process' for the definition of genre becomes clearer through Swales' explanation of what belongs to a social process, namely a community which participates in communicative events, interacts to achieve the purposes attached to these events, and has a shared understanding of their forms and functions. The concept of staging is famously demonstrated in Swales' (1990) 'move analysis' of introductions in research articles, known as the CARS (Creating a Research Space) model. In this model, Swales demonstrates the obligatory moves and steps that authors have to take in the introduction to 'establish a territory', 'establish a niche' and 'occupy the niche' (1990: 141).

Bathia, working on professional genres related to law and business, outlined seven stages for the analysis of genres. The first three steps are concerned with the situational context and the existing research on a genre; the forth requires the collection of a corpus from that genre. This is followed by an ethnographic study of the genre in its institutional context (stage 5). Stage 6 moves to the linguistic analysis of the genre which consists, according to Swales' model, of exploring the structure/moves, the rhetorical patterns of the text (e.g. use of noun phrases or citations) and lexico-grammatical features. As the last step, Bathia recommends to confirm the findings from the analysis with informants who are specialists in the genre (1993: 22–36).

Swales' and Bathia's ground-breaking proposals have determined ESP's method of genre analysis which links contexts of culture with detailed explorations of texts. In contrast to the Sydney School/SFL, which proposes broader categories of educational genres according to its target population of learners (see next section), ESP offers a high level of specificity in the description of contexts, genres and the texts associated with these genres. Both scholars have since acknowledged limitations in the original definition (see Askehave and Swales 2001 for a discussion of the concept of 'communicative purpose') and recognised the fact that genres are more fluid, complex, and subject to manipulations by expert members of the discourse community than is recognised in the initial model (Bathia, 2004). Nevertheless, the main agenda of ESP has remained to be the analysis of texts/genres in relation to the requirements of their specific contexts.

Pedagogical principles and aims

Despite targeting different learner groups, the Sydney School/SFL and ESP share the understanding that linguistic features and the social function of genres are inextricably linked, and that these links must be made explicit in order to empower learners to first understand and eventually use the genres required in their educational or professional contexts. Scholars of the Sydney School/SFL in particular saw the systematic teaching of language choices and variations in specific genres as fundamental for developing learners' critical analysis (Hammond & Macken-Horarik, 1999) as well as their ability to challenge powerful genres (Hasan, 1996).

The Sydney School/SFL's pedagogy mainly targets underprivileged learners in all sectors ranging from primary to adult and tertiary education. It has the social agenda of empowerment, based on Halliday *et al.*'s (1964: 242) concept of 'productive language teaching' which aims to expand students' abilities to create meaning by teaching them the varieties and linguistic choices that are available in a language. Inequalities in access to genres that are privileged in society, such as institutional and particularly educational genres, mean that learners from lower socio-economic or different cultural backgrounds have to be taught these genres explicitly to be able to participate fully in education and achieve social success (Cope & Kalantzis, 1993). Genre-based literacy pedagogy started from Rothery and Martin's identification of the main primary school genres, i.e. stories, histories, reports, explanations and procedures, and the analysis of their structures and lexico-grammatical features (Martin & Rose, 2008, 2012; Martin & Rothery, 1980, 1981). Later, the main instructional method of genre-based literacy pedagogy, the interactive teaching-learning cycle, was proposed by Rothery (1996). The cycle leads from teacher-supported 'scaffolded' learning to independent learning and consists of three phases. In the modelling or deconstruction phase, the genre under focus is made explicit to the learner in terms of its social context and typical structural and linguistic features. In the joint construction phase, teacher and students work together on the production of a text belonging to the genre. Finally, in the independent construction phase, students write their own texts (Cope & Kalantzis, 1993; Martin, 1999). The cycle can be accessed at any phase, depending on the need and developmental stage of the learners. The teaching and learning cycle has been widely applied in the Australian literacy interventions in primary and secondary schools and was subsequently adopted in higher education (Drury, 2004; Ellis, 2004).

ESP's main pedagogic principle is the teaching of the textual features of genres such as structure, i.e. required moves, lexico-grammar and rhetorical preferences. Its widest application is teaching English for academic purposes (EAP) to 'more advanced, often graduate-level, international students in

British and US universities' (Bawarshi & Reiff, 2010: 43); however, the model is also widely used in English-medium universities around the world. As Flowerdew (2013: 146) puts it, the tenet of ESP is 'that good genre descriptions could feed into ESP materials development and pedagogy more generally'. As a 'visible pedagogy', ESP offers to learners 'an explicit understanding of how target texts are structured and why they are written the way they are' (Hyland, 2004: 11). The model has no ideological goals of learner empowerment, a fact that is not surprising as the ESP learner groups consist mainly of educationally privileged graduate students and professionals. Although initially more text-focused, ESP has since the mid-1990s increasingly been concerned with the 'identification of the specific language features, discourse practices and communicative skills of target groups' (Hyland, 2002b: 385).

Unlike the two linguistic genre approaches, RGS scholars have been sceptical about the explicit teaching of genre and have argued that genres cannot be extricated from their real world social contexts and be re-enacted in the classroom. Drawing on Lave and Wenger's (1991) model, RGS proponents believe that genres are learned through the participation of apprentices in the community of practice, that is, in the real context where the target genre is situated. Berkenkotter and Huckin (1995: 482), for instance, proposed a model of 'enculturation' in which apprentices are socialised into the conventions of their disciplines; this model is similar to the later concept of 'academic discourse socialisation' (Duff, 2010). Freedman (1993, 1994), arguing from a second language acquisition perspective, cautioned that explicit genre teaching could not be effective, because writing teachers would not know all the genres that their students needed to learn. More recently, Devitt (2009) warned that the explicit teaching of genres would perpetuate their conventions and values and therefore 'reinforce[s] institutional and cultural norms and ideologies' (Devitt, 2009: 342). As shall be seen in the next section, this critique resonates with that raised by Critical EAP and Academic Literacies. However, Devitt acknowledges that the explicit teaching of genre, even if it is beset with problems, will help students to 'understand more about it than they would if we had taught them nothing at all' (Devitt, 2009: 341). Johns (2002, 2008, 2011) stresses that instruction should help students to develop genre awareness rather than aiming at genre acquisition. Awareness would enable students to apply their knowledge to new contexts, and would prevent them from seeing genres as fixed formats. This point will be further discussed in Chapter 4.

Critique of the Sydney School/SFL and ESP

The linguistic genre pedagogies have been the subject of critique not only from RGS scholars such as Devitt, but also from Critical EAP and Academic Literacies. Critical EAP scholar Benesch has blamed the traditional teaching of English for Academic Purposes[1] for being 'accommodationist' (1993: 714), as it prepares students 'unquestioningly for institutional and faculty expectations' (Benesch, 2001: 22). In Benesch's view, which resembles the previously discussed doubts of Devitt (2009), disciplinary and institutional norms are accepted, promoted and perpetuated by EAP. Students are expected to accommodate to the academic demands imposed by those in power, while EAP teachers are expected to 'subordinate their instruction to those demands and perpetuate a service relationship to colleagues in other departments' (Benesch, 2001: 22). This practice was labelled 'vulgar pragmatism' by Pennycook (1997) who calls for the application of 'critical pragmatism' in which existing norms are challenged. As Benesch (2001) explains, Critical EAP, while still engaging in the traditional classroom activities of teaching discipline-specific English, encourages students to question and even transform these activities as well as the contexts from which they emerged. Therefore, Critical EAP should include a rights analysis in which power relations, institutional hierarchies and the inequality between language and content teachers are investigated and challenged.

In the UK context, similar critique of EAP – or in fact both linguistic genre approaches, although this is not clearly specified – has been raised by the Academic Literacies movement. Academic Literacies is less concerned with second language learners, but focuses on 'home' students (i.e. those who finished their secondary education in the UK) struggling to write at university. In the framework proposed by Lea and Street (1998), which underpins Academic Literacies theory, all genre approaches seem to be subsumed in the category of 'Academic socialisation' (see Table 2.1); however, there is no nuanced account of the characteristics of the different genre schools. Lea and Street see 'Academic socialisation' as encapsulated in the higher order category of 'Academic Literacies', which pays attention to socio-political issues such as identities and power relations. In their view, approaches in the 'Academic socialisation' model are based on the assumption that 'the academy is a relatively homogeneous culture' (Lea & Street, 1998: 159) and therefore that students can get the impression that once they have learned the norms and practices of academic writing through text-based instruction, they 'get access to the whole institution', whilst instead 'the multiplicity of communities of practice within the academy' (Lea, 2004: 741) needs to be recognised. Lillis and Scott (2007) accuse 'Academic socialisation' approaches for their 'textual bias' (Lillis & Scott, 2007: 11) and normativity. In the same vein as Benesch, they argue that these approaches induct students into the conventions and genres of a discipline without giving them the opportunity to question them, thus perpetuating privileged standards and norms. However, in the absence of a clear description of which approaches are actually referred to under the label 'Academic socialisation', these accusations remain somewhat vague. Furthermore, Lea's as well as Lillis and Scott's comments ignore the considerable development of genre pedagogies over the last 20 years. Genre approaches are not anymore textually biased since they have made the discourse community 'a primary focus of analysis, equal to, if not more important than the actual text' (Flowerdew & Peacock, 2001: 16). As far as normativity is concerned, EAP/genre practitioners have since the 1990s rejected prescriptive teaching based on 'authoritative texts for students to imitate or adapt' (Tribble, 1996: 37). Instead of teaching genres and their features as norms or templates, 'contemporary genre studies approach textual features and functions as dynamic and multifaceted, rather than unidimensional and formulaic' (Racelis & Matsuda, 2013: 388). In the same way as Critical EAP, Lillis and Scott want students to be encouraged to challenge and critique existing conventions. They regard Academic Literacies as 'transformative', as it helps writers to consider the wider institutional and political context of writing, and to explore alternative ways of 'meaning making' (2007: 13). While I generally agree with the need for transformation in universities in order to deal adequately with student diversity (see discussion in Chapter 3), I have reservations about a transformative agenda that diminishes the importance of working with texts in the development of academic literacy. As argued previously (Wingate & Tribble, 2012), texts need to be a main focus of instruction as long as written texts remain the primary assessment tool in higher education; however, working with texts does not exclude a critical approach. On the contrary, literacy instruction can usefully combine text analysis with explorations of 'the resources that writers bring to the academy (Lillis & Scott, 2007: 9) and of issues of power and identity. In Chapter 7, I will propose a model which draws on both genre and social practice approaches and includes the development of students' critical awareness.

Summary

After the overview of approaches to researching and teaching academic literacy, and the detailed discussion of genre-based approaches, I want to finish the chapter by considering how the various approaches can contribute to a higher education literacy pedagogy that is suitable to cater for student diversity and inclusive of students from all backgrounds.

The animosity between some approaches, as seen in the criticisms levelled particularly against genre models, may have to do with the fact that traditionally the approaches have been confined to specific contexts. This confinement is certainly the reason for the absence of a literacy pedagogy that would be suitable for the mainstream rather than for specific target groups. Little consideration has been given to the ways in which approaches could complement each other, despite the fact that there are 'many points of convergence' between them (Jones, 2004: 255). In the last decade, however, efforts have been made to draw different traditions together. For example, Johns brought together scholars from the three different genre schools in the 2005 International Association of Applied Linguistics Conference; their contributions showed 'considerable overlaps' (Johns, 2006: 247). The symposium revealed that both linguistic genre schools support the development of genre awareness rather than genre acquisition; this helps to disprove the criticism that they teach genres in prescriptive and reductive ways. Unfortunately, the symposium was only concerned with second language writing, demonstrating again the tendency in genre traditions to target specific learner groups while excluding others.

Another endeavour in drawing together different approaches is a special issue of the Journal of English for Academic Purposes, edited by Coffin and Donahue (2012), which considers the contributions of SFL and Academic Literacies to English for Academic Purposes. Coffin and Donahue explain that while there are common concerns such as social justice, the main tensions exist around Academic Literacies' emphasis on practice as well as the negative connotations that some Academic Literacies scholars have with text. However, argue Coffin and Donahue, if language and text were understood in the SFL-sense as 'meaning making resources' (2012: 73), this tension could be relieved. Gardner points out that SFL and Academic Literacies are 'potentially compatible and complementary in research on student writing' (Gardner, 2012: 52), but she notices in relation to teaching that 'the problem... arises when practices based pedagogies are not complimented with a focus on the wording of the written text' (Gardner, 2012: 53). This underlines my earlier argument that social-political aspects should be considered in addition to work with texts. This is also felt by Johns, a scholar from the RGS tradition, who asserts that

> curricula should, in fact, begin with texts and their structures, particularly among novice students; but then, using some of the suggestions made by the New Rhetoricians, a curriculum must move towards an integration of theories and practices that value analysis of context, complex writing processes, and intertextuality. (Johns, 2011: 64)

Johns justifies this statement with the fact that the linguistic genre approaches to academic literacy instruction, ESP and the Sydney School/SFL, are 'the best known and the most successful in reaching their goals with L2 populations' (Johns, 2011: 64).

The development of the instructional model that I will introduce in Chapter 7 was based on my belief that an effective and inclusive academic literacy pedagogy must draw on the best aspects from the existing approaches, instead of being affiliated with one camp. I use the linguistic genre approaches as the basis for instruction, drawing on both ESP and the Sydney School/SFL. In addition to text-based work, there are many opportunities in the literacy classroom to discuss social and political aspects surrounding writing practices. Such discussions can be initiated by the teacher, or will more likely occur naturally, as 'language and literacy socialisation will almost inevitably involve the negotiation of power and identity' (Duff, 2010: 171). By taking up these opportunities, the proposed model draws on the sociopolitical approach and considers the critiques made by Critical EAP and Academic Literacies. Furthermore, within an inclusive instructional model, different levels of linguistic proficiency among the students still need to be considered, and the skills approach may need to be drawn on to a certain extent. And finally, an inclusive literacy pedagogy should include reading as well as writing instruction. The point was made earlier that reading is a neglected part of academic literacy and that all approaches discussed in this chapter are concerned with writing. As will be seen in Chapter 5, at least two of these approaches, process and genre, can be usefully employed in the development of academic reading.

Note

(1) As mentioned earlier, EAP is a common label for the genre-based approach of ESP.

3 Current Practice in Academic Literacy Instruction

Introduction

In the previous chapter, I reviewed the main models of academic literacy instruction and in this chapter, I discuss the dominant instructional practice in contemporary Anglophone universities. As shall be seen, the provision of academic literacy instruction and support has a number of limitations, particularly in relation to student diversity and inclusion. Instruction is typically focused on academic writing only, and offered in central units for students from all disciplines. In Part 1 of this chapter, I will address the four main problems related to this provision. These are the trend to generic teaching, the trivialisation and marginalisation of academic language and literacy, the exclusive targeting of specific learner groups, and the inadequate distribution of responsibilities between writing experts and subject teachers. I will also provide some evidence of the dominance of this approach, based on an analysis of the websites of 33 British universities. In Part 2, I will present a critique of the current university policies and practices in relation to academic literacy and student diversity which comes from a transformative perspective. As shall be seen, scholars who take this transformative position argue that linguistic and cultural diversity should be embraced rather than castigated.

Part 1: Limitations of Current Academic Literacy Instruction

The dominant approach to teaching academic literacy

English language support in Anglophone universities – with the exception of US universities where college composition is taught to all first-year students – is usually provided in service units catering for the whole university. Typical names for these units are 'English Language Centre', 'Writing Centre', or 'Academic Skills Centre'. In many UK universities, provision is made separately for 'home' students (who are assumed to be native speakers of English, but often are not) and 'international' students. 'International' students have access to centrally run English for Academic Purposes (EAP) courses that focus on linguistic and rhetorical features of a (non-existing) universal academic literacy. The only offer for 'home' students is usually some form of study skills instruction available in university-wide workshops, online resources or individual advice sessions. In the following sections, I discuss various problems attached to the central, extra-curricular provision of instruction.

Generic teaching of academic English

Partly because of their location in central units, academic language and literacy courses tend to be generic, i.e. not linked to the knowledge and discourses of any specific discipline. These courses are usually designed for students from all disciplines, and this explains why little attention can be paid to discipline-specific genres and conventions. Instead, the focus is on the grammar, structure, common rhetorical features and style of academic language use as well as on writing techniques. Although there is some variety in practice, two broad types of generic instruction can be distinguished; these are EAP and study skills. Both follow to a greater or lesser extent the skills approach which was presented in Chapter 2. Here, I take a closer look at EAP which, despite its origins, in its practical application often represents general rather than specific English language classes.

EAP is one branch of English for Specific Purposes (ESP) (the other branch being EOP, English for Occupational Purposes, see Flowerdew & Peacock, 2001), that has become the common label for teaching academic English and Anglophone academic culture to non-native speakers. This label is used in several countries, for instance Hong Kong, Singapore, Australia, and New Zealand (Turner, 2011). In this function, EAP has, it appears, moved away from important ESP principles, such as a clear focus on the discipline-specific genres that students need to understand and produce, specificity in the description of context (e.g. the communicative purpose of the genre and the expectations of the discourse community, see Swales, 1990), and the careful analysis of learner needs (Flowerdew & Peacock, 2001). While in ESP needs analysis would involve a detailed study of the discourse conventions and genres of the target community, in current EAP programmes this is reduced to some sort of gap analysis. The gap is between the student's current language proficiency, as attested by the obligatory English entrance test such as IELTS and TOEFL, and the requirements of a broadly conceived 'general' academic English.

As a result, the most widespread EAP format is that of English language classes delivered to non-native speaker students from a range of disciplines with the aim to improve their grammatical accuracy and use of style. The teaching content is not related to any specific academic context, but based on what Leung (2005: 127) called 'scaled-down universalism, that is, the language and communication inventory drawn up on the basis of teachers' and materials writers' knowledge of what is likely to be said'. Thus, the texts used for instruction can come from any discipline and may represent genres which are irrelevant for the students' study contexts. The preferred texts types include extracts from research journals from a range of disciplines (see for instance the sources for sample texts in Swales & Feak, 2012: 412–414), or pseudo-academic articles which do not belong to any discernible discipline (for instance newspaper articles). Although Swales and Feak (2012: xi) point out the advantages of the consciousness-raising that occurs when students experience different rhetorical conventions in the 'multidisciplinary class', research has shown that students are unlikely to regard instruction that is unconnected to their own subject as relevant (e.g. Durkin & Main, 2002). Working with generic academic texts does little to help students to learn the discourse conventions of their own disciplines. There are more sophisticated versions of EAP, for instance when students are grouped into fields (such as Life Sciences or Humanities) so that 'the materials may be broadly relevant to the students' area of study' (Morley, 2008: 127), or when EAP practitioners seek information from specialists from the students' discipline (Dudley-Evans, 2001; Dudley-Evans & St John, 1998). The usual unspecific and grammar-focused EAP format, however, whilst it may be useful for students with lower language proficiency, should not be mistaken for literacy instruction.

This generic and extra-curricular EAP and skills provision is the result of institutional policies which, as I explained in Chapter 1, still adhere to the structures of the previous elite systems. Furthermore, these policies are influenced by common beliefs about language as well as by budget limitations. The beliefs are (1) that academic literacy is a set of skills which can be learned independently from subject knowledge and, once acquired, can be transferred to any context, and (2) that students who come to university without these skills are deficient and need remedy (e.g. Ivanič & Lea, 2006; Lillis, 2001). Moreover, difficulties with academic literacy are frequently misunderstood as language problems (Boughey, 2002). In relation to university budgets, instruction for large heterogeneous groups is clearly less expensive than the design and delivery of literacy teaching for each discipline. As Hyland (2002b: 387) remarks, generic language programmes are not only cheaper, but also 'logistically undemanding, and require less skilled staff to implement'.

Theoretically, the generic form of EAP is underpinned by the common core hypothesis (Bloor & Bloor, 1986) which claims that all academic texts have core grammatical and lexical features in common, and that these need to be taught before specific language can be addressed. This belief has led to the rather absurd distinction in EAP between EGAP (English for General Academic Purposes) and ESAP (English for Specific Academic Purposes) (see for example Dudley-Evans, 2001). An obvious shortcoming of this hypothesis is that it assumes a fairly low proficiency level for EGAP, lower than non-native speaker university applicants would normally have. Moreover, as Flowerdew and Peacock (2001: 17) point out, the hypothesis 'assumes an incremental model of language acquisition', which has long been rejected by second language acquisition researchers. However, the common core hypothesis provides a convenient justification for a cost-saving approach to teaching academic language at universities. Commercial pressures are also reflected in the published EAP materials which are largely generic (and in many cases directly derived from courses within a College Composition tradition, e.g. Oshima & Hogue, 2006); clearly producing specific materials for smaller target groups is less lucrative for publishers.

Although much of the literacy instruction provided by service units in Anglophone universities is generic and skills-focused, there are various examples of units that work in a discipline-specific and curriculum-embedded manner. I will discuss some of these in the next chapter. Overall, however, it needs to be recognised that the provision of literacy instruction in central units encourages generic teaching and is problematic in other aspects, too. These aspects are considered next.

Trivialisation and marginalisation of academic language and literacy

The generic nature of instruction trivialises and marginalises the role of academic language and literacy. Trivialisation occurs through reducing diverse academic discourses to a common template, and through equating the ability to communicate in an academic context with the ability to produce grammatically correct sentences. Marginalisation occurs through locating literacy instruction outside the subject curriculum, conveying a clear message that language and literacy are subordinate to content knowledge. This message is reinforced through the fact that the instruction is often only available to those students who are marked as 'deficient', for instance because they are non-native speakers of English. Marginalisation also happens through delegating writing or skills instruction to staff members of lower ranking in the university hierarchy. As the teaching of writing is detached from academic departments and divorced from subject content, it is regarded as non-academic, low-status work (Benesch, 2001; Ivanič & Lea, 2006). Teachers 'are frequently employed as vulnerable, short-term instructors in marginalised service units' (Hyland & Hamp-Lyons, 2002: 10); their designations, for instance 'writing instructor' or 'learning developer', mark them out as inferior to academics in the disciplines. More recently, Hamp-Lyons (2011: 4) noticed that 'in 2010, there were several signs in Britain that EAP was again in a period of declining status', because several UK universities had downgraded EAP staff from academic positions to 'teaching-only' or 'support workers'. A growing number of British universities have even started to outsource their EAP provision to private companies (Ansell, 2008). According to Beaufort (2007: 31), the situation is not much different in the USA where composition courses 'are mainly staffed by PhD students in English literature'. At the same time, the actual experts in disciplinary discourses, the subject lecturers, are spared from the responsibility of supporting students' development of academic literacy. As long as the reductionist beliefs about academic literacy, which I discussed earlier, persist, it can be expected that the marginalisation of both literacy teaching and teachers will continue.

Exclusive targeting of academic literacy instruction to specific learner groups

Academic support at universities in the UK and some other Anglophone countries is typically targeted at specific learner groups, with the broad distinction being between international students who have foreign language learning needs and home students who are considered to have deficiencies in their writing performance.

As explained in Chapter 1, universities in English-speaking countries attract a growing number of international students, mostly non-native speakers of English. Since the high fees these students have to pay are becoming indispensable for university budgets, intense marketing and recruitment activities are pursued to increase the intake. A common obstacle to the admission of international students is an insufficient score in the English language proficiency test required for entry. Universities have therefore established English language support systems that facilitate the admission of students and enable them to meet the expected linguistic standards (for a discussion of the expectation that international students must accommodate to British English see Turner, 2011 and Jenkins, 2014). The typical provision consists of pre-sessional and in-sessional EAP courses. Pre-sessional courses, ranging in length from one to several months, are designed for students who did not reach the English language test score required by the programme they applied for, and received an offer of admission on the condition that they successfully complete the pre-sessional course. International students can receive further in-sessional language support after they started their degree course. In-sessional support is sometimes initiated by faculties and departments who 'buy in this specialist expertise (i.e. from writing specialists in the English Language Centre) to enhance their own programs' (Morley, 2008: 126). In some cases, in-sessional teaching is based on a certain level of cooperation with specialists in the disciplines in which the EAP teachers gather information about the subject content, discourse conventions, required genres and expectations by the subject specialists (Dudley-Evans & St John, 1998). However, the most common format of in-sessional support is centrally run classes offered to international students from all disciplines. Although students tend to recognise the merits of pre-sessional EAP courses in familiarising them with Western academic culture as well as study skills and techniques (Dooey, 2010; Terraschke & Wahid, 2011), they may not feel well prepared for studying in their disciplines. As far as the in-sessional courses are concerned, there is some evidence that students find them unhelpful because of their generic nature, and the difficulty of fitting them in with the work required in their study programmes (Jenkins & Wingate, in preparation).

Despite the shortcomings of EAP, such as its generic nature and its focus on grammar, it is often the only systematic support provision available in universities. The problem is that it is available for only one group of students, those who are, on the grounds of their geographic origins, classified as non-native speakers. This exclusive clientele is sometimes obvious in the name of the EAP unit, for example the 'English for International Students Unit (EISU)' at the University of Birmingham. Even if the unit's name does not make this restriction clear, it is usually flagged up in the introductory texts on its website. Indeed, on the websites of some universities, information about academic writing support can only be found by navigating through 'International Students' links. When it comes to the rest of the student population, the so-called home students, literacy support is patchy or simply not available. Before I look at the provision for home students more closely, I first want to further consider the inadequacy of using the distinction between 'home' and 'international' students as the basis for literacy support.

My main concern is that this distinction ignores the realities of student diversity. In universities in the UK, for instance, many 'home' students have immigrant backgrounds and are from ethnic minorities. Having gained their entry qualification in the UK's secondary school system means that they are classified in the same way as English native speakers, although English is an additional language for them and they might have been in the English education system only for a limited number of years. At the same time, some English native speaker students are from educational backgrounds that have not prepared them well for the university's literacy requirements. The language and literacy needs of these student groups are largely ignored in the current provision. At the same time, the system advantages those international students who have enjoyed a bilingual or English-medium education. These students, on the grounds that they have not completed their secondary education in the UK, are entitled to language support, while home students, regardless of their linguistic backgrounds, are not. Underpinning the different provision for home and international students is the aforementioned belief that literacy problems can be explained with weaknesses in grammar and vocabulary, areas in which particular student groups such as international students are pre-categorised as weak.

As a result of these distinctions, academic literacy support for 'home' students has been poor in many universities. If it is available, it often takes a 'study skills' approach (the model and its underlying assumptions are discussed in Chapter 2). Typically, central units tasked with the learning development of all students in a university offer remedial support, either through university-wide skills courses, online materials, or through short one-to-one sessions, sometimes called 'drop-in-clinics' (intimating the remedial approach) where students can get advice on the piece they are currently writing. In the skills courses and online materials, academic literacy (mostly academic writing) features among other skills such as time management, exam preparation, and avoiding plagiarism. Table 3.1 shows an example, from the website of the University of Bedfordshire, of what is typically on offer in learning development units. However, quite a number of universities do not even offer this level of support. As Morley (2008: 129) describes, provision is especially poor at the undergraduate level, because traditionally 'UK universities have not seen the teaching of writing as a mainstream learning activity for undergraduates'. Despite the massive expansion in student numbers since the 1990s and the associated diversity in students' backgrounds, universities have retained a support system that was originally conceived for a few struggling students.

Inadequate attribution of responsibilities

The last limitation I want to address is that, as a result of the centrally run and generically taught EAP or study skills courses, the responsibility for

Table 3.1 Study support offer at the University of Bedfordshire

Study support

It is not unusual for students to need some extra advice and guidance at some point during their studies. If you feel that you would benefit from some additional help with your studies why not contact the Professional and Academic Development team via SiD Online.

The PAD team offer support to all University of Bedfordshire students. If you are experiencing difficulties or if you simply want to develop particular skills and raise your grades, we are here to help and advise you how to do that.

We can help you in a number of ways. We can advise and help you to improve:

- The quality of your written assignments
- Your understanding of mathematical or statistical concepts
- Your organisation skills and how you approach studying
- Your time management and prioritising
- The strategies you use when reading
- Your language skills
- Aspects of your IT skills
- How you prepare for exams

(University of Bedfordshire, 2014)

developing student's academic literacy is assigned wholly to staff working in service units. These are the 'writing instructors' or 'learning developers', who, as discussed before, usually have lower academic status than academic staff in the disciplines.

The academic literacy models that see literacy/writing as social practice situated in a social context, such as the genre approaches, imply that academic literacy needs to be learned within the relevant discourse community. As subject lecturers are insiders and highly proficient members of the community, clearly they are better suited to introduce students to the community's literacy practices and conventions than writing experts from the central unit. This requirement has been explicitly stated by the 'Writing in the Disciplines/Writing across the Curriculum' (WiD/WAC) movements (McLeod, 1989; Young & Fulwiler, 1986), and, as Clark and Russell (2014: 377) put it, WiD/WAC practitioners around the world make efforts 'to support and encourage university teachers in the disciplines to attend to students' writing at the service of their disciplinary learning'. However, as Clark and Russell also note, university teachers tend to see writing as someone else's responsibility, and their reluctance to teach anything but subject content is also reported by North (2005) and Mitchell and Evinson (2006). There are several reasons for this unwillingness apart from the ever increasing workload that academics currently face, including the previously discussed beliefs about academic language and literacy, and the perception that students should learn to write before they come to university. Furthermore, subject specialists tend to feel uncomfortable with teaching language-related issues. Usually they have not received explicit literacy instruction themselves, and therefore their knowledge of the discipline's discourses and conventions remains 'tacit' and 'unarticulated' (Jacobs, 2005: 477). This situation makes the collaboration between subject lecturers and writing instructors, which Dudley-Evans and others have advocated (e.g. Dudley-Evans, 2001; Dudley-Evans & St John, 1998; Etherington, 2008), even more important. I will discuss forms of collaboration in the next chapter.

In completing this stage of the discussion, it should be noted that there are several ways in which subject lecturers have the possibility of contributing to the development of students' academic literacy as part of their routine practices. One example is formative feedback. In most Anglophone higher education contexts, lecturers are expected to provide comprehensive feedback comments on students' assignments. The feedback is supposed to be formative, that is, capable of helping students to make improvements in their next assignments. However, as a number of researchers (e.g. Carless, 2006; Weaver, 2006) have shown, feedback is often perceived as unhelpful by students, because it is too general, unconstructive, or incomprehensible. As Nicol (2010) points out, in the national student surveys such as the Australian Course Experience Questionnaire or the UK's National Student Survey, feedback consistently receives lower ratings than other aspects of teaching and learning. This means that a powerful method of subject-specific and individual literacy instruction is not used to its full potential, largely because lecturers do not have the training and explicit knowledge to (1) identify underlying problems in student writing (see Lea & Street, 1998, and Wingate 2012b, for lecturers' comments on 'argument'), and (2) express their comments in formative and constructive manner. Another way in which students' literacy development could be supported would be through the provision of more explicit information about the expected literacy practices in assignment tasks, in the associated guidelines and in the assessment criteria. This explicitness, however, is also widely lacking (e.g. Lea & Street, 1998; Morita, 2004, 2009). The provision of more systematic and helpful feedback and fuller, more explicit information about literacy requirements would be an important step towards discipline-specific academic literacy instruction. However, as long as lecturers have little literacy awareness and are not trained to offer effective feedback, the provision will remain sporadic and highly variable.

Survey of provision at UK universities

Having reviewed the limitations of the centrally-run, grammar- or skills-oriented literacy instruction, I want to substantiate my earlier claim that this is the dominant type of provision in Anglophone universities. For this purpose, Chris Tribble and I surveyed a sample of 33 universities representing 25% of the 132 members of UK Universities, the umbrella organisation of universities and colleges in the UK (UK Universities, 2013). The sample was drawn from a set of the existing university groupings; these groupings and the selected universities are shown in Table 3.2.

A search using the built-in search engines on each university's website for the term *International* students showed that all universities in the sample have the typical pre- and in-sessional provision exclusively for international students. To gain insights into the support available for *both* international and home students, we created additional searches using the terms *Academic support*, *Learning support*, *Student support* and *Academic writing*. We found that at least one of these terms would lead to the kinds of provision we were investigating, although in the case of one of the 33 universities, no information could be located with any of the terms.

Before I report the findings, it must be noted that they have to be considered with caution, as this type of survey has obvious limitations. First, we can make no claims that the web searches produced complete information,

Table 3.2 Sample from UK universities

Group	Selected universities
Russell Group (consists of 24 research-intensive universities)	Cambridge, Durham, Leeds, Manchester, Nottingham, Oxford, Southampton, University College London, Warwick,
1994 Group (operated until 2013 and consisted of 11 research-intensive universities, some of which have since joined the Russell Group)	East Anglia, Essex, Goldsmiths, Lancaster, Royal Holloway
Million+ Group (consortium of 22 post-1992 universities[1] and university colleges)	Bedfordshire, Bolton, Derby, Greenwich, Kent, Northampton, Staffordshire, West London
Non-affiliated institutions	Brighton, Hull, Reading, St Mark and St John, Teesside, University College Birmingham
Specialised universities	Harper Adams, University of the Arts/London, University for the Creative Arts

as the search terms might not have captured all aspects of a university's provision, or some information may not be available on the publicly accessible websites. Furthermore, since the searches started from the universities' home pages, the information they yielded was bound to be general and restricted to what is available university-wide. As we did not have the resources to examine individual study programmes in the sample universities, it is likely that we missed a number of discipline-specific academic literacy initiatives and activities. In the three universities where we discovered such initiatives, these were driven by central units, which explains why the relevant information was accessible through the universities' main websites. Despite the limitations, the findings are useful for highlighting dominant trends in provision. The findings are only summarised here; the list of all sample universities and their provision can be found in Appendix 3.1.

28 out of the 32 universities for which information could be obtained seem to provide only generic study skills support; in 14 cases, this support only being available online. The skills websites typically have a menu on the left side offering a choice of skills- or writing-related topics. The menu in the 'Academic skills' site of the University of Southampton, for example, includes 'Concentration and time management', 'Lectures and taking notes', 'Reading skills', 'Giving presentations', 'Writing essays and assignments'. The choice of one of these topics then leads to a new site which offers a lengthy list of tips. In other universities, the online resources are even less interactive. For instance, on the University of Staffordshire's website the search term *Academic writing* leads to a document entitled 'Academic Writing Tips'. Links to PDFs which contain study tips or simply an information leaflet with writing guidelines were found at eight universities. This type of support is offered in almost all cases as an adjunct to library and information services.

Seven universities provide university-wide skills/writing workshops, mostly in addition to online resources. A few offer workshops to exclusive target groups, such as dyslexic students (Leeds), or to home and international students separately (UCL). Oxford offers workshops for international students and staff for which a fee is charged. Two universities, Northampton and Kent, offer study skills modules which are credit-bearing. Face-to-face provision, i.e. individual drop-in sessions or sessions by appointment, is offered by seven universities. In two of them, the University of Creative Arts Canterbury, and Teesside, this was the only provision we could find. At Teesside, this individual advice service seems to be carried by just one person, a Writing Fellow sponsored by the Royal Literary Fund.

From these findings it appears that generic study-skills oriented instruction is indeed the dominant approach to supporting students in the development of academic literacy. We found evidence of some discipline-specific support only in four institutions, Cambridge, Durham, Lancaster and the University of Creative Arts in Canterbury. At the University of Cambridge (2014), the funded Transkills Project which is based on collaboration between writing specialists and academics in the disciplines, has led to the development of discipline-specific online courses for the subject areas of Biosciences, Divinity, Economics, English, Geography, History, Modern Languages and Linguistics. Topic addressed in the online courses include 'Exam writing', 'Essay writing', 'Interpreting the title', and 'Dissertation toolkit'.

Similarly, Durham also offers a semi-integrated approach. On the English Language Centre's (University of Durham, 2014) website they report:

> In 2011–12, individual academic writing sessions and programmes have been or are being delivered in a range of departments including Education, Medicine and Health, the Business School (UG Economics, UG Business Finance, MA Management, MSc Finance) and SGIA amongst others.
>
> The Academic Writing Unit has also been involved in a collaborative project with the University's DUO team and the Geography Department, designing online academic writing activities and materials.

Cambridge and Durham were the only examples where collaboration between writing experts and subject specialists was explicitly mentioned. At the University of Lancaster, student learning advisors are allocated to the Faculties of Management, Science and Technology, and Health and Medicine, where they offer academic support. However, it seems that some of the courses they offer are for international students only. The forth university which declares in their website that it offers discipline-specific writing support is the University of Creative Arts in Canterbury.

This survey, despite its limitations, underscores my earlier claim that academic literacy instruction consists predominantly of language or skills support delivered in a generic and extra-curricular manner. What is worrying in the findings is that quite a number of universities seem to rely entirely on online resources, and that some of these are just leaflets with instructions. This shows a lack of understanding of students' learning needs and the complex nature of academic literacy. The fact that most of the support is provided by libraries or study skills units with seemingly no involvement of academics in the disciplines is also unsatisfactory for the reasons discussed earlier in this chapter. Even if there is a great deal more discipline-specific activity which could not be captured by this survey, the very fact that this is not visible on university websites shows that discipline-specific literacy work is not part of the overall teaching strategy for most UK universities, and is a sporadic rather than a systematic provision.

This provision is clearly unsatisfactory for the whole student population, as it leaves the majority without any systematic instruction, and those who do participate in EAP or skills courses without access to the discourses of their academic discourse communities. It is also clearly outdated as it does not respond to the needs of the diverse student population in contemporary higher education where very few students can be expected to arrive at university with the required level of academic literacy. Based on the understanding that all students are novices to their chosen academic disciplines and therefore need to learn the specific conventions and discourses, it follows that academic literacy instruction needs to be provided to the mainstream as part of the subject curriculum. For those students who have additional linguistic needs, the existing language-oriented courses should continue to be offered, but as an additional, rather than the only option. Before I pursue this argument further in the next chapter, I want to present a more radical line of critique of the failure by current higher education systems to deal adequately with diversity. Whilst the argument presented thus far has been concerned with the instructional provision made by universities, the 'transformational' critique discussed below calls for changes in the current literacy requirements.

Part 2: Calls for Transformation of Academic Literacy Policies and Instructional Practices

Various scholars have argued that universities will ultimately need to undergo substantial transformation in order to provide fair and equal chances to students from diverse backgrounds. The requests for transformation come mainly from the fields of Academic Literacies, Critical EAP, English as an Academic Lingua Franca, and Multilingualism, and are related to different groups within the spectrum of student diversity. Academic Literacies has focused on widening participation in the UK, and has been particularly concerned with the experience of 'non-traditional' students (e.g. Lillis, 2001; Lea & Street, 2006). Critical EAP focuses on non-native speakers of English preparing to study through the medium of English, and similarly, scholars from the field of English as an Academic Lingua Franca take an interest in the experience of international students in Anglophone universities. Academics working in Multilingualism have mainly focused of multilingual students from underprivileged backgrounds.

Academic Literacies

Academic Literacies has been an influential movement in the UK since the publication of Lea and Street's (1998) seminal article which uncovered inadequacies in universities' approaches to student writing. In contrast to the widespread belief that literacy problems are equal to language deficiencies, Lea and Street showed that the difficulties student encounter with writing are less of a linguistic and more of an epistemological nature. Students have to deal with a variety of practices (the fact that there is no singular literacy practice is expressed in the name 'Academic Literacies') and have to respond to institutional and disciplinary requirements, which may conflict with their identities and previous experiences. As these practices and requirements are situated in specific contexts, academic writing cannot be taught outside the discipline as a set of generic and transferable skills in what the authors call the 'study skills' and the 'academic socialisation' approach. An Academic Literacies approach, by contrast, understands writing as a social practice which is dependent on the particular context; the approach also considers power relations and identity conflicts that impact on academic writing. More recently, some Academic Literacies scholars have promoted the model's transformational potential (e.g. Lillis & Scott, 2007). Lillis has long asserted the role of the model as a 'critical research frame' (Lillis, 2003: 195) and as an 'oppositional frame' (Lillis, 2006: 32) in relation to instructional practices at UK universities. An additional distinguishing feature of Academic Literacies is, according to Lillis and Scott (2007), that, unlike the text-focused 'EAP work' (Lillis & Scott, 2007: 12), it puts more emphasis on the practices surrounding text production. Lillis and Scott's main critique of text-focused approaches to academic writing is that these tend to be normative (for a discussion of this critique see Chapter 2). By contrast, Academic Literacies research is 'transformative' in Lillis and Scott's view, as it considers the perspectives of writers on how they are restricted through the existing conventions, and explores 'alternative ways of meaning making in academia' (Lillis, 2007: 13) with the aim to draw on, and legitimise, the resources that students bring with them to the university. In terms of literacy pedagogy, Lillis in particular (e.g. 2001, 2006) has stressed the need to 'explore ways in which alternative meaning-making practices in writing can be institutionally validated' (Lillis, 2006: 44).

Critical EAP

Critical EAP challenges the pragmatism of traditional EAP which sees its role in preparing non-native speaker students for the requirements of academic study, and where 'the traditional EAP teacher is mainly a conduit for efficient inculcation of those requirements rather than an activist who could invite students to question them' (Benesch, 2001: 51). According to Critical EAP theory, an important part of traditional EAP is needs analysis, i.e. the analysis of the discourses and genres used by the academic communities that students want to join. This analysis enables EAP teachers to develop teaching resources that respond directly to students' needs. However, as Benesch points out, as learner needs and institutional requirements are conflated in this approach, 'needs analysis naturalises what is socially constructed, making externally imposed rules seem not just normal but also immutable' (2001: 61). Therefore, she argues, needs analysis must be accompanied by rights analysis which is based on the understanding that academic rules and conventions are negotiable and that students have the right to participate in the academic community on a more democratic basis, and therefore to question these rules and conventions. In line with Academic Literacies, Critical EAP promotes a transformative agenda which raises awareness of power relations and inequalities (Morgan, 2009), and 'allows ESL teachers and students to examine externally imposed demands and negotiate their responses to them' (Benesch, 2001: 53). Linking EAP courses with content courses is a possible way of practising Critical EAP, according to Benesch. In this approach, the EAP classes would give students the time and space to make sense of the content and critically review materials and requirements.

English as an Academic Lingua Franca

English as an Academic Lingua Franca is branch of English as a Lingua Franca (ELF) which is concerned with the use of English among non-native speakers (often in communication with native-speakers) in academic settings (e.g. Mauranen, 2008). In her recent book, Jenkins (2014), a leading ELF scholar, makes a strong call for the transformation of English language policies and practices at so-called 'international' universities. As she points out, while many Anglophone universities market themselves as international in their drive to recruit large numbers of international students, there is little evidence of internationalisation in their English language requirements. Universities in the UK and US, as well as their offshore branches, remain remarkably monocultural and monolingual, expecting non-native speaker students to accommodate to Standard English and to 'native speaker' norms. Even English-medium universities in non-Anglophone regions insist on (North American or British) standard versions of English. In a website analysis of 60 English-medium universities around the world, Jenkins found that English language policies and practices in all institutions required conformity with native-like standards of academic English. These linguistic restrictions can have a harmful effect on international students' academic identity and self-esteem, as Jenkins' conversations with 34 postgraduate non-native speaker students revealed, in line with the findings of other researchers (e.g. Marshall, 2010; Ryan & Viete, 2009). In view of the fact that these universities pride themselves in being international, Jenkins argues that, 'if English is the language of *international* HE [higher education], it is not appropriate for it to be a *national* version of HE's Anglophone minority: in other words, not the kinds of English that North American or British people, academics or otherwise, use among themselves' (Jenkins, 2014: 206) (italics in original). She calls for the transformation of English language policies and practices towards a model that is appropriate to a lingua franca environment where 'the only criterion should be mutual intelligibility among the relevant academic community inside and outside the institution instead of blanket conformity to a particular version of native English' (Jenkins, 2014: 202). This transformation would require 'a change of mind-set' (Jenkins, 2014: 202) which would involve the enhancement of the intercultural awareness of staff and home students.

Multilingualism and language policy

While Jenkins argues for transformation in the interest of international students – the majority of whom are privileged in the sense that they can afford an English-medium education abroad – scholars in the field of multilingualism are more concerned with access to higher education by students from ethnic and linguistic minority backgrounds. From the large literature on multilingual students and academic literacy (e.g. Canagarajah, 2007; Preece & Martin, 2010; Thesen & van Pletzen, 2006), I will take a closer look here at two articles which demonstrate the need for a change in higher education policy and practice in the widening participation contexts of England and South Africa.

Simpson and Cooke (2010) describe the 'downwards trajectory' of a Nigerian migrant to the UK, who in his attempt to gain access to study law was prevented by various gatekeeping English language tests. Some of these tests were locally generated by the Further Education College where the student, who had already started a law degree in his home country, had been relegated to a low-prestige pre-access route typically offered to people from minority ethnic backgrounds. These tests largely focused on surface features such as grammar and spelling, and identified the student as a speaker of a 'low prestige variety of English' (Simpson & Cooke, 2010: 61). If the 'sustained attempt to orient students towards a normative standard variety of academic English' (Simpson & Cooke, 2010: 62) failed and students did not improve their written standard English in the generic, grammar-focused language classes, they were counselled out of their original aspirations and directed to lower career and educational paths by their class tutor. In Simpson and Cooke's case study, this 'sideway or downward movement' (Simpson & Cooke, 2010: 62) occurred to four out of 15 students in a pre-access class. The authors point out that UK universities invest heavily in attracting students from affluent international backgrounds, such as China, but ignore the academic literacy challenges of ethnic minority home students and keep them out by linguistic gatekeeping mechanisms.

Stroud and Kerfoot (2013) examine language policy at the University of the Western Cape (UWC), which was the first university with a non-racial open admission policy in South Africa's post-apartheid higher education system. This system is still marked by huge inequality with extremely low participation of coloured and black students, and with the success rate of black students being below 5%. The majority of students at UWC come from bi- or multilingual households, and despite the fact that in 2010 over 40% declared English as their first language, most do not have access to the variety of English expected at university. After earlier initiatives towards transformative language and literacy education, UWC reverted to predominantly remedial practices aimed at developing students' monolingual, that is, English, language proficiency, and maintained language policies that are multilingual on surface but use languages other than English 'purely as instruments of remediation' (Stroud & Kerfoot, 2013: 400). In order to respond adequately to the academic difficulties experienced by the majority of students, the authors argue that more is needed than conventional EAP programmes which in their view serve to maintain inequality. Instead, the authors call for a transformative language policy which questions monolingual norms. Such a policy would

> take voice, rather than language, as a starting point... focusing on *linguistic repertoires* rather than *languages*... on *practices* rather than *proficiency*... and on *translanguaging* rather than *codeswitching* in which students use multiple, multilingual discursive resources in achieving communicative aims. (Stroud & Kerfoot, 2013: 397, italics in original)

In other words, in a transformed curriculum that responds to the challenges, but also exploits the potential of diversity, students would be able to express their voice by drawing on all languages available to them. They would also be allowed to express themselves in new and more informal genres, for instance those afforded by social media, than previously accepted in academia. Lastly, teaching and learning would be enhanced through the use of multimodal resources, such as sound, images, and hypertext. These could afford easier access to knowledge than the conventional modes of semiosis in higher education (e.g. written and spoken texts) which benefit students from privileged educational backgrounds. While Stroud and Kerfoot proceed with concrete recommendations for transformation at the UWC, including multilingual tutors or multiple versions of lectures in different languages, their call for the recognition of students' linguistic repertoires as well as for the use of multimodal forms of communication clearly has currency for the inclusion of disadvantaged students in higher education worldwide.

Summary

Although coming from different perspectives, the scholars I referred to in this discussion broadly share two concerns. The first is the dominance of monolingual, normative language policies in Anglophone universities, which is itself based on a previous elite model which assumed a linguistically fairly homogeneous student population. The second is the expectation of one-directional accommodation to the conventions and norms; students are required to conform with the norms of the university, while universities make little effort in adapting educational practices in order to accommodate the needs of students with different linguistic, educational, and cultural backgrounds. In addition to the huge disadvantage at which some groups of students are put, the existing normativity and power relations also means that students are denied democratic participation in the academic community. Added to these concerns should be the fact that as a result of current policies, universities miss out on the opportunity to benefit from the rich linguistic and cultural resources of a diverse student body.

In summary, English-medium universities, although paying lip-service to widening participation, internationalisation and multilingualism, have been more or less continuing business as usual, preferring uniformity to diversity, and therefore perpetuating patterns of disadvantage and inequality. However, the transformation called for by the scholars cited above is unlikely to happen any time soon. It would involve fundamental changes in English language policies and practices, including access and admission, assessment and teaching. This in turn would require radical rethinking by university managers and teachers, and an agreement in the wider academic world, beyond individual institutions and individual disciplines, to loosen the sacrosanct standards and regulations of academic literacy. While this seems a distant and perhaps unachievable goal in view of the fact that there are valid arguments for adhering to standards, in the meantime it is important to find more appropriate ways of helping students to meet the expected academic literacy standards required by their discourse communities. As the following chapters will show, this goal in itself also requires substantial changes in current perceptions of literacy and diversity, as well as subsequent changes in instructional provision.

Note

(1) In the Further and Higher Education Act 1992, polytechnics in the UK were awarded university status.

4 Discipline-Specific Approaches to Academic Literacy Instruction

Introduction

In the previous chapter I presented the dominant model of academic literacy support in Anglophone universities, a model which is typically generic and taught in central units to students from various disciplines. Here, I discuss approaches which link literacy instruction to the discipline and subject curriculum, and are therefore more suited to help students with the literacy requirements in their immediate study context. The discussion consists of two main parts. The first deals with structural and organisational conditions for discipline-specific literacy instruction, namely the collaboration between writing experts and subject experts, and various levels of integration of literacy instruction into the curriculum. The second part is concerned with methods and materials used in discipline-specific literacy instruction; in that discussion I will consider the affordances of genre- and corpus-based approaches.

Collaboration and Integration

Various limitations inherent in the central provision of academic literacy instruction were discussed in Chapter 3. However, it is important to note that there is considerable variation in the ways central English language or learning development units operate. In some educational contexts, most notably in Australia and South Africa, central units have established productive relationships with academic departments and have achieved various levels of integration of literacy instruction into the subject curriculum. Evidently, the closer literacy instruction is linked to the regular subject teaching, the more inclusive it is, as it reaches all students in a cohort. As I will show below, the integration of literacy instruction into the curriculum, as well as its quality, is greatly facilitated by the collaboration between academics in the disciplines and writing experts.

Before I discuss the benefits of collaboration between writing and subject experts in more detail, I want to question the terms 'writing expert' or 'writing specialist' which are widely used in the literature in reference to staff in central units (e.g. Purser *et al.*, 2008), alongside 'EAP practitioner', 'literacy practitioner' and 'language teacher' (e.g. Dudley-Evans, 2001; Johns, 1997). The 'expertise' of staff engaged in the development of academic literacy is often a first degree in English (language, literature or both); in the US, as Beaufort (2007) explains, teachers on composition courses are often PhD students in English literature. Most English language centre staff in the UK would also have gained an English language teaching qualification and perhaps a Master's degree in applied linguistics. These qualifications alone do not make them 'writing experts', because, when they take up literacy development work, their only expertise comes from their own writing experience at university. If they do not seek information from, and cooperation with, academics from the disciplines for which they are tasked to provide literacy instruction, their teaching is likely to remain at a generic, grammar- and skills-oriented level. However, what EAP practitioners will have gained from their qualifications is the ability to analyse texts, identify linguistic and discursive features specific to genres and, subsequently, to help students to recognise these features. This is an ability that subject specialists usually do not have; nonetheless, these specialists can provide the EAP practitioner with access to discipline-specific texts, an awareness of the discipline's literacy conventions and some understanding of content. If the expertise of writing and subject specialists were drawn upon in a complementary fashion, this type of collaboration could lead to considerable improvements in discipline-specific literacy instruction.

Levels of collaboration

Some scholars, particularly those influenced by the Writing across the Curriculum (WAC) and Writing in the Disciplines (WiD) movements, have contended that subject lecturers should take larger responsibility for developing their students' academic literacy (e.g. Mitchell & Evison, 2006; Monroe 2003). The arguments in favour of this proposal are compelling: subject lecturers, unlike writing teachers, understand the content of students' writing and have expert knowledge of the discipline's discourses. Furthermore, subject lecturers are usually the ones who set assignments and assess students' writing, and part of this role is to provide explicit guidance and feedback. However, as I explained in Chapter 3, subject specialists often have only a 'tacit' understanding of the discipline's discourses and literacy conventions (Jacobs, 2005: 477); as a result, the guidance and particularly the feedback they provide may not have the necessary clarity, or indeed the information that student need to improve their performance. While inadequate guidance and feedback lead to common misunderstandings between lecturers and students concerning literacy requirements (Lea & Street, 1998; see also Chapter 6 for a discussion of 'mismatches'), this situation could be greatly improved if subject lecturers collaborated with writing experts.

There are different levels at which writing experts can work with subject lecturers, as Dudley-Evans and St John (1998) explain. The first level, which they call 'cooperation', means that the writing teacher gathers from the subject lecturer in-depth information about the discipline's discourse conventions and relevant genres. Equipped with this information, the writing expert can then analyse key texts and prepare teaching materials. At the second level, 'collaboration', writing and subject expert jointly prepare teaching sessions – to be delivered by the writing expert- with the intention of helping students with challenging academic tasks, for instance note-taking during lectures. At the level of 'team-teaching', subject and writing specialist deliver joint classroom sessions. The writing expert often prepares the materials and leads the discussion in the teaching sessions, while the subject lecturer initially advises on the materials development, and then answers subject-specific questions in the sessions. Dudley-Evans and St John see these three types as stages, and explain how writing teachers can gradually develop a working relationship with subject teachers, which helps them to move from cooperation to team-teaching. In the instructional approach that I will present in Chapter 7, we used the team-teaching format which encapsulated the previous two stages of cooperation and collaboration. To avoid confusion, I will refer to all joint activities between writing and subject experts as 'collaboration' in this book, using it as an overarching term; this use is also widespread in the literature.

Collaboration opens opportunities for integrating literacy instruction into the curriculum, and this integration in turn facilitates an inclusive approach to literacy instruction. I would argue that the higher degrees of collaboration and integration are, the more could the limitations attached to central and generic provision (see the discussion in Chapter 3) be reduced. The current trivialisation of academic literacy and the marginalisation of writing experts would considerably decrease when language and literacy are given attention in the subject curriculum and when writing experts teach alongside academics in the department. The exclusive targeting of specific learner groups disappears when writing instruction becomes part of a study programme and thus inclusive of all students on that programme. Finally, the collaboration between writing and subject teachers ensures a fairer distribution of responsibilities.

The degree of involvement of subject lecturers in academic literacy instruction is often closely related to the degree to which the instruction is integrated into the subject curriculum. Examples of different types and levels of integration are considered next.

Levels of integration

The levels at which academic literacy instruction can be linked to the subject curriculum range from independent learning formats, that is, resources which students of a study programme can access electronically or in handbooks, to workshops that are offered by the study programme on a voluntary basis, and to the embedding of instructional methods into the subject teaching. The highest level of integration is reached when academic literacy development becomes part of a credit-bearing module within the degree programme; this level represents a fully inclusive approach to literacy instruction. The various levels are presented in Table 4.1, which also includes, for comparison, the extra-curricular, generic model of literacy instruction.

The extra-curricular, generic model has been discussed in some detail in Chapter 3. Here, I offer examples of the other three models. The first examples come from a series of three studies which I carried out in a university in England to assess the effectiveness of different types of discipline-specific academic literacy support (Wingate, 2010, 2011, 2012a). The second set of examples comes from Australian and South African universities, where curriculum-linked models have made a wider impact.

The three approaches I evaluated represented different degrees of integration as well as collaboration, which I called 'additional', 'partly embedded' and 'fully embedded' provision. 'Additional' literacy support, although discipline-specific, is characterised by low involvement of the subject experts. While they may contribute texts and some insights into disciplinary practices and conventions, the main responsibility for materials development and teaching is carried by the writing expert (i.e. the 'cooperation' level in Dudley-Evans and St John's terms). Another characteristic of additional writing support is that student participation is voluntary and not monitored or even noticed by their subject lecturers. The additional provision in my study

Table 4.1 Types of academic literacy development

Increasing levels of integration →

Type	Extra-curricular	Additional	Curriculum-linked	Curriculum-integrated
Location	**Outside department** English Language/Skills/ Learning development unit	**Outside timetable** Extra resources: • Online courses • Print materials	**Timetabled** • Workshops • Presentations in designated teaching sessions	**Timetabled, credit-bearing** Assessed component of content modules
Delivery	EAP teachers	Independent (EAP teachers)	• Subject lecturers • EAP teachers	• Subject lecturers • EAP teachers
Collaboration	None	Some input from subject lecturers	Equal contribution to design and delivery	Input/advice from EAP teachers
Focus	Grammar, lexis, style, structure, referencing	• Literacy conventions • Genres • Text features	• Literacy conventions • Genres • Text features • Argumentation	• Literacy conventions • Genres • Text features • Language for the creation of meaning and knowledge
Materials	**Unspecific** General/pseudo-academic texts	**Subject-specific** Texts/tasks from the discipline	**Subject-specific** Texts/task directly linked to classroom content	**Subject-specific** Texts/task directly linked to classroom content
Participation	**Exclusive/Remedial** • International students • Students with difficulties	**Semi-inclusive** Available to all students/ voluntary	**Semi-inclusive** Available to all students/ voluntary	**Fully inclusive** Part of regular teaching, learning and assessment

consisted of an online academic writing and reading course[2] specifically developed for first-year undergraduate students of a Management programme. Staff members of the Management department had provided materials such as course handbooks, student essays and journal articles. The online course was an 'add-on' to the curriculum in the sense that students were expected to make use of it in their spare time. The course was recommended by a Management lecturer during induction week, and students were given a worksheet with instructions how to access it. Following this brief introduction, the course was not referred to by lecturers in the regular subject classes, although a few recommended it to struggling students as a remedial tool. The evaluation of the online course over a number of years showed clearly that the lack of interest and involvement by subject lecturers resulted in a low uptake. Only about a quarter of the cohorts logged in at all, and the number of repeated log-ins decreased sharply after the first weeks of the term. Responses in questionnaires and interviews revealed that most students were unwilling to spend time on not-credit bearing activities, and that weaker students in particular, who would have most needed support with academic writing, saw this provision as unhelpful, because they could not add extra work to their already great pressures (Wingate, 2011, 2012a).

The second type of support was partly embedded or 'curriculum-linked' (see Table 4.1). It consisted of workshops offered in various disciplines which were team-taught by subject and writing teachers and offered to all students in specific study programmes (Tribble & Wingate, 2013). This provision, which I will explain in more detail in Chapter 7, was highly specific to student needs, as instruction was based on student texts representing the genres that are relevant in their programme. The relevance of the materials as well as the presence of subject teachers in the workshops resulted in high levels of participation (60–80% of the cohorts took part, although participation was voluntary), and very positive student evaluations. Students particularly appreciated the fact that the workshops afforded opportunities for assessment-related discussions with the subject tutor for which there was little space in the regular curriculum. Although this type of instruction was popular with students and therefore the workshops were well attended, its voluntary nature means that it is not fully inclusive. The workshops were timetabled events in the students' programme handbook, but not assessed or credit-bearing. This again might have left out those students who, although most in need of literacy support, felt too pressured to attend.

The third approach I evaluated broadly represents the curriculum-integrated type outlined in Table 4.1. The support consisted of reading and writing instruction which was fully embedded in a first-year content module of an undergraduate programme in Applied Linguistics. The subject lecturers integrated various instructional methods into the regular teaching sessions, including the analysis of texts and identification of discourse features, group reading and writing tasks, the analysis of arguments, as well as formative feedback which was given to students on increasingly larger and complex pieces of writing throughout the term. This initiative fulfilled the criteria for inclusivity: academic literacy was part of the regular subject teaching and assessment, and as such included the whole first-year cohort. It was also successful in the sense that it was positively evaluated by the students, and resulted in improvements in most students' writing (Wingate, 2010). Nevertheless, the drawback in this particular initiative was that it was planned and carried out entirely by subject lecturers without contributions by writing experts from the central unit, resulting in unsustainable workloads, as well as in a lack of long-term planning. Thus, the instruction was confined to one first-term module, when clearly many students in the cohort would have benefited from extended training. Also, an approach driven entirely by subject lecturers would be unrealistic in other contexts, because not only does it rely on the willingness of subject lecturers to invest considerable amounts of time, but it also requires explicit knowledge of the discipline's genres and their textual features. While this knowledge was available to lecturers in Applied Linguistics, it is, as discussed previously, usually not available to experts in other disciplines. In the initiative described here, collaboration between subject lecturers and writing teachers would have been useful in that the increased workload could have been shared; moreover, writing teachers might have been helpful in identifying literacy development opportunities in the broader curriculum and ensuring that literacy instruction was sustained beyond the first term. As shall be seen later, this curriculum-related advice has been provided by writing/learning experts to faculties in Australian universities.

Curriculum integration as an inclusive approach to academic literacy development

The curriculum-integrated approach (see Table 4.1) makes academic literacy instruction inclusive of all students, because the development of academic literacy is a timetabled – and ideally an accredited – part of the curriculum. It also removes the stigma of 'remedy' that is attached to the currently dominant models of literacy and learning support. However, the curriculum-integrated approach is rarely taken in English-medium universities, and implementing it would require a mind change among university managers and academic staff as well as considerable structural changes at the institutional level. These would involve the decentralisation of literacy instruction and the attachment of writing experts to faculties or departments. Currently, although several initiatives in collaboration and integration in Anglophone universities have been reported (e.g. Morley, 2008; Foster & Deane, 2011 for some UK examples; Percy & Skillen, 2000; Dovey, 2010 for examples from Australia; and Thesen & van Pletzen, 2006; Archer, 2012 for examples from South Africa), many represent the efforts of individuals or small groups which have not made an impact beyond, or sometimes even within, the institution. However, in some contexts, for instance in a number of Australian and in South African universities, the impact has been wider, reaching institutional or even national policy level.

Examples from Australia

Academic literacy support at Australian universities is, as in the other Anglophone countries, predominantly provided through central units, which in most universities are called Academic Language and Learning (ALL) units. The role of these units has been strengthened by the Australian government's commitment to improving the standards of teaching and learning in higher education. This commitment is evident in the recently published Higher Education Standards Framework (TEQSA, 2011) which requires universities to provide 'orientation courses and transition support' as well as 'ongoing academic language and learning support' (paragraph 6.5).

While ALL units are physically located outside the mainstream curricula, and had initially offered remedial teaching formats such as one-to-one advice and generic skills courses, since the 1990s the units have worked increasingly closer with the academic disciplines (Arkoudis & Starfield, 2007). Much of the work was initiated at the University of Wollongong (Percy & Skillen, 2000) where a 'transformative model' (Skillen, 2006: 140) of integrating academic language and study skills into the disciplines was developed. This model, called 'collaborative, curriculum-integrated literacy instruction' (Purser, 2011: 30), is based on the premises that all students are unfamiliar with the special variety of the academic English used in their discipline, that explicit instruction will aid them best in learning the necessary genres and conventions, and that the instruction should not be 'peripheral but central to study in the disciplines' (Skillen, 2006: 141). The main aim of the model is to support student learning in general, and academic writing as part of it (Purser et al., 2008), which is evident in the units' name, and in the typical job designation of staff working in these units as 'learning developers'.

One aim of this transformative approach is making the role of language in academic learning visible and 'helping teachers across the disciplines recognise the linguistic nature of academic learning and teaching' (Purser,

2011: 34). The collaboration of learning developers with subject specialists is therefore not just concerned with the creation of instructional resources or workshops, i.e. the cooperation level as described by Dudley-Evans and St John (1998). It also goes beyond Dudley-Evans and St John's understanding of 'collaboration' in which writing experts are invited to departments to deliver writing classes to students (Percy & Skillen, 2000). The aim of collaboration is, as Purser et al. (2008) explain, to 'make specific changes in teaching and learning practices so that student learning is better understood and supported'. Skillen (2006: 144) explains that this approach involves 'the Learning Developer in more than the teaching of writing, and the subject lecturers in more than the teaching of their subject content'. Collaboration involves changes in the curriculum which ensure the inclusion of literacy support, as well as the revision of assessment practices which ensure that literacy issues are considered as part of the learning objectives. In the case of the University of Wollongong, learning developers joined the faculties' education committees, and also became visible and accepted teaching colleagues in the departments (Percy & Skillen, 2000). Following the example of Wollongong, collaborative curriculum-integrated literacy instruction has been increasingly implemented at other universities in Australia (Purser, 2011). There is also a trend at Australian universities to include into degree programmes credit-bearing core subjects concerned with academic and professional communication (Dovey, 2010). Publications in the journal of the Australian Association for Academic Language and Learning over the last few years bear witness to the increase in collaborative and integrative activities (e.g. Harris & Ashton, 2011; Thies, 2012). The crucial role of the language and learning units in embedding literacy development in the disciplines and raising academics' awareness of the importance of language and literacy work has been widely acknowledged in Australia (e.g. Candy et al., 1995; Threadgold et al., 1997).

According to Purser (2011), the recognition that academic literacy needs to be developed within the curriculum has also reached the national policy level in Australia. This is evidenced in the 'good practice principles' for developing the English language proficiency of international students (Department of Education, Employment and Workplace Relations , 2009, cited in Purser 2011: 32), and in the Higher Education Standards Framework issued by TEQSA (2011). The 'good practice principles' in particular put strong emphasis on integrating the development of academic language and learning into the mainstream curricula in the disciplines. To my knowledge, Australia is the only country where curriculum-integrated academic literacy instruction has become more widely endorsed at the institutional level, and has influenced nation-wide higher educational policy. This approach has emerged in response to student diversity and the large number of students who are non-native speakers of English in the Australian tertiary system (Dovey, 2010). Due to immigration and widening participation policies, Australian universities have the largest number of international students within the OECD (Arkoudis et al., 2012), and a large number of non-traditional students. Although universities in countries such as the UK and the US come close in terms of student diversity, they have so far not responded to the academic literacy needs of their diverse student populations in the same way as Australian universities. In Australia, government initiatives go even further as measures have been introduced to enhance and test graduates' language and communication skills in order to give all students a fair chance in the employment market (Arkoudis et al., 2012).

What I found missing from the literature on literacy development in Australian higher education was an account of the teaching approaches taken (e.g. process, genre, social practice; see Chapter 2). Authors writing from the perspective of learning developers such as Skillen and Purser are concerned with students' overall learning development of which literacy is only one aspect (Purser et al., 2008). It is also not revealed in their publications which linguistic theory underpins the curriculum-integrated literacy instruction offered in Australian universities. It is rather surprising that there is no reference in these publications to systemic-functional linguistics and the Sydney School's genre-based literacy pedagogy, given the influence these frameworks had at all levels of the Australian educational system.

Examples from South Africa

As a result of decades of racial segregation and stark social inequality, student diversity in the South African higher education system poses an even greater challenge than in other Anglophone countries. Despite the widening participation objectives of the 1998 Higher Education Act and the massive increase in the National Student Financial Aid scheme, access and progression of underprivileged student groups remains poor. Participation of coloured and black students is extremely low, partly as a result of the dysfunctional school system (Soudien, 2007). As Stroud and Kerfoot (2013) explain, the overall enrolment of underprivileged students in HE is 16%, as compared with up to 60% in developed countries. Of this ratio, only 12% are black or coloured students, and of these the success rate is below 5%. Examining language policies and practices at the University of the Western Cape (UWC), an institution committed to the inclusion of underprivileged students, the authors argue that the current provision remains remedial. Their point is that the university's inclusion policies are based on the principle of monolingualism and the attempt to compensate for a lack of proficiency in (academic) English. Stroud and Kerfoot argue (as do other scholars who promote transformation, see the discussion in Chapter 3) that inclusive language policies need to build on the recognition of students' multilingual and multimodal repertoires. However, these changes in policy are a somewhat distant goal, as they require a fundamental reconceptualisation of academic literacy that would need to occur in a context much wider than the UWC. Even if the use of multimodal forms of literacy and of various languages for the construction of meaning in academic discourse were to be sanctioned in the UWC, students and scholars of that institution would be isolated if this new form of literacy was not accepted in the wider academic world. As this kind of transformation is unlikely to happen soon, in the meantime universities need to develop practices that help students to succeed despite the existing monolingual policies. At some South African universities, student support has been enhanced through the collaboration of writing experts with staff in the disciplines, as well as through the integration of literacy in the curriculum.

Academic development units were developed in South African universities from the 1980s in an effort to address social inequality and cater for disadvantaged students (Archer, 2012). Best known internationally because of its research and publications profile is the Language Development Group (LDG) in the Centre for Higher Education Development at the University of Cape Town. As Thesen and van Pletzen (2006: 7) explain, 'development' in the name of the centre implies the 'recognition of the imperative to focus on systemic change across the university, rather than on designing fragile bridges for 'non-traditional' students'. The LDG has, from the beginning, rejected a remedial approach of offering EAP to linguistically disadvantaged students and emphasised partnership with departments, staff development, and the integration of academic literacy teaching in the disciplines. The group's website (UCT, 2013) shows that literacy instruction has been embedded in the Humanities, Engineering, Health Sciences, Commerce and the General Entry Programme in Science. LDG members choose a faculty or department for collaboration and develop a long-term working relationship with the departments. They teach in mainstream modules, offer tailored literacy courses and help with curriculum design in a fashion very similar to the Australian approach discussed earlier. The long-term involvement with specific disciplines provides staff from the LDC with an understanding of the disciplinary culture and discourses, and to a certain extent perhaps of the subject, and facilitates discipline-specific literacy instruction (see for instance Paxton, 2007, 2011, who worked for many years with the economics department).

Particularly innovative is the work of the Writing Centre which is attached to the LDG. Apart from providing specific workshops for departments, the

Centre offers a walk-in service to students from all disciplines where they can receive one-to-one advice on their writing. To avoid the typical de-contextualised and remedial nature of this provision, the Centre trains, on an annual basis, postgraduate students from ten disciplines to become consultants. This model has a number of advantages, as Archer (2012) describes: the Centre can provide discipline-specific advice to students from these ten disciplines, creates 'a vibrant cross-disciplinary intellectual community' (Archer, 2012: 355), and is cost-effective. The most 'transformative' aspect of the model is that it develops 'future academics who are attuned to the academic literacy practices of their disciplines' (Archer, 2012: 361). According to Archer, a substantial number of the consultants subsequently entered academic positions. Whilst the walk-in provision is very popular with students and, according to Archer's evaluation, effective in enhancing students' understanding of literacy conventions, it is an exclusive provision, dependent on (irregular) funding and the engagement of academic staff in the disciplines. As Archer (personal conversation) explained, there is a booking system and many students have to be turned away.

Summary

In the UK, I am aware of only one university, Middlesex, where collaborative and curriculum-integrated literacy instruction has been implemented across the institution (Lazar & Ellis, 2012; Middlesex University, 2013; Thomas, 2013); however, this lack of awareness may stem from the fact that other examples have not been reported in publications.

So far, I have looked at structural and organisational conditions for literacy instruction and considered how collaboration and integration facilitates discipline-specific literacy development. In the next sections, I discuss methods and content of literacy instruction.

Genre-Based Literacy Instruction

In Chapter 2, I presented genre approaches to literacy instruction and argued that work with texts and genres should be at the centre of literacy pedagogies. Genre-based literacy instruction[3] means that the features that are characteristic of a genre, as well as the link between these features and their social functions, are made visible and are explicitly taught to learners. In this section, I look at examples of genre-based literacy instruction. A useful overview of empirical studies concerned with learners' genre acquisition is provided in Tardy's (2006) meta-analysis. In addition, I will also refer to more recent studies, as well as some studies which were not considered by Tardy because she focused mainly on the North American context.

Of the 60 studies analysed by Tardy, 47 examined genre learning in practice-based, natural settings, whilst only 13 studies investigated instructional contexts. This imbalance resonates with the dominance in North America of the Rhetorical Genre Studies (RGS) model which questions explicit teaching and maintains that genre knowledge is acquired through participation in the community of practice (see the discussion in Chapter 2). As Tardy points out, despite repeated calls for the need to provide more empirical evidence of the benefits of genre instruction, studies which are not theoretical or anecdotal, but data-driven, remain sparse. Of the 13 studies into instructional contexts, 11 were carried out in higher education. Tardy groups the findings from these studies into five categories; of these, I draw only on 'Textual modelling' and 'Explicit instruction' as the most relevant for this context, leaving out findings concerned with prior experience, transferability, and dimensions of genre knowledge. However, Tardy's separation of textual modelling from explicit instruction, whilst perhaps plausible in her classification of themes, is less plausible in a pedagogical sense, as arguably modelling should be part of explicit instruction. To illustrate this point, I first discuss one of the 'modelling' studies presented by Tardy, and then examine types of models and methods of modelling which are regarded as successful in literacy instruction.

Studies into textual modelling

Textual modelling means giving learners access to examples of the genres relevant to their disciplinary study. Research has aimed at establishing how the analysis of models influences students' reading and writing performance. The three experimental studies presented by Tardy in this category all found exposure to models to have positive effects on student writing. In Charney and Carlson's (1995) research, undergraduate psychology majors were given models for writing a methods section of an experiment. The authors found that this exposure had a positive impact on the content and organisation of the participants' own texts. The other two studies arrived at similar findings. For instance, Henry and Roseberry (1998) provided six hours of genre-based instruction, including the analysis of models, to L2 management students in Brunei, and found improvements in cohesion and coherence in students' subsequent writing. These findings, however, have to be treated with caution, because, as Tardy points out, there are some methodological shortcomings in the three studies, among them the shortness of instruction and the lack of evidence of long-term effects.

In my view, further shortcomings are the absence in these papers of a proper conceptualisation of 'model' and 'modelling'. The lack of consideration of which type of model, and which method of using models, might be most suitable for genre learning is best shown in Charney and Carlson's research. In the first place, the authors do not offer a rationale for using student rather than expert texts as models; this choice seems to have been made for convenience rather than for pedagogical motives. Furthermore, the models were inauthentic: they consisted of student texts which were manipulated by the researchers to fit them in the quality categories of high, intermediate and low-achieving examples. As a result, they may have been misleading to students, because they did not reflect the real assessment processes and outcomes. The way in which the models were used in the experiment is also debatable, as the students were merely exposed to them. They were given limited time to review the models immediately before writing their own texts, and could then refer to the models during writing. No specific instruction was given, but the authors 'hoped to discover how much students could achieve on their own using various kinds of models' (1995: 113). The assumption that students could develop genre knowledge just by seeing models for a limited time seems naïve. Given the flaws in this study's design and underlying assumptions, it is not surprising that 'the results indicate that models do not have automatic benefits for the writing process' (1995: 111).

It is unlikely that genre learning can be 'automatic', based on mere exposure to models, and it seems therefore more promising to use models for detailed analysis in the classroom. In the next sections, I consider which type of model is most suitable, and which methods are most suitable for using models in genre-based literacy pedagogy.

Types of models

Swales' (1981, 1990) influential move analysis of introductions in research articles led to the wide-spread use of expert texts in genre-based literacy classrooms. An example for this approach is the well-known academic writing textbook for graduate students by Swales and Feak (2012), where the tasks are based on extracts from research articles. While the research article may be a genre to which graduate students aspire, it is less suitable as a model for students at the undergraduate or postgraduate (i.e. Masters in the UK higher education system) levels. Students at these levels are required to produce genres that are rather different from expert genres (such as the 'essay'; see Nesi & Gardner, 2012 for an in-depth account). Expert and student genres usually have entirely different communicative purposes. Many student genres serve the purpose of 'knowledge-telling' (Bereiter & Scardamalia, 1987), while expert genres aim to expand knowledge in the field. Since genre approaches aim to make visible the link between a genre's linguistic features and communicative function, genre instruction based on texts written for a different purpose and audience is unsatisfactory. As Hüttner (2008: 152) asserts, a discourse community 'is essentially the community of users of particular genres'. Therefore the discourse community for student genres are the student writers as well as the lecturers who assess their assignments, and the communicative purpose of these genres may be limited to fulfilling the assessment criteria. Hüttner (2008) argues for a methodology of analysis of student genres that is different from that proposed by Bathia (1993) for expert genres (see Chapter 2 for the stages of analysis proposed by Bathia). The steps she proposes for the analysis and teaching of student genres will be discussed in Chapter 7, as they relate closely to the instructional approach presented there.

Methods of genre teaching

The rationale behind both linguistic genre approaches, ESP and the Sydney School/SFL, is that the identification of a genre's specific features aids the development of specific teaching materials and units which aim to help students to produce these genres. However, the inherent problem of these approaches is that they can be prescriptive and normative, and this problem is linked to the way in which models are presented. Earlier EAP teaching tended to use genre models as prescriptive templates, based on the notion that a genre is a monolithic form of communication in stable disciplines (Kress, 2007). The same problem was identified in relation to the Sydney School/SFL's approach in which the key genres tend to be 'viewed as relatively fixed and prototypical for certain contexts in the dominant culture' (Johns, 2011: 61). In the teaching of these genres, their formulaic features are often presented to be memorised by learners, a method which turns literacy instruction into a 'linear transmission pedagogy' (Cope & Kalantzis, 1993: 13). There has certainly been a trend in academic writing courses and materials which purport to be genre-based to overgeneralise, and to reduce the findings of genre analysis into templates. The templates typically offered in these EAP approaches would be either a set of rules, or authoritative model texts from which the rules could be deduced. There is evidence that this pedagogy of transmission is still continuing in contemporary EAP units (see Turner, 2004 for a discussion of EAP's teaching to the test). The potentially normative nature of the linguistic genre approaches has been criticised on various fronts (see the discussion in Chapter 2).

The danger of prescriptivism has been addressed by a number of genre researchers and practitioners. Swales warned from the beginning against the use of 'rigid templates against which all texts are forced to fit' (1990: 213). He stressed the importance of raising students' consciousness of typical rhetorical structures rather than telling them how to write the genre. His argument has been strongly enforced by Johns (2002, 2011), an RGS scholar, who distinguishes between genre acquisition and genre awareness. Where genre acquisition is the goal of teaching, students learn to reproduce a text type from fixed text formats; as a result, students are only able to do 'low road transfer', that is, to apply the learned skills to a very similar context. By contrast, instruction that aims at genre awareness helps students to gain 'the rhetorical flexibility necessary for adapting their socio-cognitive genre knowledge to ever-evolving contexts' (2008: 238), that is, the ability for 'high road transfer'. Furthermore, genre awareness enables students to recognise genres as constantly evolving socially situated forms of communication, and texts as 'problem-spaces open to critique and challenge' (Johns, 2011: 61). Along with other RGS scholars, Johns recommends that genre-based instruction should encourage students to become researchers or ethnographers in the community where the genre is situated. This 'socioliterate approach' (Johns, 1997) involves exploring the social context of the discipline before analysing the associated genres. An excellent example of this approach is described by Motta-Roth (2009). Her teaching of academic literacy to graduate students at a Brazilian university is informed by systemic-functional linguistics and aims at raising awareness of the close link between specific contexts and genres. Unlike the Sydney School/SLF, and in line with the RGS approach, however, she asks students to analyse the context of a genre first. Based on a set of exploratory questions, students carry out ethnographic investigations of the social practices of the discourse community before they work with texts. This exploration equips students with a deep understanding of the nature of genres they have to produce. Ethnographic research has been used in various contexts (see Johns *et al.*, 2006), involving observations, interviews with academics, as well as the exploration of the physical sites of genre production, as proposed in Swales' (1998) 'textography'.

When it comes to the analysis and production of texts, the concept of 'scaffolding' has been influential in genre-based literacy teaching. The concept is based on socio-cultural theories, originating from Vygotsky's (1978) work on child cognition, which explain learning as the outcome of social interaction and collaboration. Scaffolding means that learners receive support by teachers or peers in the earlier stages of learning, and that the support is gradually withdrawn when the learner reaches a level of competence that allows independent learning (Bruner, 1978). The Sydney School/SFL's teaching/

learning cycle (Rothery, 1996; Martin, 1999) is probably the most widely used application of scaffolding. The cycle consists of three phases. In the first, the modelling or deconstruction phase, teacher and students analyse, on the basis of model texts, the genre's context and social purposes as well as its rhetorical patterns and linguistic features. In the second phase, called joint construction, the teacher and student collaboratively work on a text, using the insights from the first stage to produce an acceptable version of the genre. The third phase, independent construction, requires students to apply the knowledge gained from the previous phases to the writing of their own texts. The teaching/learning cycle is meant to be flexible, allowing access to any of the three phases at the point of need (Drury, 2004), and anticipating further feedback by teachers or peers on the outcomes of phase 3, independent construction. The cycle underpinned genre-based literacy pedagogy in the Sydney School/SFL's literacy projects in primary and secondary education, for instance the Disadvantaged School Program and LERN. Although it seems to be collaborative, concerns have been raised about the prescriptive use of texts in the modelling phase (Kress, 2003) which 'involves no less than telling students how they should write' (Cope & Kalantzis, 1993: 15). Cope and Kalantzis describe the teaching/learning cycle as a process in which the modelling phase presents a 'predetermined generic structure' that is subsequently internalised by the learners in the joint construction phase, and which ends in the assessment of how well the learners can realise this predetermined structure in their writing. Therefore, in Cope and Kalantzis' view, the cycle imagery which suggests that the cycle can be accessed at any phase 'belies the fact that the underlying pedagogical process is linear' (Cope & Kalantzis, 1993: 15). Despite this critique, the cycle continues to be widely used and was also adopted in higher education (e.g. Ellis, 2004; Rose et al., 2008).

Scaffolding is a prominent feature of genre teaching in the Sydney School/SFL and ESP. Hyland (2007: 160) describes group work as a typical form of scaffolding in which peers collaborate to explore the key features of a genre. This activity, according to Hyland, aids students' development of rhetorical consciousness. In literacy instruction to children, writing frames are often used to scaffold the learning of a new genre. These frames provide the structure and cohesive devices as a framework in which the learner fills the content (Wray & Lewis, 1997).

Corpus-Informed Literacy Instruction

Corpus linguistics has over the last three decades become an influential field within descriptive linguistics. Traditionally, corpus linguistics has been the computer-based quantitative examination of large collections of texts. As Stubbs (2009: 2) points out in an acknowledgement of John Sinclair's pioneering role in corpus linguistics, through technology,

> it becomes possible to observe patterns of language use which are otherwise invisible. Sinclair is one of the very few linguists who has discovered many things which people had simply not noticed, despite thousands of years of textual study – because they are observable only with the help of computer techniques which he helped to invent.

The large-scale analysis of texts has typically been concerned with phraseological trends and lexico-grammatical patterns, for instance collocations and the co-occurrence of specific lexical items with grammatical forms (L. Flowerdew, 1998). This descriptive work has led to considerable pedagogic contributions, such as the Cobuild English Grammar (1990) and the Cobuild English Dictionary (1995) which were based on the Collins Birmingham University International Database, later called the Bank of English, a corpus of over 200 million words of authentic contemporary English (Sinclair, 1991).

Limitations of corpus approaches

Doubts have been expressed over the lack of a theoretical framework in place before findings of corpus analysis are analysed, which, according to Grabe and Kaplan (1996), gives corpus research a post-hoc nature. Further doubts are concerned with the pedagogical applications to language pedagogy which were called 'indirect' by L. Flowerdew (2012). Pedagogic applications are indirect when corpus data are used to inform syllabus design as well as reference and teaching materials; by contrast, 'direct' applications involve 'data-driven learning' (DDL) when students are guided to discover typical language use and rules through the exploration of corpus data (L. Flowerdew, 2012: 197). These applications will be discussed later.

A major critique relates to claims that corpus data represent authentic language as 'an authoritative basis' for pedagogic interventions (Widdowson, 2000: 5). The mode of enquiry of corpus linguistics, so Widdowson points out, can only provide a partial view of language, because 'it can only analyse the textual traces of the process whereby meaning is achieved: it cannot account for the complex interplay of linguistic and contextual factors whereby discourse is enacted' (Widdowson, 2000: 7). Because corpus-produced accounts of language decontextualise texts for the sake of revealing frequency of occurrences in lexical and grammatical patterns, they are, according to Widdowson, detrimental if they are used to determine the content of language teaching. This decontextualised language, so Widdowson argues, must then be, in very different contextual conditions, 'contextually reconstituted in the classroom for their reality to be realised' (Widdowson, 2000: 7). Swales (2002: 151) also warned of the limitations of corpus linguistics 'working from small-stretch surface forms and then trying to fit these into some larger contextual framework'. In order to understand a genre, Swales explains, a process is needed 'which starts from macro features and only *later* tries to align these with particular linguistic realisations, and *then* looks for explanatory links between the macro and the micro' (Swales, 2002: 152; italics in original). Thus, Swales promotes, and provides examples of, corpus use that is driven by specific pedagogic needs, 'rather than out of a research project per se' (Swales, 2002: 158).

Complementary use of discourse- and corpus analysis

Since the 1990s, however, there has been a 'gradual coming-together' (Charles *et al.,* 2009: 4) of discourse and corpus analysis which had previously been regarded as opposing approaches. This came as the result of the development of small and specialised corpora in the area of ESP/EAP and the recognition that the complementary use of both approaches greatly facilitates contrastive research. Early on in this process, L. Flowerdew (1998: 541) had pointed out that small specialised corpora were needed and that these had to be analysed at a more textlinguistic level, 'if corpus linguistics is to develop further its "applied" aspect and potential for exploitation'. Some examples of specialised corpora of written academic discourse are those of published articles (e.g. Hyland, 1998) and different types of student writing such as that of non-native speaker undergraduate students in eight different fields (L. Flowerdew, 2008; Milton & Hyland, 1999), or MPhil and doctoral theses in the disciplines of politics/international relations and materials science (Charles, 2006). Typically, learner corpora have been compared with reference or expert corpora to identify novices' shortcomings in academic writing. Examples are the comparison of citational practices of apprentice writers and those of published writers (Thompson & Tribble, 2001) and the use of lexical bundles between expert published and apprentice writing (Hyland, 2008b).

A large number of corpus- and discourse-analytical studies into academic writing have revealed variations in language use between native and non-native speakers of English (e.g. Granger, 1998; Hyland & Milton, 1997), and different disciplines and genres (e.g. Charles, 2006; Harwood, 2005; Hyland, 2008b; Nesi & Gardner, 2012). Biber (1988) developed the corpus approach of multidimensional analysis to reveal statistically relevant differences in linguistic and rhetorical patterns across different genres and disciplines. A particular focus of complementary research, based on genre theories, has been on interpersonal features, namely how writers engage with their readers, a focus which has been addressed under the labels hedging (Hyland, 1998), evaluation (Hunston & Thompson, 2000), appraisal (Martin & White, 2005) or metadiscourse (Hyland, 2005).

Several edited volumes in recent years have advocated the integration of corpus and discourse approaches (e.g. Ädel & Reppen, 2008; Biber *et al.*, 2007). Charles *et al.* (2009) regard the two approaches as constituting a continuum and situate the fourteen papers presented in their edited volume at different positions on that continuum, according to their methodologies. An example of a discourse-oriented paper in this volume is that by J. Flowerdew and Forest who applied corpus techniques to the move analysis[4] of literature reviews of PhD theses in Applied Linguistics in order to examine typical linguistic patterns in the generic moves. These author's approach is hailed as valuable by Swales (2009: 293) because it moves 'from quantification, to explication, and then to revelation'. However, Swales maintains that 'we will often see that it is typically somewhat easier for discourse analysts to incorporate corpus linguistics than for corpus linguists to expand their textual horizons to encompass the discoursal plane' (2009: 294).

It is beyond the scope of this chapter to give justice to the large body of corpus-linguistic studies that have contributed to the understanding of disciplinary discourses and specific genres. In the final section, therefore, I will focus on the direct pedagogic applications of corpus analysis.

Direct pedagogic applications of corpus analysis

As explained earlier, in direct applications, or data-driven learning (DDL), students are given access to corpus data to enable them to explore specific features of the target genre. Tribble (2002: 145) has recommended a 'corpus-informed' pedagogic approach in which the linguistically-oriented analysis of corpus data is used as a complementary method or an extension of the preceding 'contextual' analysis (called 'top-down' by Swales, 2002). While the latter focuses on the features of individual, whole texts and the social context and communicative purpose of the genre, the corpus analysis looks at typical lexico-grammatical features and textual patterning across a range of texts that represent the target genre. This complementary approach is taken by Charles (2007) who begins academic writing classes for graduate students with discourse analysis tasks which aim to raise awareness of certain rhetorical functions. Following this, students investigate the pattern and the typical contexts in which it appears in two small corpora of MPhil/PhD theses. In relation to the type of corpus suitable for EAP instruction,

Tribble (1996) and Granger and Tribble (1998) have advocated the use of learner corpora for the development of teaching materials in order to give students insights into the very genres they have to produce. Particularly useful is the comparison of expert (exemplar) and apprentice corpora, which helps students as well as materials developers to identify performance gaps and learning needs (Tribble, 2011).

The direct application of corpus analysis in language and literacy classrooms has been seen as problematic when it requires students to access whole corpora through unfamiliar software and corpus tools. Although ideally students would be given the opportunity to browse the whole corpus to make their own discoveries about language use, it has been questioned whether the – potentially limited – outcomes of the analyses justify the effort of acquiring the necessary technical competence (see Römer, 2006 for a discussion). Furthermore, the approach disadvantages students with low computer literacy. As an alternative, selected corpus extracts can be presented in worksheets, but, as L. Flowerdew (2012: 197–98) explains, there have been objections to this method on the grounds that this reworked corpus data does not represent real language anymore. However, in our own research (e.g. Tribble & Wingate, 2013), we have found that presenting corpus extracts for specific linguistic patterns in worksheets was the only feasible way of giving students this exposure within the time limitations of literacy workshops.

Typical corpus methods used in DDL are the analysis of keywords and the use of concordances that show typical collocations and textual patterning in the target genre (Tribble, 2002). An well known example of the use of concordances was the 'Kibbitzers' materials developed by T. Johns (1997). In these materials, students were given a number of concordance lines in which students which show the typical environment of lexical items and structures which were found to be problematic for students.[5] Another useful approach to corpus analysis for language pedagogy is the study of what Biber (2006) calls lexical bundles, otherwise known as 'clusters' (Scott & Tribble, 2006) or 'n-grams' (Dunning, 1994), which reveals the most frequent occurence of word sequences in texts, and helps students to recognise typical phrasal expressions in a genre. An example of how lexical bundles can be used to alert students to epistemological differences between disciplines was shown by Tribble and Wingate (2013). The most frequent four-word bundles in an apprentice corpus of Applied Linguistics showed the rhetorical function of framing argument and reader engagement. By contrast, the most frequent bundles in a Pharmacy apprentice corpus were concerned with quantification. In addition to giving students a fuller understanding of discourse preferences in their disciplines, the bundles also provide them with a resource bank on which they can draw in their writing.

Finally, as there is now growing consensus that discourse and corpus approaches should be used in a complementary fashion, as well as a growing number of interventions that use selected corpus data to enhance and exemplify findings from discourse analysis (e.g. Charles, 2007), earlier problems noted by Widdowson and Swales may have been overcome. If the common direction in literacy pedagogy is from text to corpus (Tribble & Wingate, 2013), and corpus data is used to address clearly-identified student needs, then corpus analysis is another effective discipline-specific instructional method.

Notes

(1) 'EAP teacher' is used here as an umbrella term for brevity; it includes staff working in learning development or skills units who might not be language specialists.
(2) Other types of additional provision would be print resources and/or guidelines, as well as workshops targeted to the needs of students of a discipline, developed and delivered entirely by writing experts.
(3) This is the approach of the two linguistic genre models, but not that of RGS; see Chapter 2.
(4) Another example of applying corpus analysis to analyse textlinguistic features in generic moves is Upton and Connor (2001).
(5) See for examples: http://lexically.net/TimJohns/index.html. One example, Kibbitzer 17, shows that 'related' typically collocates with 'strongly', rather than 'deeply' as found in student texts.

5 Reading and Writing

Introduction

Academic literacy pedagogy has always paid more attention to writing than to reading, despite the fact that university writing, being largely evidence-based, crucially depends on effective reading. Most academic activities are of the 'reading-to-write' type (Dobson & Feak, 2001), also called 'composing from sources' or 'discourse synthesis' (McGinley, 1992). These activities require students to 'produce written compositions that display appropriate and meaningful uses of and orientations to source evidence' (Cumming et al., 2005). In a needs analysis conducted across six undergraduate and graduate courses in various disciplines and fields at a university in the US, Carson (2001) found that all student assignments required synthesis of information from texts.

Although the reading and writing nexus has been examined in various studies[1] since the 1980s (for an overview see Grabe, 2001), and the need to teach reading-to-write has long been recognised (e.g. Spack, 1988; Leki & Carson, 1994), literacy curricula have continued to neglect the reading part of the nexus and remained primarily focused on writing. This is evident in the names of instructional programmes, such as 'College Composition', or support units (e.g. Centre for Academic Writing, Coventry University), as well as in the titles of textbooks (e.g. Swales & Feak, 2012) and in online guidelines (e.g. www.uefap.com/writing). EAP has traditionally excluded writing from sources and relied on independent writing prompts (Plakans & Gebril, 2012), although changes to this situation have long been advocated, for instance by Leki and Carson:

> We are convinced that EAP writing classes need to move away from writing tasks that require students to tap into their own opinions and experiences and toward work that encourages students to integrate those opinions and experiences with external sources of information and argument. (1994: 95)

Whilst texts, particularly expert texts such as journal articles, play a role in many academic writing classrooms, they are typically used as models for writing instruction but are not considered as sources of information. Although the components of the reading-to-write process such as summarising, paraphrasing, direct quotation and synthesising materials from source texts are, as Hirvela (2001: 332) states, 'common elements of EAP writing instruction', these activities are concerned with generic techniques rather than with the purposeful retrieval of information for a specific writing assignment.

Grabe's (2001: 18) explanation for this situation is that 'many researchers assume basic reading abilities for their students or see such learning issues for reading as unproblematic'. In Dovey's (2010) view, it is the dominance of genre approaches, with their focus on the product of writing and their rejection of the process approach and its pre-writing activities that has led to the neglect of reading. In genre models, she explains, 'the key academic activity of reading to write has been largely relegated to the analysis of target genres' (2010: 48). Hirvela (2004: 3) suspects that writing teachers 'feel ill prepared to teach reading, especially in connection with writing'. Leki (2001: 202) also questions whether writing teachers are sufficiently trained to teach reading and notes that existing reading methodologies are restricted to 'quick tips, such advising students to read the subheads of a chapter first'. Another explanation for the lack of attention to academic reading may be that writing is prominent as a high-stake activity, which in most assessment systems determines success or failure, while reading, even though it is the premise for successful writing, is less visible.

As the discussion so far suggests, within the literature on academic reading, which is the neglected side of academic literacy research and pedagogy, the main focus is on the reading-to-write process. This is reflected in this chapter, of which the larger part is devoted to reading-to-write. This focus does, however, highlight another area of neglect, namely that of developing students' ability to read 'only' for the acquisition of information and knowledge. Most students, particularly at undergraduate level, would not have been expected in their previous education to learn substantial amounts of formal knowledge through independent and extensive reading. Research has shown that students find academic reading problematic (e.g. Mann, 2000), and even more difficult as academic writing (Phakiti & Li, 2011); yet at university, students' reading ability is taken for granted, and their performance of reading 'is usually left both unprobed and unaided' (van Pletzen, 2006: 105).

Therefore, I focus first on reading only and discuss the components involved in the reading process, the difficulties students experience with academic reading, as well as some studies concerned with developing academic reading competence. Next, I discuss the complexity of the reading-to-write process, and in the last section of this chapter, I present a number of intervention studies in which the teaching of reading and writing has been integrated.

The Reading Process

Until the late 1960s, reading was understood as a process in which information from texts was gathered in a bottom-up, word-by-word fashion. Since then, theorists have explained L1 and L2 reading as a psycholinguistic and interactive process (Grabe, 1991). Reading is seen as interaction between reader and text in which not only textual information but also the reader's background knowledge and conceptual abilities are drawn upon. Background knowledge, which has been explained by schema theory as consisting of content, formal and linguistic schemata (Anderson, 1984; Carrell, 1984), determines what readers expect from texts, and facilitates hypothesis-building and top-down processing. Genre knowledge is an important part of background knowledge, as it allows the reader to recognise the text's communicative purpose, rhetorical organisation and formal features, and aids not only comprehension, but ultimately also the production of similar texts (Johns, 1997).

The reading process has been explained as consisting of six component skills: (1) automatic recognition skills; (2) vocabulary and structural knowledge; (3) formal discourse structure knowledge; (4) content/world background knowledge; (5) synthesis and evaluation skills/strategies; and (6) metacognitive knowledge and skills monitoring (Grabe, 1991: 379). These six skills interact, but work at different cognitive levels. At the lower cognitive end are the abilities needed to read 'for basic comprehension' (Grabe, 2001: 18), including rapid and automatic recognition and processing of words, sentences and discourse cues. These abilities form the basis for advanced levels of reading, such as the critical and analytical reading required in academic contexts. At these levels, the reader needs to evaluate the text information while reading, and compare and synthesise it with information from other sources. Metacognitive strategies, which are concerned with the overall planning, monitoring and evaluation of an activity (e.g. O'Maley & Chamot, 1990), are needed at all levels. In relation to reading, they include (1) setting the reading goal, which in a reading-to-write task would the retrieval of relevant information, (2) choosing appropriate strategies to achieve these goals, for instance skimming the text for specific information and taking notes, and (3) monitoring goal achievement, which can entail a change of previously used strategies. As Grabe (1991) points out, beginner readers are more preoccupied with process strategies such as word identification, and they are also more likely to take a bottom-up approach to reading. By contrast, proficient readers make more effective use of their background knowledge and are able to use a top-down approach to identify the information they need.

These cognitive theories were developed through research in L1 (first language) reading and subsequently adapted to L2 (second language) reading. While L1 reading development begins in childhood and therefore the component skills are acquired in a fairly linear and gradual way, L2 readers already possess most or all of these skills in their L1, but have to acquire the basic skills anew when starting to read in their L2. This leads them to recur to the bottom-up approach and process strategies that they would not use when reading in their L1. The position of novice readers at university, whether they are native or non-native speakers of English, is not dissimilar from L2 readers. Although university students can be assumed to be experienced and proficient readers in genres that are familiar to them, their lack of subject knowledge and of academic genres can reduce their reading to the level of basic comprehension. While they are struggling to gain subject knowledge from the texts, as well as with unfamiliar terminology and genre-specific discourse features, they are at the same time required to evaluate these texts, and to identify relevant information. In the absence of sufficient subject knowledge, however, students often fail to distinguish relevant from irrelevant information or to identify conflicting points of view in the literature (Andrews, 1995). These difficulties are compounded by students' previous reading experience, their conceptions of reading and associated reading strategies, as will be discussed in the next section.

Conceptions of reading and associated reading strategies

Many students arrive at university with conceptions of reading or 'epistemologies of text' (Wineburg, 1991: 509) that are inadequate for the demands of academic reading. Schraw and Brunig (1996) found three 'implicit models' of reading in a study with 154 undergraduate students. The first is the 'transmission model', which is based on the belief that meaning is transmitted directly from the author to the reader, who is the passive recipient of this meaning. The second, the 'translation model', assumes that meaning in a text is independent from the author's intended meaning and that the reader must decode the meaning in an objective way, without recurrence to his/her own experience or the cultural and social context of the text. The third model is 'transactional' and is based on the understanding that a text is perceived differently by different readers, and that therefore the reader constructs the meaning of the text with reference to his/her prior knowledge and the cultural and social context of the text. In the same way as Bereiter and Scarmadelia (1987) distinguish between 'knowledge telling' and 'knowledge transforming' in academic writing, Schraw and Brunig describe the transmission model as leading to knowledge reproduction, while the transactional model leads to knowledge transformation and the reader's personal and critical engagement with the text. Similarly, Bakhtin (1981; 1986) distinguishes between a passive understanding of meaning in texts, which is merely the reception and reproduction of what already exists in the world, and an active understanding, which means a dialogic interaction between reader and text. In this interaction, the reader does not simply accept information from the text, but works with it, by questioning the truth of this information and using it in 'a new conceptual system' (1981: 282).

At the beginning of their studies, students tend to be guided by the transmission model of reading and unquestioningly accept the information presented in academic texts as authoritative, before they gradually develop a more engaged and critical stance (Abbott, 2013). As Abbott points out,

> [f]or undergraduate students, understanding that the text they study can be seen as arising from a particular discursive position which can be interrogated and challenged, rather than as books which offer incontrovertible pieces of knowledge, is an important threshold to cross. (Abbott, 2013: 194)

Students' conceptions of reading have been formed through their sociocultural and educational backgrounds. As Rose et al. (2008) explain in relation to Australian indigenous students, and Dreyer and Nel (2003) and van Pletzen (2006) in relation to students coming from under-resourced South African secondary schools, students from less privileged backgrounds are often particularly under-prepared for academic reading. This is because they lack the linguistic capital that mainstream middle-class students have, and are used from their previous experience to information being 'handed over... with the result that independent reading abilities are left relatively undeveloped' (van Pletzen, 2006: 106). However, it is well attested in the literature that students coming from mainstream secondary education, and even students at the postgraduate level, also have inappropriate conceptions and are unprepared for transactional reading (e.g. Jolliffe & Harl, 2008; MacMillan, 2014).

Students' initial belief in the text as the absolute authority is accompanied by inappropriate reading strategies such as bottom-up, word-by word decoding (Sengupta, 2002), and the failure to make meaningful connections beyond the text, either to prior experience, or to the wider context (MacMillan, 2014). Connections beyond the text also include the consideration of the purpose of reading, which in academic contexts is often a critical comparison of contrary viewpoints expressed in a range of texts; yet, students' conceptions and the associated bottom-up approach hamper the critical reading of multiple texts.

Van Pletzen (2006) provides a useful example of how previous encounters of genres, their communicative purposes and the associated purposes of reading interfere with students' ability to read effectively at university. She reports on research carried out with 16 first-year students in a medical degree programme at the University of Cape Town. This degree programme requires reading of 'psychosocial' texts in addition to the more factual biomedical materials. The students were comfortable with reading Anatomy texts, which resembled the kind of genres they had encountered in their previous science classes at school. These genres offer 'definite content', and reading follows the concrete purpose of extracting definite facts; thus, students had developed the concept of 'reading as a simple vehicle' (van Pletzen, 2006: 115) for the delivery of knowledge, and met this purpose by strategies such as drawing diagrams and filling them with information. The 'psychosocial' texts, on the other hand, which were 'wide-ranging in terms of discipline, genre and intended audience' (van Pletzen, 2006: 112) and presented debate and argumentation rather than concrete facts, were far less accessible for the students, as they presented unknown epistemologies and required unfamiliar strategies. Being exposed to unfamiliar genres and their communicative purposes affected, as van Pletzen describes, students' sense of identity and caused confusion and frustration.

It is likely that this example represents the experience of many students, who have been conditioned by their previous education to read in order to extract facts from the text. Since conceptions of reading are, as Schraw and Brunig (1996) explain, implicit and readers have little awareness of them, it may take some students a long time to realise that their reading approach is insufficient for academic study. To avoid the anxiety, frustration and possible failure caused by inappropriate reading models, reading instruction that focuses on students' existing text epistemologies and the need for a transactional approach should be offered early on in university programmes.

Examples of academic reading instruction

Although there are a number of academic journals concerned with reading, they usually focus on children's reading development or reading in a second or foreign language, while publications on academic reading are sparse. Even in journals that deal with English in academic contexts, such as the Journal of English for Academic Purposes, the number of contributions on reading is limited. Most of these contributions address students' reading experiences and practices (e.g. Atai & Mosayeb, 2014; Kwan, 2009) or their reading proficiency and performance (e.g. Nergis, 2013; Pritchard & Nasr, 2004). The very few articles on academic reading instruction are largely concerned with strategy training and genre awareness.

Dreyer and Nel (2003) present a course in which reading strategies were taught, as part of the university's EAP programme, to South African students with English as an additional language. The course content included cognitive and metacognitive strategies, for instance defining the reading purpose, formulating guiding questions, activating personal knowledge and monitoring comprehension. The strategies were taught through interactive study guides, contact sessions and a virtual learning environment. Pre-and post-tests showed that the students achieved significantly higher reading comprehension scores after the strategy training. The authors make a strong case for the explicit teaching of reading strategies, as students are underprepared by 'the limited task demands of high school' (Dreyer & Nel, 2003: 350) and cannot be expected to learn effective strategies incidentally.

MacMillan's (2014) study is also concerned with strategy training. She aimed at enhancing students' deep learning by improving their ability to make connections between the academic text and their prior knowledge. In an academic reading workshop, the 30 participants, who had previously been made aware of the importance of making connections beyond the text, were asked to write down the connections that they could make in relation to the given text. Analysing the connections made by the students as well as the points that triggered these connections from a phenomenographic perspective, MacMillan found different levels, ranging from surface connections (word associations) to meaning-based connections, which included the integration of text information with students' personal views as well as critique. Meaning-based connections are, according to MacMillan, likely to be related to a deeper understanding of the text. However, students are not usually aware of the importance of connecting textual information to prior knowledge, and enabling them to do so means changing their reading habits. Therefore, as MacMillan points out, it is necessary 'to rethink what we mean when we ask students to read and develop activities and assessments accordingly' (MacMillan, 2014: 951). She recommends to model the strategy of making connections in the reading classroom and to encourage students to evaluate the text within its wider context and in its meaning to the intended audience.

Genre-based reading instruction is discussed by Hyon (2001, 2002) and Sengupta (1999). Providing learners with knowledge about a specific genre equips them with prior knowledge for the reading of further texts from that genre, because knowledge of a genre's formal and functional features guides the reader's expectations towards texts (Nystrand, 1986). In a 12-week reading course for students with English as a second language (L2), Hyon introduced four genres (hard news, feature article, textbook and research article) and discussed their content, structure, style and purpose. Based on interviews with the eleven participants, Hyon (2002) concludes that explicit genre instruction facilitates the location of key information in texts, improves reading speed and gives students greater confidence. A limitation in Hyon's genre-based instruction turned out to be the almost exclusive focus on rhetorical features. This prevented adequate attention to the content of the texts, which is known to be the most difficult aspect of academic reading. When investigating the long-term effect of her instructional approach, Hyon (2001) found that genre-based teaching varies in its impact on students. While 'EAP students can remember, over an extended period of time, at least *some* genre features learned through instruction and *may* recognise those features in new texts' (Hyon, 2001: 432; my italics), there is however also the danger that students overgeneralise the learned genre features to other genres.

In a reading course with 15 Hong Kong Chinese first-year undergraduates, Sengupta (1999) aimed at raising their consciousness of how writers use rhetorical and linguistic features to address their audience and make the text accessible to readers. The long-term objective was to enable the students to become analytical readers who would eventually use in their own writing rhetorical features that are appropriate for the audience and genre purpose. The students were asked to identify 'reader-friendly' features which had made reading the required texts easier for them. The features most commonly mentioned by the students were signals (e.g. advance labelling to give the reader a preview of what was following), structure (e.g. meaningful subheadings), 'good' Introduction (e.g. stating text organisation and purpose), and 'good' Conclusion (e.g. showing how purpose was served). These features were regarded as useful because, among other reasons, they enabled the students to save time when reading, and to identify the main points more easily. Sengupta found that by the end of the reading course, more students were able to make an effective gist of texts, obviously as a result of their increased awareness of the features of successful written academic discourse. However, despite this awareness, the students were not able to apply to their own writing the rhetorical features they had identified as reader-friendly.

In the same context, i.e. reading classes for Hong Kong Chinese undergraduate students, Sengupta (2002) also sought ways of changing inappropriate conceptions of reading. She found that the students, who had not received any strategy instruction at secondary school, started off with the transmission model, which was evident in the use of strategies such as word-for-word decoding in a linear and additive manner. The change to a more transactional concept was achieved through the training of metacognitive strategies, or what Sengupta calls the 'process approach' to reading instruction. By this she means developing students' knowledge 'about the process and actions involved in reading as well as knowledge about how to monitor these processes' (no page numbers available). This approach, as Sengupta points out, helps students to acquire strategies for selective, purposeful and critical reading, and at the same time changes their initial beliefs about reading. By using these strategies, students are able to develop a reading process that would begin with identifying salient features of the text, identifying the communicative purpose and the author's intentions, and producing a gist of the text. These initial steps would then lead to a more precise reading plan and decisions as to which parts of the text need to be read more carefully. Fundamental to Sengupta's instructional approach were the classroom discussions about the reading processes that the students used to understand the main argument in the text and the difficulties encountered in these processes. The transcriptions of the recorded reading classes showed that by the last session, the students had shifted concepts from the initial getting 'correct' meaning out of texts to the active construction of meaning. They had begun to read texts critically, question content and challenge writers. However, taking a longitudinal approach, Sengupta found in follow-up interviews that the students would not use the transactional model of reading outside her reading classroom until much later (i.e. Year 3 of their study programme), as they believed that their subject teachers wanted them to read word-for-word to find correct answers.

Of the instructional approaches discussed in this section, only Sengupta (2002) addresses learners' conceptions of reading, while the other studies focus either on certain strategies or genre features. As conceptions of reading underpin reading behaviour and the choice of strategies, it is essential that reading instruction begins with raising students' awareness of their implicit conceptions, and help them to adjust these conceptions if necessary. Sengupta's example shows that conceptual change can only be initiated, but not fully achieved, in a limited number of reading classes, as students still do not want to take the risk of applying active and critical reading in their larger academic context. This demonstrates the need for embedding reading instruction into subject curricula, so that reading models and strategies are discussed as part of subject teaching and in relation to the texts that students are required to read for the subject. Embedded instruction would help students recognise the importance of reading as a core activity of academic work, and understand the transactional approach as the discipline's approved way of dealing with knowledge. If students would receive this type of instruction at the beginning of their study programme, they would be far better prepared for the more complex tasks ahead, namely that of reading multiple texts and synthesising them in their own writing.

The Reading-to-Write Process

As mentioned earlier, reading-to-write is necessary for most student assignments, and the most widely used assignment genre across the main disciplinary groups of Humanities, Life Sciences, Physical Sciences and Social Sciences is the essay (Nesi & Gardner, 2012). At the core of the essay is the development of an argument (Andrews, 2010) which must be supported by evidence from the relevant field. This clearly requires the interaction of reading and writing. The 'reading-to-write' process may appear to be linear, proceeding along the stages of (1) identification and evaluation of sources, (2) selection of relevant information from these sources, and (3) integration of that information into the evolving argument. However, although the process may initially follow this order, it becomes recursive as the writer has to go back and forth between the stages. In order to carry out the first two stages, the writer needs a clear concept of the writing goal, as well as a plan of the argument to be developed. In the last stage, the writer is likely to go frequently back to the first two, looking for additional sources and evaluating further information. Thus, the three components are interconnected, and this interconnectedness requires an integrated teaching approach, as I will discuss later in this chapter. First, I want to explore the reading-to-write process in more detail.

Variables influencing the reading-to-write process

Some researchers have investigated how certain variables influence the reading-to-write process and performance (see Grabe, 2001, for an overview). One important finding was that 'merely having reading and writing abilities is not sufficient to perform reading-to-write tasks successfully' (Ascención Delaney, 2008: 141). There are further influential factors, for instance individual variables such as educational background and literacy expertise, or external variables such as the type of task guiding the reading-to-write activity. Testing the effect of reading ability on reading-to-write performance, Ascención Delaney (2008) compared reading comprehension and writing scores of 139 L1 and L2 students and found that the scores were not significantly correlated. The pedagogical implications of this finding are obvious. Students need to be supported in acquiring reading abilities that go beyond text comprehension and involve the strategic use of texts for the identification, organisation and evaluation of information.

A series of studies in the 1980s (Newell, 1984; Langer & Applebee, 1987; Marshall, 1987; Tierney *et al.*, 1989) investigated the influence of writing tasks on students' reasoning and learning from texts. The student groups (11th graders and undergraduate level) were asked to carry out different writing tasks ranging from note-taking, answering study-guide questions, summary writing and analytic (essay) writing. The overall results of these studies show that when reading is accompanied by a writing task, students gain a significantly deeper understanding of the topic. The results also demonstrated that task type strongly influences the level of analysis and reasoning students engage in. Langer and Applebee, for instance, found that note-taking and summary writing prompted students to read the whole text carefully, but without deep engagement with the information. Similarly, answering study-guide questions instigated selective reading without in-depth processing of the text's information. Essay writing, by contrast, encouraged students to perform more complex activities and to use metacognitive strategies such as building hypotheses, goal-setting, planning, organising, and reviewing. Newell explains why essay writing aids the learning of concepts considerably better than answering study-questions. In the latter activity, writers only draw on information in isolated segments, and 'consequently, while a great deal of information is generated, it never gets integrated into a coherent text, and, in turn, into the students' own thinking' (1984: 282). Essay writing, on the other hand, requires the organisation and synthesis of ideas; this level of engagement with the information facilitates learning. Whilst these findings confirm the important role essay writing plays in students' learning at university, they also have some implications for literacy instruction. For instance, note-taking, study-guide questions and summary writing are widely used tasks in reading and writing classrooms. While these activities are certainly useful to develop reading comprehension, they have clear limitations for the teaching of reading-to-write.

Operations involved in the reading-to-write process

In addition to the variables influencing reading-to-write, the activities and complex mental operations required from the reader/writer have also been the focus of research. McGinley (1992) offers an early investigation into the processes involved in writing from sources. One of his aims was to examine the previous assumption that writing from sources is a linear process (i.e. from reading to writing). Seven undergraduate students were asked to write a persuasive essay on the basis of two articles and to think aloud during the process. The researcher observed the students during the process and asked them debriefing questions after the completion of the task. The participants' reading/writing as well as reasoning activities identified by McGinley demonstrate the complexity of writing from sources. The reading/writing activities consisted of reading the source texts, reading notes, reading drafts, reading the assignment, writing notes, and writing drafts. The reasoning activities included questioning (expressing uncertainties about content or text organisation), hypothesising (stating plans, assumptions, or predictions), using schemata (i.e. the reader/writer's existing knowledge), meta-commenting (making comments on use of information from the text), paraphrasing, citing evidence, validating (e.g. stating that the goal was fulfilled) and restating (i.e. re-reading information from the source texts or the student's written draft or notes. Analysing the distribution of activities across the reading-to-write process, McGinley found it to be both linear and non-linear. While the students spent much time reading the source texts in the initial phases, later they enacted a 'more balanced combination of reading and writing activities' (McGinley, 1992: 241), moving between the articles, their notes and their drafts. The reasoning operations were also found to be both linear and non-linear. Although initial reading-related activities such as questioning and hypothesising decreased during the process, indicating a linear trend, these activities were still used to a considerable degree in the later phases. This complexity of the recursive operations involved in the reading-to-write process highlights the insufficiency of academic literacy instruction that focuses on writing only.

Reading-to-write strategies and behaviours

Various researchers have explained that reading-to-write requires different strategies than reading for comprehension, because the choice of strategies is determined by the task (e.g. Block, 1992; Cohen, 1994; Cohen & Upton, 2007). Reading comprehension is often tested by questions; to answer them, students need to employ selective reading strategies but need not engage in any deep analysis of content (Langer & Applebee, 1987). When it comes to reading-to-write, Hirvela (2004) refers to strategies involved in the process as 'mining' and 'writerly reading'. Mining means reading for the retrieval of information that is needed for specific writing goals. Plakans and Gebril

(2012), who examined how undergraduate L2 students at a Middle Eastern university used source texts, found three types of mining, i.e. reading for gaining ideas, shaping opinion and supporting opinion. Writerly reading refers to extracting from the source texts features such as terms, phrases, or structure for the improvement of the writer's text. In Plakans and Gebril's study, students engaged in writerly reading mainly by borrowing organisational patterns from the sources to structure their own texts.

In her analysis of the think-aloud protocols of twelve L2 students' during a reading-to-write task, Plakans (2009) identified the following main categories of strategies: (1) goal setting for reading the source text, (2) metacognitive strategies, (3) global strategies, (4) cognitive processing, and (5) mining the source texts for use in writing. A goal setting strategy is for example that writers re-read the writing task to clarify what information they need from the source texts. Metacognitive strategies were already discussed earlier in this chapter. Both goal setting and metacognitive strategies were used infrequently by the participants in Plakan's study. Global strategies, called top-down strategies elsewhere, meant that the participants skimmed the text to understand the gist of it, looked for cues in the text structure, and identified main ideas. Cognitive processing occurred when the participants experienced comprehension problems and subsequently slowed their reading rate or re-read words or phrases. Mining the source texts implied that the students returned to the text to find specific information and then integrated the information into their writing through paraphrasing or citation. In line with previous reading research, Plakans found that the high-achieving students in her sample used more global and metacognitive strategies. They also engaged more in mining than the low-achieving participants.

McCulloch (2013) takes issue with the fact that much research into writing from sources, including McGinley (1992), Plakans (2009) and Plakans and Gebril (2012), uses artificial tasks 'that represent a poor reflection of the ways in which students actually read to write in higher education settings, particularly at postgraduate level' (Plakans & Gebril, 2012: 136). In the studies criticised by McCulloch, students were given two source texts; in McGinley's research with L1 students the sources were between 800 to 1000 words long, while in Plakans' and Plakans and Gebril's studies the texts had a length of only between 200 and 300 words, perhaps because the research was carried out with L2 students. By contrast, in natural reading-to-write situations, writers have to find sources by themselves, and have to deal with diverse and much lengthier texts. Equally inauthentic, as McCulloch points out, was the time constraint in these 'one-shot' (McCulloch, 2013: 137) studies, as participants were asked to complete the task in one sitting, and were therefore less likely to use different strategies than they would if they had a longer period of time to reflect and revisit their sources. Because of the unrealistic conditions, these studies may allow only limited insights into the reading-to-write process.

Addressing the dearth of research at the postgraduate level, where reading-to-write is more complex involving writing from multiple sources for literature reviews, McCulloch asked two L2 MA students to think aloud while reading-to-write for their dissertations. She found that the higher-achieving student displayed a larger variety of reading-to-write behaviours than the lower-achieving student as well as a greater range and frequency of responses to the source texts. For instance, while the lower-achieving student's agreement with source texts was entirely perfunctory (restricted to utterances such as yes, ok), the higher-achieving student tended to use elaborated agreement (e.g. yes, that's definitely right), or expressed interest in the argument of the text, thus showing not only deeper engagement, but also 'the confidence to actively position herself in relation to it' (McCulloch, 2013: 142). Furthermore, unlike the lower-achieving student, the high achiever expressed intertextual awareness by making connections across multiple sources. She also elaborated on the source texts, for instance by adding her own examples or extending the information to a new context. This high-achieving student's reading-to-write behaviour demonstrated 'an active process of dialogue with her sources' (McCulloch, 2013: 145). Descriptions of such purposeful and engaged reading behaviour are valuable for academic literacy instruction as they can help students 'to avoid some of the common pitfalls of source use in academic writing such as lack of evaluation or failure to take an authoritative stance' (McCulloch, 2013: 146).

Despite McCulloch's critique of 'one-shot' research that relies on short and preselected source texts, it seems worthwhile at this point to go back to McGinley's study which provides a detailed description of the strategies and behaviours of two students from his sample. McCulloch's study focuses mainly on reading behaviours; by contrast, McGinley's analysis of the activities of the two students offers insights into the whole process of reading-to-write. One student was a proficient writer from sources, while the other was not. The proficient student employed a range of activities in a purposeful manner and her decisions were always targeted at 'accomplishing both the local and overall goals of the composing-from sources activity' (p. 242). By contrast, the second student's decisions were 'governed by chance'. This student continually went back to re-reading the source texts, but never managed to integrate their divergent arguments into her own writing. As a result, she was not able to develop a stance. The behaviours McGinley observed in these two case studies are listed in Table 5.1 in the order in

Table 5.1 Reading-to-write behaviours revealed in McGinley's (1992) study

Successful student	Unsuccessful student
Had no initial definite opinion on topic; read source texts purposefully to identify essential information of both (pro – and con) arguments. Carefully analysed conflicting arguments. Discovered inconsistencies in both arguments.	Began reading with strong opinion on topic; changed her opinion after reading first text, and again after reading second text.
Stopped reading and wrote notes, listing the pro and con arguments 'to objectively look at both sides' (McGinley, 1992: 237).	Got trapped in the reading, viewed each argument as valid and logical; made little attempt at analysing and reconciling the different perspectives.
Stopped writing notes and brainstormed to clarify own position, and to develop arguments consistent with that position.	Was aware that note-taking is important, but unaware of which functions notes might serve.
Started writing essay. The writing helped her to articulate and better understand her own position.	Was unsure how to start writing. Re-read article beginnings and endings. Wrote dysfunctional notes.
Referred back to notes and sections in articles purposefully for information; was able to define precisely her own position.	Found notes unhelpful; resorted to re-reading texts: 'When I...got stuck, I usually reread what I had just written...but if nothing came to me I went back to the articles hoping to get some ideas. Most of the time I was just looking for something to sound appealing and to inspire me...' (McGinley, 1992: 238).
Result: Formulated a novel and convincing argument.	*Result:* Paraphrased, restated arguments from articles without developing own position.

which they occurred. This is to highlight the contrast between successful and unsuccessful strategies, as well as the complexity of the reading-to-write process.

Considering the studies discussed above, and in particular the comparisons of proficient and less proficient performance provided by McCulloch and McGinley, it is obvious that different types of reading need to be employed at the different stages of the reading-to-write process, and that the reading activities must be closely guided by the writing activity. In the following section, I discuss the different types of reading, as well as the reading strategies that students need to acquire to successfully carry out the reading-to-write process.

Types of reading required at the different stages of the reading-to-write process

The first stage of the process usually consists of reading for the selection of sources. This type of reading is absent from the artificial tasks presented in much of the reading-to-write research (McCulloch, 2013). This stage involves first compiling, and then sifting through, a body of potential sources. The step of compiling seems relatively unproblematic, as information search skills such as using databases, library catalogues and keyword searches are usually taught to students as part of their induction to university. However, Thompson et al. (2013), who conducted a longitudinal study into the source use by first-year undergraduate students from various disciplines, found that students initially rely greatly on websites and Wikipedia as their main sources. Even towards the end of their first year of study, many preferred to rely on materials provided by their lecturers. When they selected sources independently, their choices were guided more by ease of understanding than by relevance. Although the most frequently mentioned criterion for selection was that the source needed to be authoritative and reliable, students were not always aware of what made a source reliable. These selection strategies suggest that novices are likely to miss some relevant source texts. At more advanced levels of academic writing such as postgraduate or doctoral, writers usually have the problem of having to identify the key literature in a large body of publications from sometimes different disciplines with multiple paradigms (e.g. Kwan, 2008). This step requires the ability to read fairly speedily, as well as effective use of metacognitive and top-down reading strategies. Metacognitive strategies, as explained earlier, include the setting of a clear search focus which requires careful analysis of the assignment task and topic. Top-down strategies (called 'global' by Plakans, 2009) include using parts of the texts (e.g. abstract, conclusion), structure, headings and lay-out features, as well as skimming and scanning, for an overview of what the texts have to offer.

After text selection, critical and analytical reading of the texts is required. The same strategies as in the previous stage are needed. Metacognitive strategies help to create a clear reading focus, while top-down strategies help to locate relevant information within the texts. To read with a focus, students need to have an initial stance on the essay topic, if not a clear concept of the argument they want to develop. Without this focus, the reader may be unable to identify and evaluate the conflicting arguments in the sources. This was the case with the weaker student in McGinley's study who aligned herself with 'whatever point of view she was reading at a given time' (1992: 242). The problem for novice writers is that they tend to lack the confidence to take a stance, often because they feel too unfamiliar with the subject content. This lack of familiarity also creates difficulties in the area of academic attributions, as students find it hard to distinguish between what is common knowledge in the subject and which information needs to be attributed to a source.

As explained earlier, the later stages of the process, although mainly concerned with writing, still require recursive reading. In successful performance, writers refer back to either the sources or their notes with the purpose of confirming information or seeking further evidence. By contrast, less proficient students return to the source texts for ideas rather than for specific information (McGinley, 1992). Plakans and Gebril describe the difference between effective and ineffective recursive reading as follows:

> After initially reading each passage, they would begin writing, but returned regularly to the source texts. Such text consultations took on varying degrees of dependency. Some writers returned to the source texts with every sentence they wrote to find the next idea or to find words they could use, while others shaped the essays with their own ideas and only returned to find support and evidence. (Plakans & Gebril, 2012: 26)

Integrating information into the developing text is also beset by other problems, such as the attribution of sources as well as correct referencing and paraphrasing. These are not further discussed here, as the focus is on reading; however, paraphrasing is considered in the section on reading-to-write interventions.

Reading-to-write summary

The previous sections attempted to describe the complexity of the reading-to-write process and the problems that novices can encounter with it. As much of their reading is still concerned with comprehension, they tend to employ a bottom-up approach which involves word-by-word decoding and copious note-taking. Information is not purposefully selected, but often plucked from the source texts in chunks that also contain irrelevant material, and then reproduced in written notes. Some of these notes might be directly copied into the students' assignments, leading to charges of plagiarism. Furthermore, novice writers have a tendency to display knowledge and therefore tend to present much irrelevant information from their sources. The implications for literacy instruction are obvious. Students need to be made aware of the different types of reading required in the different phases of the reading-to-write process, and learn the associated strategies. In addition to reading strategies, writing-related strategies for the integration of information of sources need to be addressed as well. These include citations from source texts, summarising and paraphrasing, as well as appropriate note taking in order to avoid plagiarism that might arise from verbatim notes. All this would require instructional approaches that address the whole process of text production; however, despite the repeated calls for 'an integrated pedagogy of reading and writing' (Ascención Delaney, 2008: 148; Hirvela, 2001), there are still very few examples of such a pedagogy.

Reading-to-Write Interventions

As evident from the previous sections, much research has been concerned with the abilities and operations involved in writing from sources. By contrast, much less work is available on teaching initiatives, a fact that was also noticed by Tardy (2006; see Chapter 4). I only found four studies concerned with the teaching of reading-to-write. One of them was only a short, decontextualised intervention, while the others were curriculum-integrated teaching initiatives. These studies are discussed next.

Wette (2010) conducted an intervention with 78 undergraduate L2 students from a range of disciplines studying on credit-bearing academic literacy courses in a New Zealand university. In an eight-hour course, the students received explicit instruction in textual borrowing (e.g. direct citations and paraphrasing) in order to expand their declarative knowledge of the rules and conventions of source text use. The main aim of the intervention, however, was to create procedural knowledge and 'develop students' ability to comprehend the essential meaning of source texts, and to transform this understanding into paraphrase and summary citations' (Wette, 2010: 161). Unfortunately, little is said in the article about the actual teaching approach and materials; this makes it difficult to fully understand the results. These show that on the one hand, students' declarative knowledge of the rules governing the citing from sources had improved significantly. In addition, a post-unit writing assignment revealed that students' copying from the source text had decreased. On the other hand, it was also obvious from the assignment that the more complex aspects of writing from sources, namely comprehending difficult texts, summarising content and integrating it with the writers' arguments, remained problematic for the students. Furthermore, the researcher found that students' difficulty with identifying core meanings from sources persisted; students had often paraphrased one part of the source text but ignored other equally or more important parts.

In other words, while the students improved in the technical aspects of writing from sources, procedural knowledge could not be enhanced in this short intervention. Wette argues that the intervention was suitable for raising students' awareness of the complexity of this 'important learned academic literacy skill' (Wette, 2010: 169). While I agree with this argument, I have considerable doubts about the feasibility of teaching reading-to-write in a multidisciplinary classroom, and in a skills approach as chosen by Wette. Although the techniques of referencing can be taught generically, the knowledge of *what* to reference certainly cannot. Neither can the knowledge of what to paraphrase or summarise be taught generically. Transforming 'the essential meaning of source texts' into 'paraphrase and summary citations' (Wette, 2010: 161) is deeply contextual and inextricably linked to the specific writing topic and task. Identifying what is 'the essential meaning' requires critical engagement with the source texts and a clear concept of the argument to be developed in the written text. Without this argument in mind, the purpose of paraphrasing or summarising remains unclear for the writer – as expressed in the title of Hirvela and Du's (2013) article 'Why am I paraphrasing?'.

Paraphrasing, which (along with summary writing and citing) is commonly taught in academic writing classes to both L1 and L2 students (Hirvela & Du, 2013), is a mechanical exercise when it is taught in a generic, decontextualised manner, as in Wette's intervention. Students will simply use synonyms or structural devices to express themselves differently from the source text. Hirvela and Du found that their participants, having learned 'paraphrasing as a decontextualised mechanical process of rewording and grammatical rearrangement' (2013: 92) were comfortable in using the techniques – at the level of 'knowledge telling' (Bereiter & Scarmadelia, 1987) – but saw little value in this activity, apart from it being a way of avoiding plagiarism. Interestingly, when the participants needed to use paraphrasing for 'knowledge transforming' (i.e. writing their research papers), they were intimidated by the 'seemingly superior text produced by the original authors' (Bereiter & Scarmadelia, 1987: 96) and resorted to direct quotations in order not to have to interfere with the original text. Only through 'contextual paraphrasing' (Hirvela & Du, 2013: 88) can students understand its function in academic debate. Therefore, as the authors point out, it is important to foreground 'knowledge transforming' in the teaching of paraphrasing. This means that the writing task needs to represent an authentic context, in which paraphrasing, as well as summarising or direct quoting, are needed for a specific purpose such as providing evidence for the author's position. It also means that students' conceptions of reading need to be shifted from the transmission towards the transactional model, discussed earlier in this chapter, so that students critically interact with texts rather than taking a receptive approach.

Wette's work shows that short and generic interventions may be useful in helping students to acquire some basic techniques, but fail to help with the far more complex understandings and operations involved in writing from sources. To develop students' ability to write from sources, a long-term and subject-integrated approach is needed.

Such an approach was taken by Rose et al. (2008) in an action research project on using 'Scaffolding Academic Literacy' pedagogy with indigenous undergraduate students of health science at the University of Sydney. These students often have low or no formal qualifications and are faced with multiple literacy demands in a programme that spans science and social science disciplines. As Rose et al. explain, the traditional academic cycle requires students to independently read academic texts to gain topic knowledge before lectures, then hear an elaboration of this knowledge in the lectures, and then write an assignment to demonstrate what they have learned from the readings and lectures. These requirements, based on the assumption that students can already read and write complex academic texts when they arrive at university, typically lead to a high attrition rate in this particular student group. The 'Scaffolding Academic Literacy' approach used class time to prepare all students for the critical reading of academic texts, as well as for the writing assignments.

The four scaffolding levels for reading were (1) Preparing for reading, (2) Paragraph-by-paragraph reading, (3) Paragraph-by-paragraph text marking, and (4) Sentence-by-sentence text marking. The first level provided students with a general introduction to the content, background knowledge and an overview of the text. At the second level, key paragraphs of the text were read jointly with the teacher who offered beforehand a summary in accessible language and introduced academic terms appearing in the paragraph. After the reading, the key elements were discussed and new concepts explained. According to Rose et al., the combination of the first two levels 'provides sufficient support for all students to independently complete the [remaining course] reading with greater depth of understanding than is normally possible' (Rose et al., 2008: 169).

Level 3 prepared students to locate and highlight key information in a paragraph. Position cues were used to direct students to this information, and paraphrases and explanations were provided to aid their understanding of specific wordings and meanings. In Level 4, students were supported in identifying wordings and expressions in individual sentences, and as in the previous level, 'their understanding is elaborated with definitions, explanations or discussion' (Rose et al., 2008: 170). This procedure divided the complex task of reading into manageable steps. It enabled students to achieve a critical understanding of texts, as the four levels of scaffolding helped them to 'recognise, interpret and critique constructions of meaning at the levels of choices of wording, text organisation, field or subject matter, and ideology, and to use these understandings to make critical choices themselves in their writing' (Rose et al., 2008: 170). Based on the knowledge gained from the reading activities, students were adequately prepared for writing. This took various stages, following the Sydney School's teaching/learning cycle (see Chapter 4), from jointly writing notes to independently writing a text in a new field, but in the same genre. By the time students had to write their first assessed assignment, as a result of the scaffolded reading-to-write instruction, 'crucially the teacher can be confident that all students have been adequately prepared to complete the task successfully' (Rose et al., 2008: 170).

'Scaffolding Academic Literacy' instruction was delivered consistently in two courses per semester throughout the academic year. The texts chosen for reading instruction were part of the regular curriculum. A common objection to the use of class time for literacy activities is that subject content might not be sufficiently covered. However, as Rose et al. point out, these activities were not simply concerned with the reading and writing of texts, but also included in-depth discussions of the academic topic. Furthermore, the extensive treatment of a few selected texts in the classroom enabled students to deal with the much larger amount of required reading materials independently and effectively. This example demonstrates that literacy development and subject learning can be usefully integrated. Through systematic assessment providing quantitative measures of student learning (based on the 'Measuring the Academic Skills of University Students' [MASUS] test developed at the University of Sydney), Rose et al. were able to show significant improvements in literacy skills that occurred over the course of the intervention. The extended and consistent instruction implemented in 60 hours classroom teaching led to literacy increases 'comparable with a gain from junior secondary school level literacy to matriculation level, or from middle secondary to undergraduate level, in other words an equivalent of four years academic literacy improvement in just one year' (2008: 178).

Rose et al.'s action research sets an important example in several respects. First, much can be learned from the scaffolding approach. In most academic contexts novices are left to their own devices when they begin to read and write academic texts, and this means an unnecessary struggle for many, and failure for some. The scaffolding activities in which the teacher familiarises novices with academic genres and gradually enables them to read and write these genres independently are clearly beneficial for all students new to university, and as Rose et al. have shown, essential for students with low academic literacy levels. Equally important is the integration of these activities into time-tabled subject teaching. As I argued in Chapter 4, this integration does not only ensure that the whole student cohort receives literacy support, but also gives due recognition to the role of language and literacy in the construction of academic knowledge. Another major point to learn from Rose *et al.* is the integrated instruction of reading and writing, when, as already explained, traditional writing instruction still blends out the first stages of the reading-to-write process. Furthermore, this approach capitalises on what the students have learned from reading and analysing the relevant genre, as they are encouraged to use the genre's features and organisational patterns when composing a text in the same genre.

Two further useful examples of integrated reading-to-write instruction are Devereux and Wilson (2008) and Dovey (2010). Devereux and Wilson describe how literacy development was scaffolded throughout the four years of a Bachelor of Education programme in Australia. From the very beginning, students learned how to write from sources, and a strong emphasis was placed on critical reading. Dovey's (2010) work adds insights into reading-to-write support at a more advanced level. Similarly to Rose *et al.*, she developed and taught curriculum-integrated reading-to-write courses at an Australian university; however, her intervention was concerned with preparing postgraduate students for the complex task of writing from multiple sources for the literature review. An interesting and original aspect of Dovey's study is that she questions the supremacy of genre-based approaches to literacy teaching. Whilst it is widely assumed that genre-based instruction is the most suitable approach for teaching writing, particularly for advanced learners (e.g. Cheng, 2006), Dovey's point is that genre approaches have their limitations when it comes to the literature review. This is, she argues, because they neglect the reading-writing nexus and focus too much on the written product.

The literature review, as Swales and Lindemann (2002: 107) acknowledge, 'is one of the more difficult part-genres for an EAP writing instructor to teach', and does not lend itself to the ESP method of move analysis which works well in other part-genres of a dissertation or a research article. The literature review does not have predictable moves, but follows idiosyncratic routes determined by the varying fields, as well as the distinctive research objectives and questions. It is therefore difficult to use specific literature reviews as exemplars, as they cannot be detached from their specific research context. For these reasons, Dovey argues that genre pedagogy needs to be accompanied by the process approach (see Chapter 2 for a discussion of this approach). The process approach helps students to understand the recursive processes involved, that is, the interconnectedness between reading, referring back to sources and the evolving argument in their writing. The need to raise students' awareness of these processes for the complex task of integrating many sources into a literature review is also highlighted by Swales and Lindemann's (2002) study. The authors asked their multi-disciplinary cohort of graduate students to create a tree diagram of how they would organise the information of nine abstracts into a coherent discussion, and found, predictably, that the routes taken by students varied greatly according to the participants' different disciplinary backgrounds. While Swales and Lindemann, faithful to the ESP genre school, used the exercise to raise awareness of discipline-specific variations, Dovey points out that this exercise was in fact a process-oriented activity which could have been usefully exploited to illustrate decisions made in the process of drawing together information from a number of sources.

The first version of Dovey's reading-to-write intervention was based on genre pedagogy. The students learned the different sub-genres that make up a literature review, first through analysing models in the classroom and then through independent writing. They subsequently had to produce a summary of one paper, followed by annotations of a number of papers, a critical review of another paper, the introduction of a literature review and finally the complete review. Dovey found that there was little improvement in performance from one task to the next. One reason was that the individual writing tasks were not purposefully guided by a particular focus or research project (they were not even on the same topic) and therefore remained disparate. Another reason was that 'exposure to sample LRs (Literature Reviews)... did not provide insight into the recursive processes that had generated the categories evident in the finished product' (Dovey, 2010: 52).

The course was consequently redesigned to create a fully integrated reading-to-write assignment in which all writing tasks were directed by the target genre, a literature-based report. While genre-focused activities still played a role, the teaching aimed at scaffolding the processes and strategies involved in writing from sources. To enable students to manage the selection and organisation of information from sources more effectively, they were asked to create graphic organisers. Initially, the organisers referred to the information from one text only; then they were gradually developed into concept matrices which included all sources to be used in the report. The advantage of these visual representations, which were an assessed part of the students' work, is that students reorganise (instead of reproduce) the content of sources according to the requirements of their writing task. The graphic organisers are arranged in a way that reflects the argument that students are developing in their writing. The organisers therefore render the processes involved in the selection of information from texts and its rearrangement in the production of a new text. Dovey found that this genre- and process-focused approach led to significant improvements in student writing and that, unlike in the previous disparate activities, learning was now incremental and transferred from one task to the next.

Summary

In this chapter I have argued that reading and reading-to-write, although key academic literacy activities, are not given much attention in literacy pedagogy. Several reasons for this situation have been named, for instance that academic writing, as a high-stake activity, is more visible than reading, that EAP teachers might not be trained to teach reading, and that students' ability to read is taken for granted (Swales, 2002). Although the need for integrated reading and writing instruction has been repeatedly pointed out, only the writing-oriented components of the reading-to-write process are addressed in the typical EAP classroom. These include the so-called 'skills' of referencing, paraphrasing and summarising, which, as I explained earlier, cannot be effectively taught or learned without an authentic reading-to-write-context.

There were only three accounts of a curriculum-integrated reading-to-write instruction, all from Australia and influenced by the scaffolding approach of the Sydney School. These interventions were carried out with students at different levels, ranging from 'non-traditional' undergraduate students to postgraduate students, and resulted in considerable improvements in students' performance. This work shows the importance of teaching the reading-writing nexus holistically, of integrating this instruction into a timetabled course, and of providing the instruction over an extended period of time. In addition, it illustrates the benefits of using visual representations to help students to manage the processes of organising and synthesising multiple sources. It is clearly time for this approach to take hold in universities beyond Australia. Whilst not all reading-to-write initiatives need to be of the scale of Rose *et al.* (2008) or Dovey (2010), extending over a whole semester or academic year, it is essential that they are embedded in the disciplinary context and concerned with the real reading-to-writing that students are required to do in their subject.

Note

(1) The majority of publications refers to L1 reading and writing; however, as explained in Chapter 1, in relation to academic literacy instruction I wish to avoid the distinction between native and non-native speakers of English.

6 Academic Literacy Development and the Student Experience

Introduction

In the preceding chapters, I have considered academic literacy from the perspective of instructional provision. In Chapter 2, I discussed the range of approaches to literacy instruction which have evolved over the last five decades. Then, in Chapter 3, I looked at the limitations of the existing types of academic literacy support at Anglophone universities, followed by examples of provision that is more specifically targeted at students' needs, presented in Chapter 4. Chapter 5 provides a thematic link between instructional provision and student difficulties, as reading and reading-to-write were discussed from both perspectives. This chapter focuses entirely on the student experience and considers the various difficulties that can be involved in learning academic literacy.

In examining what I call 'academic literacy development', I was guided by language socialisation theory. As explained in Chapter 1, language socialisation refers to the process in which novices gradually become competent users of the language of a specific community (Ochs, 1986). In this process, they are assisted by expert members who socialise the novices into the communicative practices as well as the underlying values and ideologies of the community (Duff, 2007). Language socialisation theory is informed by sociocultural theory and the community-of-practice (CoP) model, and the shared understanding of all three theories is that learning is dependent on human interaction and assistance provided for the learner by more knowledgeable/competent persons. Language socialisation in the context of students entering university and acquiring communicative competence in their disciplines has also been termed 'Language Socialisation into Academic Discourse Communities' or 'Academic Discourse Socialisation' (Duff, 2010). Regardless of the name, this theoretical framework is in my view the most suitable one for analysing and explaining students' transition into a study programme within an academic discipline, their acquisition of community-specific literacy practices and conventions, and the support they receive from expert members such as lecturers or more experienced peers. The framework is particularly useful as it acknowledges the potential for conflict and power struggles as well as the need for identity adjustments brought about by differences in status, values and beliefs among community members.

I will first offer an overview of previous research before I report the findings of a study I conducted into the experience of undergraduate students with the literacy requirements in their discipline, Applied Linguistics.

Part 1: Overview of Research into Academic Discourse Socialisation and the Student Experience

In this section I focus on the process of academic discourse socialisation and the difficulties students may encounter in this process. Given this focus, I exclude from my review those studies that look at student difficulties from the perspective of needs analyses, which have been conducted either through large-scale surveys (e.g. Evans & Green, 2007), interviews (e.g. Evans & Morrison, 2011) or both (Phakiti & Li, 2011).

There is a rich literature on students' experiences and difficulties in the process of developing academic literacy. As discussed in Chapter 1, the majority of publications, including at least two academic journals, are concerned with academic writing, and of these, the vast majority focuses on non-native speakers of English. A number of recent books (e.g. Jenkins, 2014; Turner, 2011) and articles (e.g. Kim, 2011; Hennebry et al., 2012) are also devoted to international students and their experiences with the language requirements in English-medium universities. In the literature on international students, it is striking how many publications are focused on Asian, and particularly Chinese students (e.g. Spencer-Oatley & Xiong, 2006; Tran, 2009; Iannelli & Huang, 2013; Leedham, 2014). This is not surprising given that China, India, and Malaysia dominate the demand for English-medium education (Li et al., 2010). There are various studies that, reporting from the students' perspective, identify English language proficiency, particularly in academic writing, as the greatest problem for non-native speakers (e.g. Dooey, 2010; Kim, 2011; Terraschke & Wahid, 2011). Similarly Li et al. (2010) found that English writing ability was the key predictor for the significantly lower achievement of Chinese students in a large Management programme. By comparison, the number of publications on the academic literacy development of 'native-speaker' or 'home' students is rather small; these publications also tend to focus on specific groups, such as 'non-traditional' students (e.g. Lillis, 2001; Rose et al., 2008). Very few studies investigated the student experience and instructional provision without making the distinction between specific student groups (e.g. Lea & Street, 1998; Wingate, 2012a, 2012b).

As a result, this literature review is heavily oriented towards the experience of international students. To present fairly up-to-date research findings, I selected empirical studies published in the last ten years, and excluded publications that are conceptual in nature. These studies explore problems in academic discourse socialisation from the student perspective. The main topics covered in the literature can be broadly grouped into the following categories (1) mismatches; (2) critical thinking and argumentation; and (3) student identities.

Mismatches

Mismatches typically exist between students' levels of academic literacy knowledge and institutional requirements and expectations. There appears to be a widespread lack of awareness of what novice students know and what they need to learn, and as a result, literacy instruction is often inadequate. Even worse is the fact that the requirements are often not made explicit to students, a shortcoming that has been called 'institutional practice of mystery' by Lillis (1999). For instance, much of the guidance provided to students, typically in the form of writing guidelines of feedback comments, is phrased in a way that is obscure to novices. As Lillis and Turner (2001) observed more than a decade ago, the expected conventions are 'communicated as if they were common-sense and transparent' (Lillis & Turner, 2001: 58), and this situation does not seem to have changed. Carless (2006: 227) found in a large-scale survey across eight universities in Hong Kong that 'assessment criteria and the unpacking of its discourse seemed to represent a barrier to student understanding of the required standards'. Another example of confusing guidance is provided by Foster and Deane (2011), who report that undergraduate law students were asked to 'apply appropriate legal English', 'construct clear legal arguments and evince sound legal reasoning' (Foster & Deane, 2011: 90). For novice students (of whom the drop-out rate was around 20% in Foster and Deane's context), such phrases are meaningless, as they do not know what 'appropriate legal English' and 'sound legal reasoning' is. Investigations into students' perceptions of assignment feedback have shown that feedback comments are often perceived as unhelpful, either because students cannot understand the way in which they are phrased, or they do not provide sufficient explanation (Walker, 2009; Weaver, 2006). Carless (2006) found a striking difference between staff and students' perceptions of the usefulness of feedback; not surprisingly, lecturers believed their comments to be far more useful than they were perceived by students. These findings highlight the mismatch between student needs and the institutions' understanding of these needs. The resulting lack of adequate support impedes students' academic discourse socialisation.

A further example of the mismatch between novices' literacy needs and instructional provision is given by Abasi and Graves (2008). The authors investigated the influence of plagiarism policies on the academic writing of four international graduate students in a Canadian university. Drawing on interviews with the students and some of their professors, an analysis of policy documents and student texts, as well as classroom observations, the researchers found that the institutional plagiarism policies had a negative influence on the students' epistemological understanding and the development of criticality in their writing. The information conveyed to the students through guidelines, assignments and verbal instructions 'prompted the students to think that academic attribution was more about avoiding plagiarism than responding creatively to the ideas of others' (Abasi & Graves, 2008: 230). No guidance was provided about the epistemological and rhetorical nature of academic attributions. Abasi and Graves conclude with the warning that this lack of adequate institutional information has a particularly negative impact on students who 'may have less experience with the argumentative literacy tradition so dominant in North American academia' (Abasi & Graves, 2008: 230).

There are also mismatches between lecturers' and students' understandings of the genres that students have to produce. Bitchener and Basturkmen (2006) interviewed four postgraduate international students and their supervisors about the 'Discussion of Results' (DRS) chapter that the students had to write for their thesis. They found that there were disparities in students' and lecturers' understanding of the functions and features of the DRS which, according to the student participants, had not been explained to them. There were also different perceptions of the type of difficulties students experience when writing the DRS. While the students believed they had linguistic problems at the sentence level, the supervisors saw the problems occurring at the level of discourse and genre, for instance students' inability to hedge statements or to develop an argument. Interestingly, while the two articles discussed previously offer examples of lecturers' limited understanding of students' literacy needs, the lecturers in Bitchener and Basturkmen's apparently understood these needs but did not address them during the supervision process.

Critical thinking and argumentation

A key requirement of academic work, particularly at the postgraduate level, is that it is 'argumentational as opposed to merely expositional and that it possesses a critical dimension' (Andrews, 2010: 206). In the literature, problems with criticality and argumentation are typically ascribed to Asian students.

It is a widely held prejudice that critical thinking, taking a stance and expressing one's voice in an argument is particularly difficult for students who come from Confucian Heritage Cultures (CHC). The argument runs that people from CHC backgrounds tend to have collectivist rather than individualist orientations, and value harmony, deference and cooperation, whilst opposing or critiquing others is not regarded as acceptable behaviour (Wu & Rubin, 2000). By contrast, in Western cultures, people are thought to be socialised as individuals and encouraged to recognise their right to criticise and argue, as well as their ability to create knowledge. In such a view, collectivism and individualism bring with them rather different attitudes towards knowledge, and to the bearers of knowledge, i.e. the teacher or the written text. Ballard and Clanchy (1991) called the Western intellectual approach as 'knowledge extending' as opposed to the Eastern approach of 'knowledge conserving'. As students from collectivist cultures are believed to have considerable problems with being critical, some earlier researchers argued against the requirement of critical thinking at Western universities (Atkinson, 1997; Atkinson & Ramanathan, 1995). Turner (2011: 187) also discusses the struggle of students who are not familiar with the 'rhetoricity of being critical'. Criticality, she argues, requires specific linguistic and rhetorical resources, which are the result 'of the deep-seated cultural embedding of ways of using language and interacting with others in debate that is grounded in the Western intellectual tradition' (Turner, 2011: 185). Wu and Rubin (2000) provide an overview of the differences between Eastern and Western writing styles identified by Contrastive Rhetoric scholars. These researchers conclude that Chinese writers prefer indirectness and are therefore unlikely to follow the English topic-led organisation of texts (e.g. Kaplan, 1972). According to Hinds (1990), the level of indirectness makes texts written by Chinese writers look incoherent to Western audiences. Hinds also holds that Chinese writers' preference for expressing their ideas through metaphors contributes to the Western reader's perception of indirectness. Furthermore, it has been claimed that writers from CHC backgrounds, in contrast to North American writers, tend to be reluctant to exhibit self-disclosure, i.e. expressing personal emotions, achievements or views (Scollon, 1991). For example, Eastern writers may find it more difficult to acknowledge their own contribution to knowledge, which is expected in Western empirically-based dissertation or article writing. The orientation to the collective rather than the individual self is, as Wu and Rubin report, directly reflected in Chinese writers' preferred use of the plural first person form 'we' instead of the singular 'I'. Finally, Chinese writing, in comparison to Western writing, exhibits a certain lack of assertiveness.

In contrast to the broader findings of Contrastive Rhetoric scholars, other researchers have found considerable variations in Eastern writing that led them to deny the existence of fundamental culturally based differences in style as well as the simplistic claim that indirectness is purely due to Confucian culture (e.g. Mohan & Lo, 1985). While some comparative research, particularly early Contrastive Rhetoric studies, was premised on assumptions of monolithic cultures and therefore prone to stereotyping, Wu and Rubin (2000), on the basis of their comparison between Taiwanese and US students, stress the variability that exists within cultures and warn of simplistic cultural essentialism. Phan (2009), through content and style of her own writing, challenges the:

> taken for granted view that English academic writing is linear, relevant and logical, demonstrating well-articulated arguments reasoning and critical thinking...This view implies that academic writing in other languages, specifically Asian languages, is illogical, circular and irrelevant lacking argumentative and analytical ability and critical discussion. (Phan, 2009: 136)

Tran (2009), who investigated Vietnamese and Chinese postgraduate students' writing in an Australian university, also challenged stereotypical cultural assumptions. For instance, one of her participants seemed to use an indirect approach to expressing her ideas which is typically attributed to CHC. However, in a 'talk around text' discussion with the student, it emerged that the indirect style was not the result of her cultural disposition. This student, who had been exposed to some Western-style education and was aware of the preferred linear style, had consciously employed an indirect approach as a way of self-positioning and in order to 'lead the reader step by step to her argument rather than jumping directly to it' (Tran, 2009: 280). Similarly, Cheng (2006) describes the engagement of a Chinese graduate student with academic criticism in his discipline, electrical engineering, and his conscious employment of direct criticism in his own writing. This writing behaviour would be regarded at odds with the student's CHC background from an essentialist perspective against which Cheng warns, stressing 'the need for a more nuanced view of the influences of national culture on students' academic literacy learning' (Cheng, 2006: 279). As a matter of fact, it can be expected that essentialist assumptions of this type will be increasingly weakened by educational globalisation, when fewer individuals are influenced by only one culture, but 'may relate more to global sub-cultures for their sense of self' (Turner, 2011).

In the meantime, however, the tendency to prejudge certain student groups as lacking the ability for critical thinking extends beyond students from CHC backgrounds, as a recent publication, *Risk in Academic Writing* (Thesen & Cooper, 2014) reveals. Thesen (2014: 2) describes the dominance of '"northern" Anglophone knowledge production' in historically white South African universities where students who come from the 'periphery', i.e. non Anglophone educational backgrounds, are generally considered 'at risk' (Thesen, 2014: 13). The experience of international students in South Africa (these are often students from other African countries with English as an additional language), who were labelled as 'not able to think critically', is discussed in the chapter by Hunma and Sibomana (2014: 115). The authors themselves, who had come from francophone African countries to South African universities as doctoral students, experienced the effects of being categorised as 'other', i.e. outsiders from Western scholarship. Trying to meet the requirement of criticality involves, as Hunma and Sibomana explain, uncertainty and considerable risk, as students do not know, particularly in the absence of explicit advise from their lecturers, 'how much is permissible' (Hunma & Sibomana, 2014: 115), and prevents students from expressing their ideas in writing. The negative impact that this categorisation and the rejection of students' previous knowledge and experience has on student identities is further discussed below.

Whilst it cannot be denied that students from CHC traditions and other non-Western educational traditions may find certain Western literacy conventions difficult to adopt, it would be wrong to assume that difficulties typically associated with epistemologies in Anglophone academia are only experienced by students from the outside. However, problems with criticality and argumentation experienced by students from Western educational backgrounds have received far less attention in the literature. Earlier work on argumentation established that students struggle considerably with the argumentative essays required at university (Andrews, 1995), yet argumentation is not explicitly taught in most undergraduate programmes in the UK

(Mitchell & Riddle, 2000). Several studies revealed that both lecturers and students have fuzzy concepts of argument (e.g. Lea & Street, 1998; Mitchell & Riddle, 2000). In their feedback to student writing, lecturers use the term argument vaguely to indicate 'different deficiencies from reasoning, to referencing to structure and style' (Mitchell & Riddle, 2000: 17). I found in a survey of undergraduate students that most students, because of their earlier experience of writing persuasive essays at secondary school, understood argument as consisting of two sides, one of which reflects their personal opinion that needs to be persuasively justified in face of a counter-argument (Wingate, 2012b). Only a minority understood argument as involving multiple views, and as a gradual development of the writer's position throughout the text. The guidance provided to the students, either through handbook instructions or lecturer feedback, showed a lack of awareness of novice students' often inappropriate concepts of argument, as well as lecturers' inability to explain the nature of argumentation in academic writing.

As mentioned previously, research into difficulties with academic literacy tends to focus on student groups that are different from an assumed norm (i.e. the 'traditional' home student). The main focus is on international students, but there are also a few studies concerned with disadvantaged student groups. Kapp and Bangeni (2009), for example, examined the development of 20 black undergraduate students in a historically 'white' South African university. The researchers interviewed the participants regularly over the period of their three-year degree course. They found that the students moved from initial alienation with disciplinary discourses and a dislike of 'this critical analysis thing' (Kapp & Bangeni, 2009: 591) to a growing allegiance with their disciplines. This process, however, involved constant re-positioning, detachment from their home cultures and negotiation of their identities. For instance, when the students found that their own experiences and voices were not valued by markers, 'they yielded authorial presence in favour of an uncritical mimicking of the discourse which enabled them to pass' (Kapp & Bangeni, 2009: 589). Although the participants eventually developed criticality and an authorial stance, they were overall less successful than their fellow students from more privileged backgrounds, and none of them achieved the grades needed to go on to postgraduate study. The authors call for student support that caters 'for both the academic and affective dimensions of their transition' and draws 'on the knowledge and experiences that students bring from their home environments' (Kapp & Bangeni, 2009: 595). If knowledge, experiences, as well as the languages that students bring with them were used as a resource rather than being subjected to deficiency discourses, students would certainly not encounter the identity conflicts described by Kapp and Bangeni and other authors.

Student identities

The literature concerned with academic literacy and identity is also dominated by the experience of students from 'other' linguistic, cultural and educational backgrounds. The studies discussed in this section are theoretically framed by language socialisation (see Morita, 2004, 2009), sociocultural theory (see Leki, 2006), and the CoP model (see Fotovatian, 2012; Kim, 2011; Morita, 2004, 2009). All these studies investigate the identity constructions of one or several, mainly Asian and mainly postgraduate, students in Anglophone universities.

Identity has long been understood as multiple and shifting according to situation as well as social and power relations (Norton, 2000). Individuals vary in their response to different groups and draw on their multiple identities to employ adequate discourses (Angelil-Carter, 1997). Ivanič and Camps (2001: 6) use the term 'voice types' to refer to the ways in which individuals choose 'culturally recognisable' linguistic resources to represent themselves in specific social groups. Thus identities are constantly negotiated through social interaction. When students enter an academic discourse community, their own histories and values may be at conflict with the community's privileged ways of communicating. As Hawkins (2005: 62) explains,

> newcomers to these communities enter into a complicated dance in which they present themselves as certain sorts of people (either consciously or unconsciously), while being invited or summoned into certain categories and positions, in part based on how their self-presentation aligns with reified categories.

Depending on whether they manage to align their previous values and understandings of literacy with those of the community, students will negotiate an identity that either makes them successful participants or marginalises them. From a community of practice perspective, the experts in the discourse community, i.e. lecturers and more experienced peers, play a crucial role in helping novices to understand, and align with, the privileged values and literacy practices. As Leki (2006: 138) states, 'a key player in negotiations over identity is the course teacher who consciously or not helps to make institutional identity categories available to learners in the lopsided power configuration of schooling'. However, lecturers in the disciplines more often than not fail to provide this help, for reasons which were already mentioned in the previous sections.

One reason, discussed in the category 'Mismatches', is lecturers' insufficient knowledge of students' previous experiences, backgrounds and values, and their lack of awareness of the identity changes and conflicts that students may have to undergo when joining the new community. A more significant reason is that lecturers, as well as peers, tend to assign identities to students according to their nationality (Leki, 2006) or gender (Morita, 2009). Students from CHC backgrounds, for instance, are not only assumed to be more indirect and less assertive in their writing, but are also categorised as reticent and passive in classroom interactions. The a priori attribution of such characteristics to students can force them into specific identities, as Morita (2004) demonstrates through the experience of a Japanese graduate student in a US university. This student developed different identities in different courses. She felt encouraged by one instructor who did not regard her silence as problematic, whilst the attitude of another instructor who she felt ignored and marginalised international students made her remain completely silent. Leki (2006) who conducted a case study of four immigrant and international students in the US also found instances of the imposition of essentialised identities according to students' nationality. In some of these instances, students were asked to 'act as spokesperson' for their nation or culture with regards to the topic under discussion (Leki, 2006: 144).

International students may also be prejudged as less competent in terms of English language proficiency, with possibly detrimental consequences for their identities. Such deficit-focused stereotyping of Asian students is reported by Phan Le Ha (2006). Jenkins (2014), in a survey of academics' perspectives on their universities' English language policies and practices, involving 166 participants from 24 countries, found strong evidence of the attribution of low standard and poor performance to non-native speaker students. Even though the language proficiency of international students is a widespread concern among lecturers in Anglophone universities (e.g. Carroll, 2005), it is problematic when they are categorically perceived as less competent. The studies by Morita (2004, 2009) and Fotovatian (2012) show how international students develop identities of deficiency and marginalisation which are co-constructed by the students' self-perception as well as the perceptions and behaviours of other members of the discourse community.

Insights into the role of self-perception in identity construction are provided by Morita (2004) who observed how four female Japanese graduate students negotiated discourses and power relations 'so that they could participate and be recognised as legitimate and competent members of a given classroom community' (Morita, 2004: 583). A common identity among these students was that of being, as non-native speakers of English, less competent than other members of the discourse/classroom community. This identity was partly constructed through real difficulties experienced with reading materials and lectures. Because of their perceived lack of proficiency in

English, the students were also reluctant to contribute to classroom discussions. Their lack of participation resulted in the feeling that they might be regarded as ignorant or unintelligent, which added to the identity of incompetence. This identity is often reinforced by peers who fail to integrate international students in classroom and social interactions (Fotovatian, 2012; Kim, 2011; Morita, 2009). Kim's participants, for instance, felt the need to emphasise their subject knowledge in the interviews, noting that it was not recognised in the classroom due to negative perceptions by their peers. Their deficiency identity was reinforced by 'professors acting in a way that unconsciously imposes their power on students and leaves students powerless' (Kim, 2011: 289).

Power relations have a strong influence on identity construction. Leki (2006: 145) found that her participants 'had little power to dictate the circumstances of their relationship with powerful others' in their community of practice. Similarly, Tran (2009) describes how the Chinese and Vietnamese students in her study conformed with institutional and disciplinary conventions, such as writing in a direct style, although these conventions were sometimes in conflict with their own values and perceptions of sophisticated writing. As a result of power relations, Tran concludes, 'what is often taken for granted as institutional conventions may contribute to silencing or marginalizing the possibilities for alternative approaches to knowledge and prevailing the seemingly homogenous nature of institutions' (Tran, 2009: 281).

An example of how institutional power can suppress students' professional identities is provided by Paxton (2014). In her study, power is enacted through research supervisors who decide, based on the assessment of students' research proposals, whether the students can continue their studies. The context is a health science postgraduate programme for health practitioners in an 'Afropolitan' South African university (also discussed by Thesen and Hunma & Sibomana, see above) that was historically white but 'has a mission to reach out to other countries in Africa, and is beginning to look for ways to cater for the needs of (mostly) foreign-language students from Africa' (Paxton, 2014: 154). Paxton presents the case studies of two senior maternal and child health care professionals from Malawi and Zambia, who were both running the risk of not being permitted by their supervisors to complete the programme because of shortcomings in their proposals. One of the reasons why the Malawian student was advised to discontinue her studies was that she wanted to conduct her research in her own workplace, a labour ward, which was suspected by the supervisor as being a possibly 'no scientific milieu' (Paxton, 2014: 156). The Zambian student wrote with a strong personal voice, which was appropriate in her professional context but rejected as unscientific by her supervisor. The supervisor also disapproved of the student's reference to personal experience, although it was effective in setting the context for the proposed research and even 'crucial' (Paxton, 2014: 162) for readers' understanding of the relevant sociocultural practices. While the supervisors in Paxton's study tended to have difficulty in explaining the criteria for the research proposal, they nevertheless had the power to enforce students' compliance with rigid genre conventions, deny them the expression of their professional knowledge and thus devalue their considerable experience and identity as senior professionals. The disregard for mature students' professional experience and the suppression of their 'experiential voice' in the context of another postgraduate programme at the same South African university are also discussed by Cooper in the same volume (Cooper, 2014).

All the studies discussed in this section describe how students eventually manage, through identity shifts and accommodation, to integrate in their discourse communities. However, this integration may come at a cost as identity changes are enforced by institutional requirements; students have no choice if they want to avoid failure. As Fotovatian (2012) found in his study of four Asian students studying for a PhD in Education at an Australian university, they succeeded in gaining 'institutional identities' and membership of the discourse community. However, 'part of this identity was imposed by the institution through institutional labels' (Fotovatian, 2012: 581) such as 'international student'. While three of his participants were successful in constructing the required institutional identities, the fourth retreated to a 'self-isolating approach', which prevented her from benefitting from the interaction necessary for academic progress. Based on these findings, Fotovatian warns that the 'labels, such as "international" and "local", can amplify the social, cultural, and even physical space between students, constructing two separate identity groups' (Fotovatian, 2012: 585).

Summary for Part 1

This review of recent research into students' experience in the process of academic discourse socialisation has highlighted some shortcomings in the way in which Anglophone universities integrate diverse student groups and support them in their academic literacy development. The shortcomings are caused by a lack of awareness of, and flawed assumptions about, student backgrounds and learning needs. In relation to international students, Jenkins (2014) explains how universities that promote themselves as international have in fact little interest in their international students' cultural and linguistic resources, requiring them to assimilate to the English language practices and discourses of the institution. Internationalisation is thus a unidirectional process with often harmful effects on student identities. However, this lack of awareness and interest, and the subsequent lack of investment into student support do not only affect international students. 'Home students', as a result of their school education, are conveniently assumed to be well prepared for the university's literacy requirements, and therefore receive less attention by researchers and even less institutional support than international students. In the next section I present a study which I have conducted with undergraduate 'home' students; this study provides some insights into the academic discourse socialisation of this so far under-researched student group.

Part 2: Undergraduate 'Home' Students' Academic Literacy Development

As discussed in Chapter 3, the term 'home student' refers to students who have completed secondary education in the UK and are therefore regarded as native speakers of English. However, particularly in the multicultural environment of the study reported here, this assumption could be considered to be based on a false overgeneralisation. Thus, of the two cohorts involved in the research at a London university, although 91% of the students came from English secondary schools, 23% of this population also came from ethnic minorities and were therefore likely to speak languages other than English at home.

The research represents a case study of the experiences of students in an undergraduate programme which, for various reasons, cannot be seen as particularly representative within the diverse English higher education sector. The study was conducted in a Russell-Group university[1] that has a selective intake and requires high grades in school-leaving certificates. Furthermore, it was carried out in an Applied Linguistics programme which means that students gained their entry qualifications in language-oriented subjects and were therefore likely to be more sensitive to the linguistic features of academic literacy, and better prepared to adapt to the literacy conventions of the discipline than students in other fields might be. The programme is also untypical in the sense that it offers a relatively high level of embedded literacy support, as a result of the lecturers' expertise in teaching language and literacy. Advice on academic writing is provided in an induction workshop, and a further lecture is devoted to referencing and plagiarism. In addition, students are given the opportunity to write an unassessed formative essay, on which they receive written comments. As a follow-up, all students are invited to individual tutorials in which the feedback comments are discussed. The formative essay is written early on in the first year so that the students can use the feedback for later assessed assignments.

The aim of the study was to monitor the students' transition into the required practices of their new discourse community within their first term at university by investigating (1) their preparedness, i.e. previous literacy experience and expectations of the requirements at university; and (2) their experience of writing the first assignment at university, including their perception of the support they received. It was assumed that the research context with its high levels of literacy preparedness and instruction would offer valuable insights into the ways in which undergraduate students' academic discourse socialisation can be supported.

The research was carried out with two cohorts with a total of 117 students. To examine their previous literacy experience and expectations of the programme's literacy requirements, they were given an 'Academic Literacy Questionnaire' in their first week at university. To gain insights into the experience of writing the first assignment, students were invited to keep a diary during the process of writing. Six students from the first cohort and five students from the second volunteered to participate in the diary study. Furthermore, 16 interviews were conducted with volunteers from the two cohorts, in order to obtain in-depth information about their experience. One focus of this study was the teaching and learning of argumentation. The questionnaire and the diaries had been previously analysed for this aspect of literacy, and the findings were reported elsewhere (Wingate, 2012b). For the study reported here questionnaire and diary data were analysed with the broader focus on students' overall experience and academic discourse socialisation, and the interviews formed an additional data source.

Students' previous literacy experience and expectations towards requirements

The questionnaire consisted of a number of closed-response questions to gain information about the students' background, as well as of two open-ended questions which aimed to elicit more detailed information about previous writing experience and the expectations concerning the language and literacy requirements at university. The closed-response questions were analysed through frequency counts, while the open questions were subjected to 'qualitative content analysis' (Berg, 2009; Dörnyei, 2007: 245–246), which means that 'latent' meanings were sought through identifying emerging themes in the answers.

One hundred and one questionnaires were sufficiently completed to be included in the analysis. Of these 101 respondents, nine came from a different route than the A level qualification which is current in England, Wales and Northern Ireland. Four had attended an access to higher education course, a route for people without traditional entry qualifications. Five had gained the International Baccalaureate (IB) which has a wider range of subjects and includes a broader writing experience though the requirement of a 4000-word 'extended essay'. These nine students, unlike most other participants in the sample, all stated that they felt 'well prepared' for literacy requirements at university.

Previous literacy experience

The first main questionnaire item asked students in which subjects they had written assignments in their previous education, and of which type and length the assignments were. All participants apart from three had written assignments in more than two subjects, and the subjects were mostly language oriented and/or in the field of the social sciences, such as English Language, English Literature, History, Sociology, or Psychology. A smaller number had written in other fields such as Religious Studies, Law, or Business Studies. All participants had been required to write essays, and for 50% (50 students) this was the only type of writing they had done. The other half (51 students) had also written reports (41) and/or other genres such as portfolios or dossiers. The fact that the students had writing experience in various subjects, and half of them in more than one genre, suggests that they had an awareness of different epistemologies, conventions and styles.

The next questionnaire item, consisting of closed categories asked about the extent of advice they had received on different aspects of writing. The vast majority of students stated that they had received either 'a lot' or 'some' advice concerning referencing, structure, developing an argument, and writing style. Only 18 participants had received no advice in some of these categories. The follow-up open question invited more elaboration on the advice received, and the analysis of the 48 available answers yielded two themes, that of 'spoon-feeding' and 'restriction'.

'Spoon-feeding' was explicitly mentioned as a term by eight students, and was implicit in the answers of another 17. According to their comments, the teachers told them step by step what to read, and how to plan and write the assignment; students would also receive comments on various drafts. Closely linked to spoon-feeding is restriction, which was directly mentioned or implicit in the answers of 28 respondents. Their teachers would prescribe at least the structure of the assignment, but usually also content. As one student reported, 'essays in history always came with a bullet pointed list of structure and content'. Other students commented that teachers imposed strict regulations on writing style, structure and content in response to the external exam board requirements. In relation to argumentation, several respondents reported that they were taught to defend their opinion and 'persuade the reader of your opinion'. As the following comments show, little leeway was allowed for individuality and independent thought:

> We were informed about the necessary steps to get the highest marks, although often this went against our personal styles and ideas.
>
> All of my course-work was spoon-fed to me. My teachers often re-phrased sentences or added to paragraphs. Also from the start we were told exactly how to structure the content, and the indicative content itself. I don't feel it was truly my own work or a reflection of my ability.

Some students expressed their hope that writing at university would allow them more freedom.

Expectations towards literacy requirements

Another questionnaire item asked in which areas students thought writing at university would be different from writing at secondary school, and what they thought this difference would be. This was an open-ended item but several categories were provided, including 'Referring to sources', 'Structuring the assignment', 'Expressing your views/developing an argument' and 'Writing style'. Most students did not provide information for all categories, and some students provided answers such as 'more in-depth, detailed, explicit' which were too general to be included in the analysis. The categories 'Structuring the assignment' and 'Expressing your views/developing an argument' produced rather vague answers which suggests uncertainty about these areas. In relation to expressing their views/developing an argument, a few students expected that these would need to be based on evidence. A third of the students (34) believed that developing an argument meant 'stating your personal opinion'.

In the categories 'Referring to sources' and 'Writing style', more than half of the respondents (58) expected that they would have to use more sources when writing at university. Some students were more explicit, stating that their source use would need to be 'more accurate', that the type of referencing might be different, and that fewer internet sources should be used. 23 students mentioned that they would have to find their sources independently at university. Most interesting perhaps were the expectations towards the required writing style. Of the 63 students who commented in this category, in 18 cases the comments included 'more mature' or 'more sophisticated'. Almost all answers showed that students expected to have to offer 'more' of something, e.g. specialist, complex, formal, or containing more 'technical terms', or 'special vocabulary'. A number of students elaborated further, stating that their writing at school had been 'fairly immature', and that they expected to have to change their style considerably.

Overall, while the answers showed awareness of some aspects of academic writing, they also revealed much uncertainty. Particularly in relation to writing style, the answers disclosed students' feeling of inadequacy, such as being not mature and sophisticated enough in their current writing. This is underlined the fact that 83% of the respondents stated they were 'somewhat' rather than 'well' prepared for writing at university. The uncertainty and inadequacy felt by the majority of participants highlights the importance of providing students with literacy information and support early on in the study programme.

Students' experience with writing the first academic assignment

Information on this experience was drawn from the student diaries and the interviews. The 11 students who had volunteered to keep a diary while writing their first assessed essay had been asked to keep a record of the process of their writing, covering the four week period between receiving the essay title and submission. Only eight diaries could be used for the research, as three students made no more than a few initial entries. The interviews were held with 16 students, eight from each cohort, who were not identical with the diary writers. The interviews, which lasted between 15 and 26 minutes, were conducted after the regular individual feedback session in which the first assessed essay was discussed. It was assumed that at this stage, after some literacy instruction and after having written a formative and an assessed assignment, the students would be able to provide useful insights into their experience. There was no interview schedule but only the broad prompt to comment on the writing process and the support provided to them. The diaries and interviews were subjected to qualitative content analysis in which initial coding was followed by second level coding when the codes were organised into themes. These were subsequently analysed to uncover 'latent' meanings (Dörnyei, 2007: 246). Four broad themes emerged; the first three, 'Time management', 'Using sources' and 'Structure', were concerned with difficulties the students encountered. The fourth theme, 'Resistance', comprises students' reaction to the literacy conventions and the instruction they received. In the following sections these themes as well as latent meanings uncovered through deeper analysis are discussed.

Time management

In most interviews and diaries, difficulties with completing the essay in time for the deadline were mentioned. Typically, students would start work too late and then had to finish the essay in a great rush, as the following diary extract shows:

> I managed to write the conclusion this morning [submission date], and I rushed it and wrote some minor facts about xxx. I thought at the end, this is not the right conclusion for the essay, it doesn't sound right at all. But the conclusion was only 300 words, so hoping I will not get marked down for 300 words out of 4000 (D 3).

This statement was previously discussed in relation to argumentation (Wingate, 2012b), which is indeed the underlying problem for the student. The statement demonstrates the surface level of the problem, that is, weak time management which left not enough time for the last part of the essay. In the student's view, time management would be the reason for her rather weak performance (she actually received a low pass grade). In the data analysis, the statement was initially assigned to the theme 'time management'; however, second level analysis disclosed the student's lack of knowledge of how the construction of argument is supported by the macro structure of the text. In other words, the student had no understanding of the important role of the conclusion in argumentation; otherwise, she would probably not have left this part to the last minute. The statement was subsequently assigned to a new theme, 'argumentation', which only emerged from the second level analysis.

There were numerous statements in both the diaries and the interviews that showed that time management was only the surface problem behind which a more complex problem was hidden. In their accounts, the students would typically only recognise the surface problem. A common reason given for delays in starting the essay was that books were not available, for instance:

> Due to having no books to read, whilst waiting for the requested books to arrive, I was stressing about the assignment because I still had not formed my views and arguments on the subject (D 7).

> All the books were gone so I was stuck because I didn't have a clue what to write (I 13).

In these and other statements it appeared that the real reason for difficulties was not, as the students expressed and perhaps felt, the unavailability of books and the resulting time pressure, but students' reluctance to think deeply about the topic and develop an initial stance which would then help them to read the literature more purposefully. Instead, many participants made themselves completely dependent on the books and delayed any engagement with the topic until they had received them. Without having developed an initial stance on the topic, the students were unable to read these books critically and effectively, as the next section will show. Thus, a problem that was initially classified as time management needs was, after closer analysis, assigned to the theme 'Using sources'.

Using sources

Difficulties with selecting relevant information from sources were widely mentioned in the diaries and interviews. Reading without a focus or critical lens has been identified by researchers as a main reason for unsuccessful performance in writing from sources (McGinley, 1992; McCulloch, 2013; see Chapter 5 for a discussion). The problem described by McGinley, namely that a student would align herself with 'whatever point of view she was reading at a given time' (1992: 242), was mentioned by almost half of the participants. As one interviewee stated,

> I got completely bogged down by the reading – too much and I didn't know any more which direction to follow (I 2).

The following diary entries show how unfocused reading created a further difficulty, that of too many, but unhelpful, notes.

> Made tons of notes. I typed all the notes on a word document and totalled 11 pages, which stressed me terribly. I get a feeling that I am going off the topic (D 7).
>
> I had already prepared many notes from my readings. The problem was that when I was reading, I copied what I thought was relevant, without proper understanding it, so I was not fully prepared for this section (D 1).

Another dilemma students encountered in the use of sources was between the requirement to be critical and their deference to published literature. In the instruction they had received so far, students had been made aware of the need to show criticality in their writing. Guidelines and feedback would advise them to 'approach critically the ideas about which you have read', 'develop your own argument', and warn them not to 'reproduce the ideas and frameworks from the sources' (Wingate, 2012b: 152). However, several students perceived criticality as having to criticise the texts they were reading, and felt too inexperienced to do that. As one interviewee said,

> I've just started, I know nothing. How can I criticise someone who has written a book? (I 10).

There are obviously mismatches between the instruction offered to students and their level of understanding. Also, a second level analysis of the comments attributed to the theme 'Using sources' revealed that there were underlying identity issues. When faced with published sources, students carry the identity of novices lacking in knowledge and competence. Part of this identity is the feeling that they have nothing to contribute, as everything was already said by experts, expressed by two students as:

> It is impossible to write anything that is original and new (D3).

> What is there left for me to say? (D 4).

As will be seen below, this feeling is coupled with students' frustration over limitations to developing their own voice.

Structure

The difficulty of structuring the essay was repeatedly mentioned in six diaries and ten interviews. The frequency in which students' concern with structure was expressed was certainly related to the fact that structure was very often declared as a problem in lecturers' feedback comments. Closer analysis of the student statements showed that structure was a surface problem covering more fundamental issues, as the following diary extract shows:

> I have all the information about around 20 theories and approaches, and what I am missing is a structure by which those are to be presented. I was keen on discussing them rather than simply presenting one by one without a link (D 7).

As in most other statements in which structure was identified as the problem, the underlying problem was ineffective use of sources which resulted in too much but largely irrelevant information. Ineffective source use, as discussed in the previous section, is typically caused by a lack of initial position, which also makes it difficult to develop a structure. Another problem with structure, mentioned by five participants, was that they did not know what to do in certain parts of the essay. This problem was also, on second analysis, assigned to the theme of 'argumentation'. One student was unsure what to write in the Introduction, and four were uncertain about the Conclusion. As one student wrote,

> I hate having to write a Conclusion. Nothing new to say, I just have to repeat what I've already said in the main part (D 6).

This comment is similar to the diary extract (D3) presented earlier under the heading 'Time Management', and further highlights novice students' lack of understanding of the essay genre, and of the fact that in an argumentative essay the structure not only supports, but also mirrors the development of argument. The fact that 'home students', who are assumed to have been socialised into the conventions of argumentative essay writing at secondary school, have in fact little knowledge of the genre underlines two claims that I have made earlier: first, that it is inappropriate to expect abilities such as critical thinking and argumentation from students with a Western educational background while students from other backgrounds are prejudged as lacking these abilities; and second, that explicit genre instruction is needed by students from all backgrounds at the beginning of a study programme to enable them to understand the genre requirements. In the examples presented here, explicit instruction would have helped the students to recognise that both the Introduction and the Conclusion have crucial functions in the argumentative essay. The instruction would need to clarify the role of the Introduction as setting the scene and preparing the ground for the development of an argument in the 'Main Body', and the role of the Conclusion as summarising or restating the argument and confirming the writers' position.

Resistance

This theme subsumes students' expressions of frustration with the rules imposed on them, and the way in which the rules were communicated. Quite a number of comments were – often implicitly – critical of the literacy instruction that the students received. In several cases, the criticism surfaced only through second level analysis. The overt response of most interviewees was that the literacy instruction had been very useful. The most frequent reason for frustration and resistance was the students' sense that they were not allowed to say their opinion. Apparently, the guidance students had received had resulted in considerable confusion over the requirement to develop their own argument and the requirement to write in an evidence-based, not opinion-based manner. This is obvious from the following statements:

> I think I'm just frustrated that we don't seem to be able to write stuff that's actually ours (I 2).

> It's going to take a long long time before I can accept these rules. At the moment we are all panicking and trying not to say what we think (D 4).

These students understand academic conventions as restricting their own voice and identity. Anxiety about these conventions and fear of power were frequently expressed, for instance:

> One thing worries me slightly, which is that my views – even though scientifically proven – are coming from a religious perspective and from the Muslim holy book, which may mean that a teacher may not accept it as academic writing, even though I would have reasons to justify my position, but it may be hard to argue as a student against it (D 2).

Some students also resisted the feedback they had received from lecturers. Several comments were concerned with the tone of the feedback:

> But the feedback on my EE [exploratory (i.e. formative) essay] kind of made me feel that marking here is tough and harsh, and they will pick on little details (D 2).

In an earlier study (Wingate, 2010), I discussed the need to consider more carefully the tone and style of feedback comments in order not to demotivate lower achieving students. In this study, the detrimental effect of negatively phrased feedback was also apparent. Students feel particularly aggrieved when they are unable to understand negative feedback comments, as was the case for the participant who found the comment 'This is not relevant' in the margin of his essay:

> Exactly, why isn't it relevant? 'cause like for me it is relevant 'cause I've got like what I want to say in my head and I can justify it in my head. But then 'it's not relevant' I can't see why it's not relevant (I 12).

This and the following statement show the potential shortcomings of lecturers' written feedback:

> And the feedback was quite disappointing, and other comments were not explained to me properly, like your conclusion does not match the reasons you gave. And I would be left hanging there trying to figure out how it did not match. I read it twice and it made perfect sense to me, which kind of disappointed me because I still cannot see where some of my mistakes are (D 8).

As comments written in the margin of student texts or on comment sheets are typically truncated, they tend to point out a weakness without explaining the reasons for the weakness. Thus they may not only fail to be helpful and formative for subsequent assignments, but they may be even counterproductive as they confuse and alienate students.

Summary for Part 2

This study has shown that even in a literacy-and support-oriented programme, the difficulties involved in academic discourse socialisation and the extent of students' learning needs may be not fully understood. Despite the high level of expertise and awareness on the lecturers' part, the literacy instruction was not fully adequate. A main shortcoming was the mismatch between students' knowledge and the lecturers' expectations; this type of mismatch was discussed earlier in this chapter as one of three main categories of student difficulties.

The lecturers had obviously assumed that students would understand the nature of criticality and argumentation. As a result, these requirements were stated in writing guidelines and feedback without any further explanation. The survey, however, established that many students' perception was of argumentation being opinion-based and persuasive, showing that there was a need to teach the role of argumentation in academic debate. Earlier, I discussed the assumption that students from Confucian backgrounds have difficulty with being critical and taking a stance. More worrying perhaps is the fact that there is also an assumption that 'home students' will be able to be critical and take a reasoned stance, when the evidence seems to be that this is not the case for many. Perhaps as a result of this assumption, what is meant by criticality and argumentation was not explained by lecturers in this study, and it is therefore not surprising that the students were unable to recognise the real nature of their difficulties, but mistook them for problems with time management and structure. The instructional shortcomings also had an adverse effect on some students' identities, making them feel that any personal experience or opinion were not welcome instead of explaining that these might form the initial stance in an argument which subsequently needs to be confirmed or refuted through the consideration of other viewpoints . As certain conventions were not explained from an epistemological perspective, they were perceived by students as rules imposed on them. Furthermore, for a lack of understanding, some conventions became distorted, incomprehensible and therefore frightening. The academic convention to provide evidence for claims, for example, was distorted to the idea that students were not allowed to 'write stuff that's actually ours'. The mismatch between students' knowledge and the lecturers' expectations is also evident in the feedback comments issued by lecturers. As shown earlier, some students did not understand the feedback, or did not find it justified. Findings of this type show the need for more 'student-writer/tutor dialogue' as suggested by Lillis (2001, 2006: 43), which would help to alleviate the mismatches discussed earlier and would certainly accelerate students' academic discourse socialisation. Most universities, however, do not allocate the necessary time to staff to engage with students on a one-to-one basis.

Considering the fact that the programme in this study offered a substantial amount of literacy instruction, fewer difficulties experienced by students might have been expected. The findings demonstrate the complexity of academic discourse socialisation and the need for instruction to go beyond technical aspects such as referencing and structure, and to address the conceptual and epistemological underpinnings of academic literacy. The findings have two more implications. First, it is likely that undergraduate students need more time than just one term to understand and acquire academic literacy, as the requirements are starkly different from secondary school. Moreover, if, as the survey results suggest, students get such close guidance in their writing at school, perhaps some more individual support is indeed needed at university, at least initially. However, suggestions of this type are likely to be rejected as unfeasible by universities on the grounds of budget restrictions as well restrictions on the part of academic staff, who, as discussed previously, may not have the expertise or inclination to teach academic literacy. In the next chapter, I will propose a model that attempts to address the limitations of the current instructional provision.

Note

(1) The Russell Group consists of currently 24 prestigious research-intensive UK universities.

7 Towards an Inclusive Model of Academic Literacy Instruction

Introduction

In previous chapters, I have discussed the broad traditions of teaching academic writing, as well as the shortcomings of the extra-curricular model of instruction that is dominant in Anglophone universities. Based on the argument made by scholars from various traditions that literacy instruction cannot be separated from disciplinary knowledge and subject content, I have then considered various aspects of discipline-specific literacy instruction, before discussing typical difficulties that students encounter in the process of their academic discourse socialisation. In this chapter, I propose a model of inclusive curriculum-integrated academic literacy instruction that draws on 'best aspects' of existing literacy models whilst avoiding some of their shortcomings. By including all students, the model would be better able than existing ones to cater for student diversity. By being closely linked to, if not part of, the subject teaching, the instruction could deal with literacy activities that are notoriously difficult for students, such as writing from sources or argumentation, which can only be learned in the authentic subject context. The model will be explained in detail in the first part of this chapter.

Implementing the model would require substantial changes in current perceptions of academic literacy as well as in institutional structures. Such changes can only be achieved if there is sufficient evidence to convince university managers and academics of the feasibility and value of the instructional approach. Although there are examples of successful discipline-specific and curriculum-integrated language and literacy instruction, for instance in

Australian universities (see the discussion in Chapter 4), not enough detail is reported in the relevant publications on teaching content and methodology. I therefore want to offer some examples of discipline-specific teaching content which we[1] developed in an intervention study conducted across four disciplines, Applied Linguistics, History, Management and Pharmacy, in a UK university. The intervention study, although small scale and restricted by the current university policies and practices, aimed at making first steps towards the proposed model by developing an instructional approach which applied some of the model's principles and by evaluating the associated teaching content and methods. In the following sections, I will first discuss the overall model, before focusing on the teaching content that we developed for the interventions in the second part of this chapter. In the third part, the teaching methodology, as well as the implementation and evaluation of the instructional approach will be reported. Recognising the limitations of our small-scale intervention study, I will discuss necessary further steps towards the model of inclusive curriculum-integrated academic literacy instruction in Chapter 8. In the last couple of years, I have been invited to present the inclusive model of academic literacy instruction and our intervention study at various seminars and symposia. A link to the most recent presentations can be found at http://www.frankfurtlodge.co.uk/wingate-powerpoints.rar.

Proposing an Inclusive Model of Academic Literacy Instruction

The proposed model is based on a number of arguments made earlier in this book. One is that in view of increasing student diversity and the currently unequal and inadequate academic literacy support, it is timely that universities replace their existing remedial and exclusive provision and adopt inclusive policies and practices. Another argument, made in Chapter 4, is that literacy instruction, in order to be inclusive of all students and targeted to their needs, needs to be discipline-specific and integrated in the subject curriculum. This integration, it was further argued, could be best facilitated through collaboration between writing and subject experts. As can be seen in Figure 7.1, these conditions are required in three of the four principles which underpin the model. Principles 2–4 are concerned with the context of literacy instruction, that is, institutional provision. The first principle, by contrast, is concerned with the content and methodology of literacy instruction, which is the focus of this chapter. As the upper box in Figure 7.1 shows, I draw on 'best aspects' of five existing academic literacy models for the instructional content and methodology. Before I discuss these, I will first explain all four

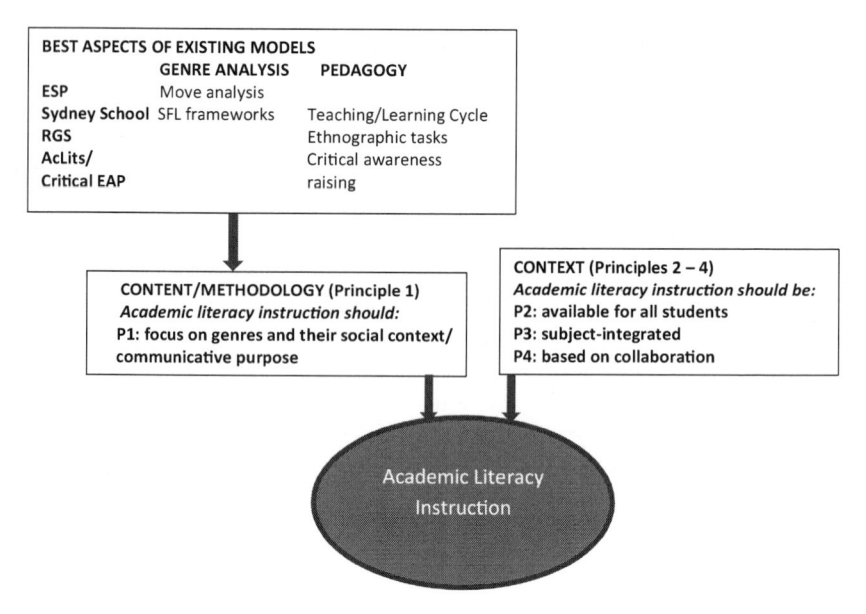

Figure 7.1 An inclusive model of academic literacy instruction

principles. Although this chapter deals mainly with the first principle, it is important to mention the other three, as they make clear the organisational structure and delivery mode necessary for inclusive instruction.

Principles of inclusive academic literacy instruction

As already mentioned, the four principles bring together a number of arguments made in previous chapters.

Principle 1

Principle 1 requires that academic literacy instruction needs to be fundamentally different from the type of instruction typically offered in EAP programmes, the limitations of which were explained in Chapter 3. Current EAP programmes tend to be focused on grammar and concerned with features of a non-existing universal academic language that is not situated in any specific context. While quite a number of students may need additional help with linguistic difficulties, the mainstream, i.e. all novices to academic literacy, need to gain an understanding of how academic language is shaped by the discourse community and its epistemologies, conventions and communicative requirements. Therefore, literacy instruction should focus on the genres that are relevant to students and make their specific social functions and communicative purposes in the discourse community visible. The fact that in academic contexts these functions are related to the construction, presentation and debate of knowledge and are performed through genres was already explained in Chapter 1. It was also argued in Chapter 1 that academic literacy comprises an understanding of the discipline's epistemology as well as of the socio-cultural context. Academic literacy instruction should provide students with what Johns (2008, 2011) called 'genre awareness', helping them to recognise how genres reflect and communicate epistemological and cultural content. It should deal with questions such as the communicative purposes of genres, the 'roles and relationships they assign to writers and readers' (Paré, 2014: A-91), and the ways in which authors agree with, or distance themselves from, other authors. Evidently, in this approach literacy teaching needs to be closely linked to the teaching of subject knowledge. The approach would also require more attention to reading and the use of sources in knowledge presentation, areas which have been neglected in EAP and other existing approaches although they are, as shown in Chapter 5, problematic for students.

Principle 2

The second principle relates to my earlier argument (see Chapter 3) against instructional provision which exclusively targets specific learner groups (such as non-native speakers of English) on the assumption that their academic English must be deficient. The principle requires that academic literacy instruction becomes an entitlement for *all* students, regardless of their backgrounds. It is based on the understanding that all students are novices in their chosen academic disciplines, and therefore need to learn the relevant discourses and conventions. While it is certainly the case that some students need additional support with linguistic problems or with managing their learning at university, the EAP or skills courses that respond to these needs cannot remain the only provision made by universities. Linguistic and skills support should be available *in addition* to academic literacy instruction.

Principle 3

The obvious consequence of the first two principles is that academic literacy instruction needs to be integrated with subject teaching. The third principle, therefore, requires an instructional format that goes beyond offers of 'additional' or 'curriculum-linked' discipline-specific materials and workshops (see Chapter 4 for the distinction between these approaches). Literacy teaching should take place alongside, or arise from, content teaching. To give an example: when new information or knowledge is dealt with in the classroom, attention could be paid to the textual evidence of how the new information builds on previous knowledge through references, citations, and the author's argumentation. Integration would be fully achieved if academic literacy became an assessed component of the subject curriculum, as is the case in several Australian universities. While this level of integration calls for considerable changes in beliefs, policies and practices, it is the only way in which the importance of language and literacy would be given full recognition. It is also the only way to ensure that all students can learn disciplinary discourse conventions in their genuine communicative context. Furthermore, integration eliminates the workload pressure created by 'additional' literacy instruction, a workload pressure which affects weaker students in particular.

Principle 4

The integration of subject and literacy instruction cannot be achieved by subject lecturers on their own, because they usually have neither an explicit awareness of their discipline's literacy conventions (see Chapter 3 for discussion), nor the expertise and meta-language to teach them. Therefore, the fourth principle is that academic literacy instruction needs to be underpinned by collaboration between writing experts and subject experts. The writing experts need to be involved in the identification of opportunities for literacy work in the subject curriculum, the analysis of the genres that students will encounter, and in making genre features visible to students. The subject expert is needed to help the writing expert understand the social context and communicative intentions of the discipline's genres.

The discussion in previous chapters has shown that there are only a few instances of instructional practices that broadly incorporate the four principles; these are mainly found in the 'collaborative, curriculum-integrated literacy instruction' (Purser, 2011: 30) offered in many Australian universities. Nevertheless, as mentioned in Chapter 4, details concerning the actual methods of literacy teaching used in the Australian approach have not been published; therefore it is unclear to what extent Principle 1 is followed there. In general, however, the instructional reality in Anglophone universities is far removed from the principles I propose, and it is not helpful that researchers and practitioners tend to be restricted by a specific model and a specific context, as discussed in Chapter 1. Not enough effort has been made to look for convergence between different literacy models and bring together their best aspects. Nor has there been much concern for the literacy needs of the diverse 'mainstream' student population for whom academic literacy instruction has therefore remained inadequate. Therefore, for the instructional content of the proposed model, we have drawn on various literacy models, their theoretical concepts and pedagogical methods. This is in my view the best way to develop a rich instructional approach that considers both linguistic and contextual factors, and is suitable for students from all backgrounds.

The Content of the Instructional Approach

Figure 7.1 shows that the content of the instruction is based on genre analysis. The importance of genre in literacy instruction has been stressed by members of the three main genre schools, and, as Motta-Roth (2009: 324) puts it, 'in order for students to become writers in their field, they need to become discourse analysts'. Genre, according to Hyland (2008a: 543) is a 'robust pedagogical approach', as it identifies the organisational patterns and typical linguistic features in texts and makes explicit how these relate to the communicative purpose of the genre and are therefore expected by the members of the discourse community. We have drawn on the linguistically-oriented genre models, ESP and the Sydney School/SFL, which provide the analytical tools for explicit genre descriptions.

However, we have also drawn on social practice approaches to ensure that students fully understand the social contexts and communicative purposes of genres, as postulated in Principle 1, and develop critical awareness of the practices influencing text production. Social practice approaches also help to avoid prescriptivism of which the linguistic genre approaches have been previously accused. In a prescriptive teaching format, texts are presented as templates or models to imitate, which, as RGS scholar Johns pointed out, leads to reproductive, non-transferable 'genre acquisition' rather than to 'genre awareness' or 'high-road transfer' (2008: 238; see discussion in Chapter 4). For this reason Johns makes a strong case for the development of genre awareness which enables students to recognise genres as constantly evolving socially-situated forms of communication. Therefore, in the methodology of the instructional approach we followed recommendations from RGS, as well as from Academic Literacies and Critical EAP. Lastly, in the selection of 'best' aspects from existing literacy models, we chose the Sydney School/SFL's teaching/learning cycle as a suitable instructional format. In spite of earlier criticisms of the use of the cycle for prescriptive modelling of texts (Cope & Kalantzis, 1993; Kress, 2003; see discussion in Chapter 4), we believe that it offers a useful instructional format that enables constructivist learning. I discuss the ways in which the five models were used in the following sections.

Genre analysis

Having explained why literacy instruction should be based on genre analysis, I will briefly discuss the choice of student genres as models for instruction, before I move on to the specific analytical methods. The most widely used models in EAP have been expert texts; however, alongside with Hüttner (2008), I have argued that the genres that students have to produce should be the focus of instruction (see Chapter 4; Tribble & Wingate, 2013). One reason for the use of student genres is that their communicative purpose, and consequently their textual features are different from expert genres. Giving students models of the genre they have to write responds directly to their need to understand the expectations and requirements attached to that genre. Working with student genres is therefore a key element in the proposed instructional model. To analyse student genres, Hüttner recommends a methodology that is different from Bathia's (1993). Bathia had proposed seven stages for the analysis of expert and professional genres, including the examination of situational and institutional context, compilation of a corpus of prototypical text, and linguistic analysis (1993: 22–36; see Chapter 4). Hüttner recommends a methodology consisting of three phases. The first is the compilation of a corpus that includes either all or randomly chosen members of the target genre. In the second phase, linguistic analysis looks first for quantitative evidence of typical features. Qualitative evidence is then sought in third phase, when expert informants are consulted on the appropriateness and acceptability of the text exemplars. The linguistic analysis proposed by Hüttner is carried out on the texts' move structure and their lexico-grammatical features and relies on corpus tools that establish the frequency of occurrence. In the case of lexicogrammar, this means that key phrases and keywords are identified and then compared with reference corpora.

While Hüttner offers a valuable methodology for literacy teachers to explore student genres in preparation for teaching, for the literacy classroom we prefer qualitative analysis over computer-driven frequency counts. The reason is that, as I will show in Part 2 of this chapter, qualitative analysis enables discussion and constructivist learning. Furthermore, qualitative analysis is essential for the development of genre awareness, as it means working with whole texts or sections of text and identifying typical features, instead of identifying differences between genres by analysing short sequences from across a large range of texts. For the qualitative analysis, it is useful to begin by analysing the macro-structure, i.e. the expected rhetorical moves of a genre or sub-genre. However, as Chang and Schleppegrell (2011: 141) have argued, whilst recognising a genre's rhetorical moves offers 'only a general orientation to, or guidelines for writing a subgenre', the move analysis 'can be enriched with the specific language features needed to achieve the expected rhetorical structure'. The next levels of analysis, therefore, need to focus on the discourse-semantic and lexico-grammatical features which enable the development of the text's argument. SFL offers the most fine-grained tools for these analyses, and we have used some of these to examine argument development and linguistic choices in student texts. However, in the learning resources the rather complex and technical SFL terminology was avoided and translated into a much more simply phrased commentary. In the following sections, I discuss how the various analytical tools were applied in the instructional approach presented in this chapter.

Move analysis

Move analysis examines the internal organisation of the components of a genre (such as the Introduction or Literature Review), also called part-genres or sub-genres (e.g. Swales, 1981; Swales & Lindemann, 2002). A key concept in genre theory is that each genre has a specific schematic structure (Rose & Martin, 2012), or follows certain stages, called moves and steps by Swales (1990), to achieve its communicative purpose. The pedagogic value of move analysis lies in the explicit descriptions of the stages or moves expected in a genre. Following Swales' seminal analysis of moves in the introductions of research articles, there has been a proliferation of research analysing other sub-genres such as abstracts, results, discussion and conclusion sections (e.g. Bunton, 2005; Hopkins & Dudley-Evans, 1988; Thompson, 1993). Much of this research was carried out on expert or graduate student genres such as research articles or PhD dissertations, and subsequently used for the design of learning materials (most notably Swales & Feak, 2012). These genres usually have a clear structure, often in the IMRAD format of introduction, methods, results and discussion, and the moves within these sections appear in a more or less regular order. When it comes to student genres such as the argumentative essay, it has been found that they do not lend themselves easily to move analysis, as texts are staged more idiosyncratically depending on assignment task, the function required in the task (such as 'describe, define, compare, hypothesise') as well as the assessment criteria of specific study programmes (Dudley-Evans, 2002).[2] For this reason, rather than using move analysis for identifying what is prototypical in a sub-genre, we used it to describe what writers of successful and less successful texts did (or did not do) to achieve the communicative purpose of the sub-genre. As can be seen in Tables 7.1 and 7.2, this description is presented in a commentary next to the text, and within the text, the moves are signalled through numbers in square brackets. Thus, while in sub-genres, such as the Introduction, the moves are fairly predictable and the commentary is similar across texts, in other sub-genres, for instance the 'Main Body' of the argumentative easy, the commentary is distinctive to the individual text and resembles a summary of content. This description of what is going on in the text, however, helps students to recognise discourse-semantic features such as the development of argument within and across paragraphs. The types of move analysis we used are further discussed in relation to the two examples below.

The example in Table 7.1 is one of multiple text exemplars provided to students in a set of learning materials that we developed for MA students in Applied Linguistics. The 3500-word assignments in this particular programme are expected to have neat structures signalled by headings and sub-headings, and therefore offer clear units for move analysis. The commentary shows that

Table 7.1 Example of move analysis of an essay introduction (Applied Linguistics)

Assignment title: *What counts as validity in formative assessment?*

Introduction	
[1] [1.1.] The role of assessment in language teaching and learning is complex and often politically-charged. [1.2.] In recent years, many researchers have promoted a more socially and democratically equitable conception of assessment (i.e. Shohamy 2001, Lynch 2001), that is non-psychometric and non-standardised. This has led to the promotion, endorsement and implementation of various classroom-based alternatives, many of which have shared characteristics and concerns (cf. Leung 2005: 870 for a brief overview). [1.3.] Despite this change in tide, however, a number of old questions rightly persist. In particular the issues of validity and reliability, which Leung (2005) refers to as 'the quality and soundness' of the assessment approach, are still prevalent (pLeung, 2005:. 869). [1.4.] Interestingly, these questions are posed by those spearheading this new movement in an attempt to ensure theoretical, empirical and epistemological robustness (i.e. Leung 2004).	**1. Establishing context** 1.1. Hyper-Theme 1.2. Refers to recent debate and changes 1.3. Narrows focus to the essay topic 'validity' 1.4. Expands further on background of essay topic
[2] [2.1.] In this discussion I shall address the issue of validity in regard to Formative Assessment (FA). [2.2.] In the first section, I shall define, examine and then problematise the central tenets of FA; this problematisation will raise three key questions in regard to validity in FA. In the second section, I will begin by briefly delineating some of the underlying assumptions of validity in conventional assessment practice. [2.3.] Following this, I shall return to the three crucial and interrelated questions previously identified, through which I argue for a reconceptualised understanding of validity in FA that acknowledges its complex and contingent nature. In my conclusion I shall argue that subscription to this viewpoint will enable FA to attain a more prominent position in educational assessment.	**2. Outlining essay** 2.1. Macro-Theme 2.2. Outlines next two sections/Hyper-Themes 1 and 2 2.3. Announces own argument/stance/Hyper-Theme 3

there are two main moves ('Establishing context' and 'Outlining essay') that would be expected or obligatory in the sub-genre 'Introduction', and describes the steps the writer took within these moves. This text also demonstrates skilful use of lexico-grammatical features such as cohesive devices. In this case, they were analysed in the classroom; in other learning resources, cohesive devices were also highlighted in the commentary, as the next example shows.

The example in Table 7.2 is from the learning materials for a Management programme. The label of the assignment was 'Critical Review', belonging to the genre family of 'Critique' (Nesi & Gardner, 2012), in which students had to evaluate a marketing concept using a typology with four criteria. The material development was based on our analysis of twenty 1500-word model texts. Unlike the Applied Linguistics assignments, the critical reviews had no headings to signal the structure, and the move analysis was therefore carried out on the texts' paragraphs.

Table 7.2 Example of move analysis of paragraph of critical review (Management)

	PARAGRAPH FUNCTION: Applying Hackley's typology/Criterion 1
[7] Alternatively, O'Shaughnessy & O'Shaughnessy (2009) argue that the intellectual validity of the SDL and the co-creation of value are unfounded and merely conceptual. **[8]** More specifically, Echeverri & Skalen (2011) state that 'it does not explain, or offer, a framework suggesting how interactive value formation takes place in practice'. Furthermore, the notion of co-destruction is highlighted by Echeverri & Skalen (2011), whereby 'interactions with providers may sometimes be perceived negatively by customers'. The downside of the SDL seems to go unnoticed in a lot of the key literature, which instead portrays the ideology as being positive and unproblematic (Echeverri & Skalen, 2011). **[9]** Another point to consider is the use of the word 'service', which in itself can be misleading and insinuates a different meaning to that which the paradigm act stands for; in which case the terminology used to portray the theory is put into question (O'Shaughnessy & O'Shaughnessy, 2009). Additionally, Brown (2007) highlights similar prior theories that have been developed and that are said to be more articulate, notably the Concept of Customer Value by Morris Holbrook (1984).	[7] Negative evaluation of concept, following previous positive evaluation ['*alternatively*'] [8] More arguments supporting negative evaluation, based on one source ['*more specifically*', '*furthermore*'] [9] Additional evidence, based on two sources ['*another point*', '*additionally*']

As this genre required rather short texts with an argumentative structure, each paragraph represents a move towards building the argument. The assignment task makes the following moves obligatory: (1) the introduction of the concept to be critiqued, (2) the introduction of the typology used for the critique, (3) the application of the typology's four criteria, and (4) the overall evaluation resulting from the application of the criteria. The move analysis by paragraphs served the discourse-semantic purpose of demonstrating the function of the paragraph in the overall argumentative structure of the text. For this reason, we provided each paragraph with a heading that described its function. As can be seen in the next section, further tools were used for the analysis of the texts' argumentative structure. The steps taken within the paragraphs are less predictable than the moves. They are described because they demonstrate the conceptual development of ideas, which is further discussed in the next section. The commentary also signals the cohesive devices which serve to organise the text within (e.g. 'additionally') and across paragraphs (e.g. 'alternatively').

Details of how these learning resources were used are given in the second part of this chapter. It should be noted here that in order to avoid prescriptivism students are always given a number of exemplar texts for comparison instead of one 'model'. An example for this is presented in Appendix 7.1, which shows an extract of the materials we developed for Pharmacy. We carried out a move analysis of the macrostructure of ten high achieving and five low achieving student texts, which were 8000-word laboratory reports. The structure of the successful reports represents the moves that are expected in this genre, that is, Introduction, Materials and Methods, Results, Discussion, Conclusion, References. The extract shows the moves of one high-achieving and one low-achieving report, where the author of the latter has considerably digressed from the expected structure. As I will discuss later, it is the comparison of several texts that helps students to develop awareness of the genre expectations.

Discourse-semantic analysis

This type of analysis is concerned with the development of argument in written texts, and the way in which this development is signalled across the text. In our analysis of student genres in four disciplines, we followed Ravelli's (2004) study of relations between paragraphs, and hyper-Themes in student genres. Ravelli's work was particularly helpful for our project, as she analysed management and history essays, i.e. two of the disciplines we covered in our study.

Relations between paragraphs

The analysis of relations between paragraphs is based on Halliday's (1994) description of two types of logico-semantic relations, projection and expansion.

As Ravelli explains, expansion is the more important type to consider in the analysis of a text's argumentative structure, as its three categories, elaboration, extension, and enhancement, serve to create 'chains of reasoning' (Ravelli, 2004: 107). While a detailed account of the occurrence of these categories in student genres is useful for identifying differences between disciplines – as Ravelli did for management and history – for instructional purposes this level of distinction seems unnecessarily complex and loaded with terminology. We therefore took a simpler approach to illustrating to students the development of argument. In the same way as Ravelli, we created both linear and synoptic descriptions of paragraph relations in a text. The example in Table 7.2, shown above, is an extract of the linear description; the students are presented with the move analysis of all paragraphs in the text, and the inserted headings describing the paragraph functions help them to recognise the argumentative structure. The accompanying synoptic view of the text (see Appendix 7.2 for an example) aims to visualise this structure. This analysis of the 'higher-level structuring of texts' (Ravelli, 2004: 104) is then followed by an analysis of how logico-semantic relations are signalled across the text and within the paragraphs. The SFL framework of Theme is useful for this analysis.

Themes

Martin (1992) stresses the predictive function of themes and distinguishes between (1) Theme, which represents 'the point of departure' (Halliday, 1985: 38) at the clause level and (2) hyper-Theme which 'is an introductory sentence or group of sentences which is established to predict a particular pattern of interaction among strings, chains and Theme selection in the following sentences' (Martin, 1992: 437). Lastly, the broadest category is (3) macro-Theme which is defined by Martin (Martin, 1992: 437) as 'a sentence or group of sentences (possibly a paragraph) which predicts a set of hyper-Themes'. While the macro-Theme in a text always points forward to the development of the text, Ravelli explains that hyper-Themes do not only predict the reasoning chains of the upcoming text, but also refer back to previous sections, and in this function signal 'a shift in the conceptual development of the text as a whole' (Ravelli, 2004: 113). Hyper-theming, in Ravelli's words, enables the student writer to establish 'retrospective and prospective connections to the argumentative framework' (Ravelli, 2004: 105), and thus reach the level of objectivity and abstraction expected in academic discourse. Most importantly, hyper-Themes are needed for the level of textual organisation expected in academic genres.

Many students struggle with this aspect of academic writing, and therefore, as Ravelli puts it, 'basic control of conceptual structure, as well as its signalling, is one of the key areas for literacy development' (Ravelli, 2004: 117).

In our instructional approach, we use different methods to alert students to the important role of macro- and hyper-Themes in signalling the development of argument, and to enable them to recognise and use the associated lexico-grammatical resources. In the move analysis of texts, for instance, these themes are highlighted in the commentary either by directly mentioning them (see Table 7.1), or by highlighting the organising vocabulary (see Table 7.2). As the example in Table 7.1 shows, in Applied Linguistics we used the SFL terminology; for the less linguistically schooled students in Management, History and Pharmacy, we replaced macro-Theme with 'outline' and hyper-theme with 'opening statement'; expressions that signal the organisation of the text or paragraph were called 'signposting', as shown in Table 7.3.

Lexico-grammatical analysis

In addition to highlighting themes in the commentary of the move analyses, the learning resources also present specific paragraphs for a closer examination of the lexico-grammatical devices used for textual organisation. An example is shown in Table 7.3. This analysis focused on the organising vocabulary, mainly the cohesive devices, as well as the use of grammatical metaphor.

Furthermore, short text extracts are presented to demonstrate to students the use of grammatical metaphor. This concept was explained by Halliday (1993) as creating the same meaning with different grammatical choices, for instance by expressing through a noun what was previously described by a verb. A grammatical metaphor typically rephrases what has been previously said in a more concise manner, and at the same time also has the discourse-semantic function of indicating the beginning of a new argument. According to Schleppegrell (2004: 176), 'the resources of grammatical metaphor enable the proficient writer to achieve the technicality, reasoning within the clause, text-structuring, and authoritativeness that instructors value'. While these resources are rarely explicitly taught, their absence in student texts is often criticised by instructors as 'wordiness', and lack of conciseness (Schleppegrell, 2004: 177). Below are three examples of grammatical metaphor (underlined in the examples) which appear in the learning resources.

> Example 1/History: Against expressed wishes of his ministers, George IV insisted that a "Bill of Pains and Penalties" be introduced to the House of Lords as a means by which he could rid himself of the wife he deplored. His will prevailed, but whilst the Bill passed its third reading, it did so only by the slightest of margins, and thereafter was withdrawn.
>
> Example 2/Pharmacy: After being swallowed, any drug contained therein must go into solution in the gastric fluids before it can be absorbed and exert a systemic effect. The rate and extent of absorption may therefore

Table 7.3 Organising vocabulary in paragraph of critical review (Management)

Paragraph function: Summarising Criteria 1 and 2	Comments
[1] This criticism shows elements of both intellectual and functional critiques. **[2]** First, it can be argued that the model is limited intellectually as it fails to accurately explain how all firms internationalise. The fact that it only selectively describes how some firms venture abroad shows its lack of internal coherence and depth. **[3]** Furthermore, it assumes a slow learning process, high uncertainty and a lack of knowledge, all of which have been challenged with recent technological advancements and other developments discussed above, meaning that these factors no longer seem to relate to the world the model is seeking to explain.	[1] Linking back to previous paragraph where criticism was explained [2] Signposting structure, introducing first argument [3] Expanding first argument
[4] Second, the model's validity as a managerial tool is being challenged by evidence showing that firms leapfrog stages in the chain. **[5]** This functional critique, **[6]** therefore, highlights the model's limitations which can have significant implications for managers. Using the establishment chain to determine a firm's internationalisation strategy, for example, may result in disadvantages as competitors may enter key markets faster by skipping stages. This may lead those players to gain first-mover or other competitive advantages in the foreign markets. **[7]** Based on the evidence discussed one can argue that this model is simplistic and does not account for firms which take their products to market in unpredictable and creative ways.	[4] Signposting structure, introducing second argument [5] Linking back to previous paragraph where this critique was explained [6] Summarising the previous two arguments [7] Summarising the argument of this paragraph and linking back to evidence provided in the previous paragraph

depend critically on the rate of disintegration and dissolution of the drug from the table.

Example 3/Applied Linguistics: In this chapter, issues in the design of a small-scale mixed-methods case study will be discussed. Data collection instruments <u>will be created</u> for the identification of informants' source use and factors involved in that source use. To ensure the *creation* of the most effective research design, issues of sampling, recruitment and ethics will also be considered.

Example 2 illustrates how the use of the grammatical metaphor 'absorption' leads to the level of abstraction and technicality that is, as the subject expert confirmed to us, expected in lab reports in Pharmacy. All three examples show the role that the grammatical metaphors play in text-structuring and the development of argument, as they refer back to and encapsulate a previous argument (e.g. 'George IV <u>insisted</u>') and at the same time mark a starting point for expansion or a new argument ('<u>His will</u> prevailed, *but* . . .).

Genre analysis: Summary

In the previous sections I have discussed the analytical tools from ESP and SFL which we used for our own analysis of student texts and for the learning resources that underpin genre analysis in the literacy classroom. Nevertheless, our work on this approach is ongoing, and we recognise that further areas need to be addressed. For instance, in order to help students to develop voice and stance in their academic writing, we will have to include the analysis of how interpersonal meanings are created. Work on interpersonal meanings has been done under different labels, such as 'evaluation' (Hunston & Thompson, 2000), 'stance and engagement' (Hyland, 2009), and the SFL-based Appraisal system (Martin & White, 2005). Chang & Schleppegrell have used the component 'Engagement' from the Appraisal system to help student writers recognise the linguistic resources they can employ to 'project themselves, incorporate and manage different voices or sources of voices' (2011: 141) and thus achieve an appropriate balance between own assertion and acknowledgement of existing knowledge. As Chang and Schleppegrell (2011: 141) point out, novice writers need 'explicit scaffolding' to gain control over these linguistic resources.

So far I have discussed genre analysis as the content of the proposed instructional approach and provided examples of the materials we developed. The next section focuses on the teaching methodology.

The Methodology of the Instructional Approach

The preceding presentation of annotated text exemplars can easily lead to the impression that an approach was taken against which scholars from RGS, Critical EAP and Academic Literacies have long warned: prescribing text models in a 'normative' manner (Lillis & Scott, 2007: 11), thus reinforcing institutional norms and values (Devitt, 2009) and asking students to accommodate to them (Benesch, 2001; see discussion in Chapter 2). We have avoided these pitfalls by designing a teaching methodology which facilitates text comparison, discussion and critique, leading to critical awareness of literacy practices and genre awareness rather than acquisition (Johns, 2008). Before we explain this in more detail, it is necessary to describe the context in which the approach was developed and implemented.

Context: Academic literacy interventions

The work began with an intervention study in our own postgraduate programme in Applied Linguistics. It was prompted by student needs that we had observed over a number of years, and that were also frequently expressed by students. For example, we had observed that a substantial number of students received low grades in the initial assignments, affecting their overall result, before they gradually managed to improve. This situation suggested a lack of adequate initial support which was also mentioned by students. They felt that the writing guidelines provided in the handbook were not sufficient to help them to understand what was required, and that they had to go through several rounds of assignments and feedback before they reached this understanding. A common complaint was that they never got to see examples of the assignments they had to write. On this basis, we began to compile a databank of student assignments by asking student cohorts at the beginning of their study to give us permission to use all texts they produced during their study for research and teaching purposes. It was then easy to collect the texts of those who gave us permission as all assignments are submitted electronically. From the databank, we selected a set of high- and low-graded assignments for the preparation of the learning materials. While the genre-analytical approach in the design of the materials was already explained, I will discuss their pedagogical rationale and use in the classroom in the next section.

The materials focus on the sub-genres that occur in assignments and dissertations and were combined into a 'Writing Guide', the contents of which are shown in Appendix 7.3. Academic literacy workshops were then arranged which focused on specific sub-genres, and were strategically timed. The first one, focusing on Introductions and Conclusions (Units 3 and 5) was offered while students were in the process of writing their first assignment, whilst the last/third, focusing on the genre of dissertation, dealt with presenting and discussing findings from empirical studies (Unit 8) and was conducted just before student began working on their dissertations.

The evaluation of the intervention showed high levels of student participation and satisfaction, as well as improved understanding of literacy conventions and practices. As a result, and as part of an ongoing search for discipline-embedded methods of literacy instruction (discussed in Wingate, 2012b), we obtained funding to apply our instructional approach to three other disciplines. Pharmacy, Management and History were chosen because we had contact to subject lecturers in these disciplines. These lecturers had recognised a need for literacy support in their programmes and were willing to collaborate. We asked them to identify a key genre, i.e. one that was most important in their programme, and/or most problematic for students. This turned out to be the laboratory report in Pharmacy, the critical review in Management, and the essay in History. Next, the lecturers were requested to provide us with a minimum of five low scoring (45–55%), five mid scoring (56–69%) and five high scoring (70% or higher)[3] exemplars of these genres. This process was not without complications as written permission had to be obtained from the student writers, and students who had achieved low scores tended to be reluctant to grant this permission. To guide our analysis of the student texts, we asked to be provided with the comments that assessors had made on the texts. During the development of the learning materials, we regularly consulted the subject lecturers. The lecturers also provided detailed feedback on the materials before they were presented to students in academic literacy workshops. As already mentioned, the learning resource developed for Applied Linguistics was a writing guide covering several sub-genres (Appendix 7.3). A similar guide was created for Pharmacy, which provided text examples with commentaries on the following components of the laboratory report: Introduction, Definitions and Descriptions, Describing the Experiment (these are parts of the move 'Materials and Methods), Presenting Results, Discussing the Results. The resources for History and Management presented whole texts rather than focusing on sub-genres, as the assignments in theses disciplines had much lower word limits.

Pedagogical design

Our instructional approach was underpinned by social constructivist theory (e.g. von Glaserfeld, 1987; Vygotsky, 1978) which understands learning as occurring through social interaction, and knowledge as constructed by learners through building on their own and others' experience. This understanding of learning is reflected in the design of the materials, as well as in the organisation of the literacy workshops.

As discussed earlier, the learning materials offered a description of the moves as well as discourse-semantic and lexico-grammatical features presented in a commentary next to the text. The purpose of the commentary was to foster learning through discovery and discussion, or in other words, to enable students to understand the genre requirements by reading and discussing the genre descriptions. In addition to the commentary, the learning resources contained the grades and assessors' comments for each exemplar, as well as a selection of stronger and weaker texts. It was expected that the analysis of this information and the comparison of texts would help students to develop a good understanding of the genre requirements. Each unit (in the case of Applied Linguistics and Pharmacy there were several units on the various sub-genres) of the learning resources consisted of the following parts:

(1) Two or three high-scoring text examples with commentary.
(2) One high-scoring text example where commentary needs to be provided by students.
(3) A notes section.
(4) Two low-scoring text examples with commentary.
(5) A reflection section.

The academic literacy workshops are based on the socio-cultural principle of scaffolding, and follow the Sydney School's teaching/learning cycle. In the first phase, Deconstruction, the students work in small groups with the learning materials, discuss the high- and low-scoring exemplars and their commentaries, and reflect on the features that make texts in the genre successful. The second phase, Joint Construction, also takes place in the classroom and immediately follows the first. The participants are invited before the workshop to bring with them the electronic version of an extract of their current writing in the relevant unit (for instance Introduction). In light of what they have learned in the Deconstruction phase, students work in their groups to revise each other's extracts. The last phase, Independent Construction, takes place outside the classroom, when the students make further amendments on their own texts, or work independently on further units of the learning resource. Three types of scaffolding occur in this approach. The first is provided through the design of the learning materials which support learning through the commentary and the contrast between strong and weak exemplars. The second is created by student discussions and joint explorations in the small group work. The third is provided by the subject lecturer and the writing specialist who are available throughout the workshops for advice and consultation.

This instructional design favours the development of genre awareness and critical awareness in at least two ways. First, the group discussions during the genre analysis inevitably lead to critical questions about conventions which students find problematic or difficult to accept; typical examples are the use of the personal pronoun 'I' (which is discouraged in some disciplines) or the extent to which evidence needs to be provided. In these situations the presence of both the writing expert and the subject lecturer is important and enables the student-tutor dialogue recommended by Lillis

(2001, 2006). In these dialogues some of the genre requirements can be clarified and confirmed, others can be critiqued, and students can find out how much leeway they may have with some conventions. Even more important is the presence of the subject lecturer for raising students' genre awareness. Several scholars have recommended committing students to ethnographic activities to develop their understanding of the social context, role and communicative purpose of a genre (Beaufort, 2007; Johns, 1997; Motta-Roth, 2009). While time limitations do not allow the integration of such activities in the literacy workshops, the subject lecturer can be drawn upon as a source of information on the genre's social context. In addition to providing insights into the discourse community's social practices, the subject lecturer can also encourage students to examine other genres used by the discourse community, thus developing their sensitivity to different communicative purposes and their linguistic realisations.

So far, we have conducted 15 literacy workshops in Applied Linguistics, and four each in Pharmacy and Management. The History department has used the learning resource for induction workshops and graduate teacher training without our participation. We have not been able to evaluate this process, but received positive feedback from the collaborating lecturer. The department has also asked for further collaboration in order to use the learning resource in future online applications. In the next section, I present some findings from the evaluation of our approach.

The Evaluation of the Instructional Approach

The instructional approach was evaluated by (1) student perceptions, (2) instances of learning observed during the deconstruction and joint construction phases, and (3) a preliminary assessment of improvements in student texts. Student perceptions were elicited through questionnaires administered immediately after each workshop, and conversations with a small number of workshop participants. To identify instances of learning, in most workshops the discussions during the Deconstruction and Joint Construction phases of one or two volunteering groups were audio-recorded. The audio-recordings were subsequently transcribed and coded for utterances and exchanges that showed developing understanding of genre features and requirements, as well as mutual scaffolding. Improvements in student texts were evaluated in two ways. First, during the Joint Construction phase, when the groups worked on electronic version of their own texts, they were asked to use the 'Track Changes' function in Microsoft Word, and provide us with the word documents of the amended versions. Altogether we gathered 28 hours of recordings and 32 amended texts, and this data set offered valuable insights into students' learning and the immediate impact this had on their writing. The results are reported in the following sections.

Student perceptions

So far, we have received questionnaire responses from 242 workshop participants. The questionnaire elicited students' assessment of the learning resource, the quality of the workshop, and invited them to comment on individual aspects (sections of the learning materials, features of the workshops) with suggestions for improvements. Almost all respondents regarded the materials as very useful/useful for writing their next assignments. Concerning the quality of the workshops, most respondents appreciated the group work and regarded the presence of the writing and subject tutors as essential. Critical comments addressed the limited time available for reading the text exemplars and commentary, and for discussion with the subject expert. This is a valid concern, as the workshops were usually scheduled for two hours and attended by more than 30 participants. Deeper insights into strengths and shortcomings of the instructional approach were gained from conversations with individual students. In the same way as Jenkins (2014), I had 'conversations' with the students rather than conducting interviews. This approach is based on Talmy's (2011) discussion of interviews as social practice where meaning is co-constructed by interviewer and interviewee. Thus there were no pre-determined questions apart from the broad prompts 'How did you find the workshops and the materials?' 'How did they help you with your own writing?' Students could then determine the course of the conversation, and I only asked questions for clarification. So far, I have analysed the data from conversations with 10 students from Applied Linguistics, five from Management and four from Pharmacy. The dominant themes that emerged from the analysis were (1) use of student texts, and (2) presence of subject lecturer.

Almost all participants expressed their appreciation of being given student texts as models. Some had been advised by their lecturers to pay attention to the writing style of the published literature in order to learn how to write. This they had perceived as 'intimidating', as they felt that they could not write at that level. Student texts were seen as much more relevant, and as one student put it:

> It's just so important to see them [essays written by previous students] and as I said you can never get hold of them. We've asked several tutors but they say they can't give them to us.

Equally valued by the participants was the fact that they were given both strong and weak texts. This was also apparent in the questionnaire responses; in the final section where respondents had been invited to suggest improvements, 38 (16%) had made requests along the line of 'more bad texts'. As one student explained, seeing the difference between 'good and bad writing' along with the assessor's comments was especially helpful for learning how to write. Our analysis of the recordings of the group discussions also showed that students constantly compared high-scoring and low-scoring texts and seemed to learn much from this comparison.

Having access to a subject lecturer in matters of writing was also highly rated and mentioned by more than half of the participants. This opportunity, according to students from Pharmacy and Management, is not available outside the literacy workshops. Consequently, the subject tutors were in constant demand during the workshops and the students felt that there was not sufficient time for discussions with them. Another, but related, limitation mentioned by Pharmacy and Management students was the one-off nature of the literacy workshop, as they felt they needed more sustained support. However, as one student pointed out, this was 'at least some help, whereas we got nothing ever before'.

Observed instances of learning

The analysis of the recordings yielded plenty of evidence of how the students made sense of the commentary and developed an understanding of genre features through discussion, consultation with the writing expert and the subject lecturer, and implemented new knowledge into their own writing in the joint construction phase. Some examples of the learning instances were reported elsewhere (Wingate, 2012a; Tribble & Wingate, 2013). Here, I provide a synopsis of the areas where learning was most frequently taking place and relate this to my earlier discussion of the genre-analytical approach we took in the development of the learning resources. From the 28 hours of recordings, I identified 121 exchanges that I called 'learning instances'; these ranged from short four-line exchanges of only two students in a group to extended (up to 35 lines) discussion involving several group members, and exchanges with the group and either the writing expert or the subject lecturer. I classified these exchanges as learning instances if an agreement or a conclusion was reached that showed that the group had understood a genre feature. An example of a longer exchange involving the subject lecturer is given in Appendix 7.4. This example not only shows an instance of learning but also of students being able to express critique and negotiate practices with the lecturer.

The learning instances were most frequently related to the move analysis (61%). In many, it is evident that the comparison of texts aided students' understanding of the requirements. In the following extract from one learning instance in Applied Linguistics, the group members are discussing whether the Introduction needs to contain references.

Extract 1 (Applied Linguistics):
S1: You thought just one reference in the intro is enough, but it's not, you have to cite enough reference to prove the academic background.
S2: But Example D has no citation at all, so I guess it must be a low-scoring one.
S3: But it is among the high-scoring ones. I wonder if you need to reference in the case of D, because this has been said so often it's become common sense.
S2: Maybe but usually I think you have to give evidence right from the beginning, otherwise it sounds like your opinion.

The remaining 39% of learning instances were concerned with discourse-semantic features and the related lexico-grammatical features. The next extract is from a Management workshop, where the students observed that the paragraph development and signposting (highlighted in the commentary, see Table 7.3 for an example) was absent from a low-scoring exemplar text.

Extract 2 (Management):
S1: Look at 3 [exemplar text] , para 3, there is the opening, about intellectual critique, then point 1, point 2, point 3 to support it, then the links, 'hence', 'in light of this critique'. And then look at the first para in 5, nothing like this, he's just wandering around.

These examples underline the point made earlier, that the comparison between strong and weak texts is extremely useful for the development of genre awareness.

Improvements in students texts

Although the learning instances indicate that the instructional approach leads to students' understanding of genre features and requirement, more research is needed to show that the approach also leads to improvements in students' production of these genres. At present, I cannot provide this evidence, as I have only a small database of texts which show the changes made during the joint construction phases. Considering that so far more than 250 students participated in the literacy workshops, the amount of 32 amended texts seems negligible; furthermore, these texts came entirely from Applied Linguistics students. In the other disciplines, where we did not have direct access to the students, they could either not be enticed to bring their passages of their own writing, or the timing of the workshop did not coincide with them working on an assignment. In the 32 texts, improvements were found, and the changes made in these texts related to the learning instances recorded during the group discussion. One example is offered in Appendix 7.5; this relates to the learning instance reported in Extract 1 above, where students came to the conclusion that evidence needed to be provided in an introduction. As a result, they inserted a number of references in one student's introduction.

However, to be able to make valid claims about improvements in students writing as a result of the instructional approach, much stronger evidence is needed, and a longitudinal study as well as a systematic analysis of student texts before and after the intervention would be appropriate. This was, given our limited resources and access, not possible beyond our own discipline, and only to a limited extent within. Despite this limitation, however, the overall results of the evaluation were encouraging. The student feedback as well as the learning instances confirmed the adequacy of the design of the learning resources as well as the pedagogical set-up.

Summary

At this point it is necessary to situate our instructional approach in the wider context and evaluate it in light of the model of inclusive curriculum-integrated academic literacy instruction which I proposed at the beginning of this chapter. For this purpose, it is important to recall the chapter heading '*Towards* an inclusive model of academic literacy instruction', and to remember that any individual initiative can only make tentative steps *towards* the proposed model which requires considerable change at the institutional level. However, individual initiatives are important for exploring instructional methods suitable for an inclusive provision. As there are few detailed reports of inclusive literacy instruction available (for an example see Rose *et al.*, 2008), I hope that our initiative contributes to the larger model some insights as to how some aspects of existing literacy models, for instance genre analysis or collaboration, can be usefully employed in literacy instruction in the disciplines.

Considering the overall model, our instructional approach has obvious shortcomings. It fared rather well in relation to Principle 1, as it did present genres and their communicative functions and succeeded in raising students' awareness of the associated genre requirements. Addressing Principles 2 and 3 was clearly not possible in an individual initiative. These principles asked for making literacy instruction an entitlement for all students by integrating it fully into the subject curriculum. In the interventions, the literacy workshops were an 'add-on' to the subject curriculum rather than a component. Participation was on a voluntary basis, and although all workshops were attended by more than 60% of the student cohorts, it is likely that some students who much needed support were left out. Collaboration with subject experts, as required in Principle 4, was achieved to a certain extent, but not without difficulties. Lastly, our instructional approach is also limited with respect to the literacy needs discussed in previous chapters, for instance students' difficulties with reading, writing from sources, and argumentation. These important aspects of academic literacy could not be addressed within the scope of our initiative. This underlines that in order to address the complexity of academic literacy in a holistic manner, instruction needs to be part of regular subject teaching, as postulated in the proposed inclusive model of academic literacy instruction. In the next chapter, I will consider ways of implementing this model.

Notes

(1) I use the pronoun 'we' in this chapter when I refer to this intervention study which I jointly developed and carried out with my colleague Chris Tribble.
(2) This is due to the slippery nature of the term 'essay' which is vaguely assigned to most student assignments (for a discussion see Johns, 2011). From an SFL perspective, it can be said that the genre essay has many more registers, i.e. contexts of situation, than other genres.
(3) In the assessment system in English universities, the pass grade for postgraduate programmes is 50%; grades of 60–69% are at 'merit' level, and 70% and higher are at 'distinction' level.

8 Towards the Implementation of an Inclusive Model of Academic Literacy Instruction

Introduction

In the last chapter, I proposed an instructional model that is based on four principles. The first principle is concerned with the content and methodology of academic literacy instruction and requires that instruction should focus on relevant genres and their communicative purposes within a specific discourse community. I also described an instructional approach which aims to follow this principle and discussed how this approach was applied in interventions in four disciplines. In this chapter I will look more closely at the other three principles; however, I first refer to some limitations of the instructional approach which were briefly outlined in Chapter 7. These limitations were caused by the absence of the necessary contextual factors requested by Principles 2–4,[1] and here I want to make the point that that the implementation of inclusive literacy pedagogy requires institutional commitment and structural changes.

In terms of teaching methodology, a major limitation to the interventions was that instruction could only be delivered in 'add-on' academic literacy workshops instead of being integrated into the subject curriculum. This contradicts the model's aim of inclusion, since participation in the workshops was voluntary and may have left out students who either did not recognise their literacy needs or were too hard-pressed to engage in extra activities. Inclusion can obviously not be achieved in small-scale initiatives, as it requires institutional transformations which will bring about the integration of literacy instruction into the subject curriculum, a major change which has to be encouraged and supported by departmental and institutional leaders. A further limitation was the way in which the collaboration worked. As the subject lecturers participated outside their usual work remit, motivated by their individual interest in enhancing their students' literacy but with little or no institutional support, their contribution to the project was often low on the list of their priorities, and their input in the development of the learning resources smaller than desirable.

In terms of content, the main limitation was that the instruction was predominantly focused on academic writing. Other important aspects of academic literacy, most notably reading, writing from sources and argumentation, could not be addressed due to the constraints of a small-scale initiative. These literacy activities also require subject-integrated instruction, so that the whole literacy process leading to text production can be modelled within the real context of the study programme and in relation to the genuine literacy tasks given to students.

It seems that the changes requested by Principles 2–4 can only happen if there is a radical change in the mind-sets of academics and academic leaders in relation to the nature of academic literacy and student needs. This may appear a remote goal, given the fact that two decades of relevant publications on academic literacy and student diversity have brought about little change to the prevalent and persistent model of generic, extra-curricular literacy support. However, it is likely that the rapidly changing higher education market will force universities into taking new approaches more seriously. As the intake of international students and of 'non-traditional' students (those who were previously underrepresented in higher education; see Chapter 1) increases, the existing support structures will become increasingly insufficient and their inadequacy will become ever more obvious. Similarly, the pressure on subject lecturers to somehow deal with the needs of diverse student intakes – a situation for which they are not specifically trained and do not receive support or workload allocations by their universities – may become unsustainable. At the same time, there is a growing competition among Anglophone universities for the recruitment of international, that is, high-fee paying, students. In England, similar competition exists for home students whose tuition fees have trebled in the last decade. If universities want to be successful in this competition, they need to be seen as providing adequate student support. For these reasons, university managers may become increasingly open to changes that enhance student support and thus student satisfaction. To promote the inclusive model of academic literacy instruction, the following argument, which I laid out in Chapter 1 and developed throughout this book, should be put forward to university managers:

(1) As a result of a widespread misconception of academic literacy and its associated learning needs, students are not adequately supported in today's universities. The available support, (generic English language and study skills classes) is merely remedial and addresses the needs of only selected student groups to only to a limited extent. Therefore, the academic literacy requirements of their study programme remain mysterious to many students for too long, and this impedes their progress and success.
(2) Academic literacy needs to be learned by *all* students new to university, regardless of their backgrounds. Academic literacy is different from language proficiency or study skills, and involves an epistemological and sociocultural understanding of the discipline. Hence, the development of academic literacy cannot be separated from the teaching of the subject.
(3) For these reasons, academic literacy instruction needs to be integrated into the subject curriculum. This integration can be best facilitated through the collaboration of English language/writing experts and academic staff in the disciplines. Subject-integrated academic literacy instruction has the benefit of including all students, enhancing their understanding of the requirements and avoiding long periods of uncertainty.
(4) Subject-integrated literacy instruction requires structural and organisational changes as well as investment in staff development. The investment is worthwhile as this provision will most certainly result in a lower attrition rates, better progress for many students, and greater student satisfaction.

Assuming that this argument has been accepted, more detailed proposals for the implementation of an inclusive model of literacy instruction are needed. In light of this, in the following sections I will discuss the institutional changes necessary to integrate academic literacy instruction into subject curricula. In the second part of this chapter, I consider the pedagogical design of subject-integrated literacy instruction.

Institutional Changes

The integration of literacy instruction into the subject curriculum would require that a considerable part of the instruction is carried out by subject lecturers. I will explain later that this does not necessarily imply the addition of new components to the curriculum or a massive increase in lecturers' workloads; rather, it implies a more strategic and effective use of regular teaching and assessment practices. However, as discussed in Chapter 3, many subject lecturers lack the training and literacy awareness to provide this instructional support, and many do not see this as their remit. Thus, making subject lecturers take responsibility for students' academic literacy development would be a major shift which needs to be supported by management-driven changes in the institutional culture and structure. The cultural changes would include recognition of the epistemological role of academic language and literacy as well as a greater acknowledgement of teaching (rather than research) achievements. Subsequent structural changes would need to involve both incentives and staff development measures. Incentives would include making adequate workload allocations that allow lecturers to devote time to academic literacy support, and offering teaching awards for successful examples of integrated literacy instruction. Staff development measures are essential in light of the current misconceptions of academic literacy and the lack of explicit literacy knowledge among lecturers. Therefore, academic literacy instruction would have to become the concern of continuous professional development courses; it also should become a component of the postgraduate teaching certificate programmes which are in most universities compulsory for new lecturers. In this way, change would be a gradual, bottom-up process which nevertheless would only be possible through top-down commitment and investment.

The necessary structural changes also involve the 'redeployment' of so-called learning developers and English language/writing experts in order to facilitate their collaboration with subject lecturers. As neither of these labels is appropriate for the role these experts would play in the proposed model of academic literacy instruction, I will henceforth use the term 'literacy expert'. As discussed in more detail in Chapter 4, the main benefits of collaboration are that the expertise of the literacy expert is useful for the analysis of target genres and subsequent preparation of learning resources, whilst subject experts can contribute their knowledge of the discourse community's discourses and literacy conventions. In addition, literacy experts can support subject experts by identifying opportunities for literacy instruction within the curriculum and regular subject teaching.

Collaboration can be implemented at different levels of intensity, matching the three types described by Dudley-Evans and St John (1998). Each level requires some degree of structural change. The lowest level, 'cooperation', means the literacy expert gathers discipline-specific information from the subject lecturer, but develops materials and teaches literacy independently from the subject lecturer. This represents some form of discipline-specific instruction and is thus preferable to the prevalent generic instruction. However, this type of instruction tends to remain at the level of 'additional' or 'curriculum-linked' instruction (see Table 4.1, Chapter 4) and is therefore not fully inclusive. The institutional structure required for this provision would remain similar to the existing one, with literacy experts working from a central unit. However, their time allocation would need to change, as they would spend less time teaching generic classes and more time working with a particular faculty or – more effectively but also more costly – department. This way, they could gradually develop an understanding of the discourse community and its conventions. An example of this type of collaboration is the Language Development Group at the University of Cape Town, where staff members have developed long-term collaborations with departments.[2]

The next level, called 'collaboration' by Dudley-Evans and St John, means that literacy expert and subject lecturer prepare teaching materials and sessions together, but the instruction is delivered by the literacy expert. This also carries the risk of not being inclusive, because the instruction is not integrated with the subject teaching. Instead, it is offered as an addition to the regular curriculum which often takes the form of online/independent materials or voluntary workshops. It might therefore be regarded as more effective to implement 'team-teaching', the highest level of collaboration in Dudley-Evans and St John's terms. However, unlike Dudley-Evans and St John, I would not consider joined teaching activities as the most important feature of effective literacy instruction. Instead I argue that it is the full integration into the regular subject teaching and assessment that makes literacy instruction most effective, for reasons that I have explained in detail in previous chapters: not only is this integration necessary for the inclusion of all students, but it is also the only way in which communicative competence in a specific discourse community can be developed.[3] In terms of structural changes, this level would require that the literacy experts would have most of their time allocated to one specific discipline/department, or ideally would be fully assigned to it. At first sight this might seem a very expensive provision, because a larger number of literacy experts would be needed. In the long term, however, this approach might be cost-effective for universities, as it would enhance the quality of literacy instruction and ensure that all students receive adequate information and support as part of their programme. As a consequence, the provision would reduce the need for many generic language or skills courses offered by central units. While central units will always play an important role in providing language teaching to students with linguistic needs, this provision should be an extra to the curriculum, whilst literacy needs to be part of it.

An example of this level of provision is the 'collaborative, curriculum-integrated literacy instruction' (Purser, 2011: 30) model at Australian universities. Learning developers there are integrated into the disciplinary community and work along subject lecturers for the enhancement of literacy and learning. However, the publications on this collaboration have not given much insight into the content of instruction and the methodologies that were employed. In order to promote the inclusive model of academic literacy instruction, it is essential to put forward some proposals and recommendations for the pedagogical design, such as the content and teaching methodology. This I will do in the next sections.

Pedagogical Design

I have argued earlier that a major weakness of existing academic literacy models and teaching initiatives (including our own initiative presented in Chapter 7) is that they focus entirely on writing, when in fact writing is only the last stage in a complex literacy process. My main concern in this section is therefore to propose a holistic instructional approach that addresses the whole process and enables students to successfully carry out all activities involved. The content of academic literacy instruction must therefore go beyond writing-focused activities and should in particular include academic reading and the reading-to-write process (see Chapter 5 for a discussion of the different types of reading involved in this process, and Rose *et al.*, 2008, for an integrated reading and writing pedagogy). I also will consider in this section how the proposed holistic approach can be integrated without substantial additions to the curriculum and without substantial additions to lecturer workloads, by making effective use of regular teaching and assessment activities and collaboration. For this purpose, literacy instruction needs to be distributed across the range of teaching, learning and assessment formats, such as classroom sessions, personal tutoring, independent and e-learning, and be delivered in complementary fashion by lecturers, personal tutors and literacy experts. Literacy experts can be instrumental in designing the overall approach and ensuring that the different activities complement each other and lead to comprehensive and progressive literacy learning. I will discuss in the following sections how the different teaching, learning and assessment formats can be used.

Lectures and seminars

Classroom sessions in which new knowledge is introduced and discussed offer good opportunities for 'literacy windows', i.e. phases in which attention is paid to the ways in which this knowledge has been communicated. Lecturers can demonstrate how the information is presented and debated in the literature, for instance by giving students extracts from articles dealing with the information, and pointing out how authors make claims, build arguments, refer to and agree/disagree with other authors. The literacy expert can be useful in preparing such activities by highlighting relevant linguistic features and preparing associated learning resources. Another important 'literacy window' would be to allocate a certain amount of lecture/seminar time for explaining and discussing the requirements of student assignments. Although this is certainly being done already, it is possible that this activity can be exploited more systematically and effectively. For instance, it can be used for explaining the expectations attached to specific assignment tasks (such as 'compare and contrast', 'outline and evaluate'), for providing advice on reading and reading-to-write, and for clarifying the assessment criteria. Certainly, additional strategies are needed to develop complex abilities such as reading-to-write, as I will discuss later, but it is important that initial discussions about the selection and evaluation of sources are held with the lecturer who sets the assignment and understand the topic. A common concern among subject lecturers is that lecture time is limited and subject content cannot be covered if time is spent on literacy activities; however, this concern can be countered by the argument that (1) some subject content can be shifted into independent or e-learning, and (2) the literacy activities can foster a deeper understanding of the new information and its epistemological context (see Wingate *et al.*, 2011 for an example).

The integration of literacy windows into timetabled lectures and seminars should be at the core of the instructional model. One obvious reason is inclusion. Furthermore, and referring back to the argument made in Chapter 1, only in relation to real subject content and in the 'particular social situations' (Ochs & Schieffelin, 1994: 470) in which knowledge is typically communicated can students develop the epistemological and sociocultural knowledge that forms the basis of academic literacy. Also, the attention paid to academic literacy by the subject lecturer will raise its importance for the students. However, given the complexity of academic literacy, the lecture- and seminar-based instruction needs to be complemented and followed up by other methods.

Follow up tutorials and e-learning

The 'literacy windows' used by lecturers for explaining and discussing the requirements of student assignments could be usefully followed up with tutorials or workshops of the type presented in Chapter 7. The literacy experts could use exemplars of the required genre, i.e. assignments written by previous students, and prepare learning resources for which they might draw on move, discourse-semantic and lexico-grammatical analysis in the way we have suggested. The tutorials could follow the teaching methodology that we used in our intervention, based on the teaching/learning cycle and moving from scaffolded to independent learning. Once the learning resources were introduced in a tutorial and students became familiar with the methodology (i.e. learning about requirements and conventions from the commentary and through the comparison of high- and low-scoring texts), the resources could be made available on the e-learning platform for independent study. The online format would also allow for the presentation of a large number of exemplar texts. As I explained in Chapter 7, giving students exemplars of the genre they have to write is an effective means of developing their understanding of the expected features. Having access to examples of textual realisations of a target genre was highly appreciated by the participants in our intervention. Tutorials using this methodology are particularly helpful when they follow the above mentioned lecture-integrated discussions, which would address more generally the discourse community's expectations and the genre's social and communicative functions. This sequence enables students to understand the broader genre context before they engage in the analysis of its specific linguistic and rhetorical features.

Personal tutoring

Most universities have a system in which every student entering the university is assigned a personal tutor who provides pastoral care and is usually also responsible for monitoring and advising on academic progress. In many institutions the personal tutor system has a clear structure which includes regular meetings between student and personal tutor, particularly in the first year of study. However, there is evidence that students tend to forego these meetings if they feel they have not got a personal problem to discuss (e.g. Owen, 2002). Some of these regular meetings could be well used for additional literacy support and for follow ups on other instructional methods. For instance, students could be encouraged to seek further clarification on genre requirements or on the feedback they received on their assignments. Equally, they could ask for advice with individual problems they face with reading and writing. It is likely that students would make better and more strategic use of personal tutorials if they knew that academic literacy support was available in them.

Assessment and feedback

The importance of formative assessment for student learning has long been acknowledged (e.g. Black et al., 2003), and giving students the opportunity to receive feedback on initial work that helps them to improve subsequent work is therefore an essential component of academic literacy instruction. In previous studies, I have described two types of formative assessment; in the first, students received explicit written and oral feedback on a short 'explorative' essay which was not formally (i.e. summatively) assessed (Wingate et al., 2011), and in the second, the three written assignments for a module were designed and timed in a way that the feedback of one could be used for improving the next one (Wingate, 2010). However, in particular the first type is labour-intensive and may not be feasible in programmes with large student cohorts; as Sadler (2010: 536) points out, even though feedback should be specific and comprehensive, it must be 'also provided within the available resources, especially time for academics to give feedback to individual students'. Nevertheless, given the fact that assessment and feedback already form a substantial part of lecturers' regular workloads, the crucial question seems to be how the associated activities can be more effectively used for academic literacy development.

As Black and Wiliam note, 'the quality of the feedback provided is a key feature in any procedure for formative assessment (1998: 36). While written feedback comments are potentially a powerful instructional method providing lecturers with the opportunity to respond to student needs and communicate with students on an individual basis (Ferris, 2008), there is plenty of evidence that feedback comments leave students confused and dissatisfied (e.g. Carless, 2006; Walker, 2009; Weaver, 2006; see the discussion in Chapter 6). This is because the comments tend to be 'ambiguous', 'too general or vague', 'too abstract', 'too cryptic', and/or are presented in an unfamiliar discourse (Nicol, 2010: 507). Nicol therefore recommends that feedback must be a dialogic process involving lecturer-student and peer interaction and active student engagement. As to peer interaction, Nicol proposes to create a dialogue among students about the assignment criteria through the comparison of good and poor genre exemplars. In our literacy interventions, we created exactly this dialogue on the basis of text analysis and comparison, and the results were positive in terms of student perceptions and learning outcomes. Furthermore, Nicol stresses the need to achieve a shared understanding between lecturers and students of the assessment requirements, which, in the approach I am outlining here, should be achieved through the literacy windows in lectures and seminars. Another way of creating dialogue around feedback is, as explained above, through personal tutoring, giving students the opportunity to discuss and clarify the feedback they received with their personal tutor. The most essential aspect of effective feedback, however, is the quality of the comments provided to students.

It seems that two main factors determine the quality of feedback, namely focus and formulation. Quite commonly, the focus of feedback comments is on surface features of writing, such as grammar, rhetorical issues and structure,[4] and it has been reported that lecturers tend to comment on these features when they are unable to identify underlying epistemological problems (e.g. Lea & Street, 1998; Mitchell & Riddle, 2000). This type of feedback is not formative because it fails to recognise students' real learning needs and can therefore not lead to improvements. As to formulation, the point has already been made that comments are often perceived as unhelpful. In addition to using vague or incomprehensible language, lecturers also tend to make comments of the categorical type, which consist of a one-word imperative such as 'Structure!' written in the margins of student essays (Mutch, 2003). Weaver (2006) also found that students were dissatisfied because the feedback was unrelated to the assessment criteria. These findings indicate that practices need to improve in order to use feedback as an effective method of academic literacy development.

As part of the proposed holistic approach to academic literacy instruction, feedback comments would need to be aligned with the other instructional methods, and it would be necessary to ensure the consistency of the language used across these methods. The genre requirements and assessment criteria would be first discussed in a lecture or seminar, further clarified in follow-up tutorials and restated in the feedback on students' assignments. Consistent language use would obviously improve the quality of feedback comments, because it would demand lecturers' deeper engagement with the assessment criteria and student learning needs. I have already mentioned that staff development measures would be necessary to achieve this provision; in addition, as I will explain below, it requires cooperation of the lecturers involved as well as effective coordination.

Modelling of the literacy process

In Chapters 5 and 6, I discussed students' difficulties with essential components of the literacy process which are hardly addressed in conventional instruction. Students struggle in particular with the identification, evaluation and integration of sources, as well as with the under-explained requirement of critical thinking and argumentation. A holistic instructional approach would therefore need to model the whole process of writing an assignment, involving the following components:

(1) Analysing and contextualising the assignment task. This includes situating the assignment topic within the wider context of the subject/discipline, and clarifying the genre's communicative purpose.
(2) Showing appropriate ways of selecting and evaluating sources. This involves demonstrating to students how to establish a reading focus, and how this requires careful thinking about the topic and possibly taking an initial stance on the topic. It also involves showing students how to recognise and eliminate irrelevant sources.
(3) Demonstrating with text examples how authors build arguments based on the evidence from sources.
(4) Showing students how the process of argumentation is used to establish the writer's position (Wingate, 2012b), and how the development of argument is signalled through textual features such as structure, headings and signposting devices.

Although some of these components would also be addressed in some of the teaching activities discussed above, ideally the whole literacy process should be modelled with one clear example at the beginning of the study programme, for instance with a non-assessed 'exploratory' assignment, or with the first assessed assignment. This would achieve much in reducing students' uncertainty and anxiety (particularly around issues of critical thinking and argumentation) and in giving them a good chance for success in subsequent assignments. This modelling would be best integrated into the literacy windows in lectures and the follow-up tutorials proposed earlier, but as this might be difficult because of time constraints, it might have to be offered as a separate unit within the curriculum.

Managing an inclusive model of academic literacy instruction

As I have shown in the previous sections, the proposed model is a package of different methods distributed on various parts of the curriculum, and most methods can be integrated into the regular subject teaching and assessment. This distribution means on the one hand that the work and responsibility are shared by a number of staff and that nobody is unduly burdened by an increased workload. On the other hand, it carries the risk that the instruction becomes disjointed into a series of individual, and even one-off, initiatives. To ensure that the instruction is holistic, ongoing and progressive and that the various methods complement each other, the package has to be carefully designed and coordinated. This is where the literacy expert plays a crucial role. As Skillen (2006) and Purser et al. (2008) have explained in relation to the Australian model of curriculum integrated literacy instruction, literacy experts can make significant changes in the teaching and learning practices of departments. With their typical background in English language education and learning development, literacy experts are best capable of advising subject lecturers how and where to integrate literacy instruction in the curriculum. Their expertise would also be needed to introduce a consistent use of the meta-language for the instruction, ensuring that the terminology and expressions used in explanations and feedback comments are intelligible, unambiguous and aligned to the assessment criteria. Once the package is implemented, the literacy expert is needed to coordinate the instruction, offer ongoing advice on instructional details to subject lecturers and collaborate with them in some of the instructional methods (for instance the follow-up tutorials). It is possible that in the long term, when the instructional model is firmly established within a department, the coordination can be taken on by a subject lecturer; however, for the design and implementation the literacy expert seems to be indispensable.

Conclusion

In this book I have tried to achieve a number of objectives. First, I wanted to contribute to a better understanding of what academic literacy is and what it requires students to learn. Using the definition of academic literacy as the ability to communicate competently in an academic discourse community, I have argued that this competence includes knowledge of the discipline's epistemology and socio-cultural context, that *all* students will have to acquire this communicative competence and that therefore existing remedial approaches to literacy teaching that target certain student groups are inadequate. Whilst the shortcomings of current approaches to literacy instruction have long been criticised by various scholars (e.g. Boughey, 2002; Ivanič & Lea, 2006), the debate so far has been almost entirely focused on academic writing. By contrast, I have tried to raise awareness of the fact that writing is only one component of the literacy process and that if instruction is to be effective, it has to address the whole process rather than the end product only. For this purpose, I have devoted a chapter to reading-to-write, and another chapter to common difficulties experienced by students, such as critical thinking and argumentation – as these abilities tend to be neglected in academic literacy research and publications.

A second objective in this book was to examine the existing models of literacy/writing pedagogy and consider what they can contribute to an inclusive model of literacy instruction. As some approaches have been much confined to specific contexts and have therefore failed to cross-fertilise, I have tried to demonstrate how features from a range of approaches can be usefully brought together. The third objective was to propose an inclusive model of academic literacy instruction. Originally, when planning the model, 'inclusive' meant to me that literacy instruction should be provided to all students in a study programme. However, as the model and my thinking developed further, a broader concept of inclusion evolved. The concept also entails that literacy instruction is included in the subject curriculum, which is necessary in order to reach all students in a cohort on the one hand, and to address all aspects of academic literacy on the other hand. The latter aspect then represents the third meaning of inclusion, namely that literacy pedagogy has to include every aspect of communicative competence and take students through the whole literacy process that leads to text production. To provide some evidence for the feasibility of the proposed model, I have presented an intervention study in which aspects of this model were applied. Despite the small-scale nature of the intervention and the limitation that the instruction could not be integrated into the subject curriculum, there was evidence that the approach, which combined features from a range of models of literacy pedagogy, resulted in high student ratings and improved genre understanding.

Finally, in this chapter I have discussed institutional changes that would be necessary for the implementation of the inclusive model of academic literacy instruction, and I have described the possible content and teaching methodology of this approach. Although the required changes seem quite substantial, they may well be unavoidable in the long run. As I have explained above, market forces such as growing competition for students and expectations by high-fee paying students will increase the need for universities to provide effective support and instruction for students. Growing numbers of students from diverse backgrounds, for instance international or non-traditional students, may make the need for an inclusive literacy pedagogy more obvious; as I have stressed repeatedly, however, this instruction is needed by all novices to university even if in the common understanding they are not from 'other' backgrounds. To bring about the needed changes, more evidence of interventions and successful practices – such as the practices reported from Australian universities – may have to be presented to university leaders. The good news here is that this evidence may already be in the making. In the last couple of years there have been several reports at literacy-related conferences of collaboration between English language/learning development staff and academic departments, indicating a trend for central units to work in a more subject-specific manner.[5] The more such initiatives get systematically evaluated and published, the more can be learned about different approaches to inclusive, subject-integrated literacy instruction, and the stronger the argument for this type of instruction will become.

Notes

(1) Principle 2 requires that academic literacy instruction becomes an entitlement for *all* students, Principle 3 calls for the integration of literacy instruction into the subject curriculum, and Principle 4 states that literacy instruction should be based on the collaboration of writing experts and subject experts.
(2) See Chapter 4 for a more detailed discussion of this and the following example and the different types of collaboration.
(3) See Chapter 1 for the definition of academic literacy as the ability to communicate competently in an academic discourse community.
(4) This is despite the fact that surface features are not usually part of the assessment criteria, given that they are not mentioned in the overarching subject benchmarks issued by the Quality Assurance Agency (QAA) which emphasise higher order abilities such as argumentation and critical evaluation.
(5) For a few published examples, see Ryan, 2013, and Yakovchuk and Ingle 2013 in the Proceedings of the 2011 BALEAP Conference.

Appendices

Appendix 3.1 Academic Writing/Study Skills Provision at 31 Sample Universities

Institution	Provision
1994 Group	
Sussex	Generic (online, workshops)
Goldsmiths	Generic (online)
Royal Holloway	Generic (online)
Lancaster	Field-specific (e.g. Science, Management) (face-to-face, workshops)
Essex	Generic (online)
Million+ Group	
Greenwich	Generic (online, face-to-face, workshops)
Northampton	Generic (online, face-to-face, workshops, 1 credit-bearing module)
Bedfordshire	Generic (online)
Bolton	Generic (online)
Derby	Generic (online)
Staffordshire	Generic (online)
West London	Generic (online, workshops)
Kent	Generic (credit-bearing workshops)
Non-affiliated	
College of St Mark and St John	No information could be located
Teeside (but only one tutor for the whole university)	Generic (face-to-face)
University of Reading	Generic (online)
University of Brighton	Generic (online)
University College Birmingham	Generic (one workshop)

Russell Group

Cambridge	Discipline-specific (online)
Durham	Discipline-specific (online, workshops)
Leeds	Generic (online; workshop for dyslexic students only)
Nottingham	Generic (online)
UCL	Generic (separate workshops for home and international students)
Warwick	Generic (online, face-to-face, workshops)
Southampton	Generic (online)
Manchester	Generic (online); peer-assisted study skills session within Faculties
UEA	Generic (online, face-to-face)
Oxford	Generic (workshops for internationals staff and students; paid service)

Specialised universities

University of the Arts	Generic (workshops)
University for Arts (Canterbury)	Generic (face-to-face)
Harper Adams	Generic (online)

Appendix 7.1 Extract from Move Analysis (Pharmacy)

Optimisation [Grade 71]

1 Introduction to Optimisation
2 Materials and methods:
 2.1 Determination of a suitable surfactant blend to be used in a cream base formulation:
 2.2 Formulation of a cream base with varying paraffin concentration and HLB
 2.3 Quality control tests
 2.4 Measuring the spread ability of cream base formulations
 2.5 Stability testing of cream formulation
 2.6 Regression analysis
 2.7 Calculating the amount of surfactant mix needed for the formulation of a cream base according to the results of the Nelder-Mead Simplex optimization.
 2.8 Addition of a co-surfactant
3 Results
 3.1 Regression analysis for viscosity of cream base formulations
 3.2 Regression analysis for stability:

Optimisation of High Dose Paracetamol Tablets by Direct Compression [Grade 52]

1 Introduction
2 Materials
3 Methods
 3.1 Experiment 1): Choosing Excipients for Formulation of Paracetamol DC Tablets
 3.2 Experiment 2): Experimental Design – To Identify the Independent Variables
 3.3 Experiment 3): Paracetamol DC UV Assay
 3.4 Experiment 4): Review of the Excipients of Paracetamol Tablets
 3.5 Experiment 5): Factorial Design of Formulation
 3.6 Experiment 6): Mixing Tablets Powder (API and Excipients) for manufacturing
 3.7 Experiment 7): Manufacturing of Paracetamol Tablets by Direct Compression
 3.8 Experiment 8): Assessment of the Manufactured Paracetamol Tablets Quality – Uniformity of Weight. 2
 3.9 Experiment 9): Assessment of the Manufactured Paracetamol Tablets Quality – Friability. 3

Optimisation of High Dose Paracetamol Tablets by Direct Compression [52] continued

 4.5 Experiment 9): Assessment of the Manufactured Paracetamol Tablets Quality - Friability
 4.6 Experiment 11): Assessment of the Manufactured Paracetamol Tablets Quality -Disintegration Time
 4.7 Experiment 12): Model-Dependent Methods (Regression Analysis) for Deciding the Optimum Formulation
 4.8 Tablet Friability
 4.9 Model-Independent Methods (Nelder Mead Simplex Optimisation) for Choosing the Optimum Formulation
5 Discussion
 5.1 Uniformity of Weight
 5.2 Friability
 5.3 Tensile strength
 5.4 Disintegration Time
 5.5 Nelder Mead Simplex Optimisation for Choosing the Optimum Formulation
 5.6 The two optimisation methods used

3.3 Contour plots
3.3.1 Conclusion
3.4 Nelder-Mead Simplex optimisation
4 Discussion
4.1 Viscosity test of aqeous cream base formulations
4.2 Spreadability test for aqueous cream base formulations
4.3 Stability test of aqueous cream bases
4.4 Subjective test of aqueous cream base formulations
4.5 Results assesment
4.6 Nedler Mead simplex optimizations Vs Regression analysis
5 Conclusion
6 Bibliography
7 Appendix

3.10 Experiment 10): Assessment of the Manufactured Paracetamol Tablets Quality – Hardness (Tensile strength)
3.11 Experiment 11): Assessment of the Manufactured Paracetamol Tablets Quality –Disintegration Time
3.12 Experiment 12): Model-Dependent Methods (Regression Analysis) for Deciding the Optimum Formulation
3.13 Experiment 13): Model-Independent Methods (Nelder Mead Simplex Optimisation) for Choosing the Optimum Formulation
4 RESULTS
4.1 Experiment 3): Paracetamol DC UV Assay
4.2 Experiment 5): Factorial Design of Formulation
4.3 Experiment 7): Manufacturing of Paracetamol Tablets by Direct Compression
4.4 Experiment 8): Assessment of the Manufactured Paracetamol Tablets Quality – Uniformity of Weight

6 Conclusion
7 References

Appendix 7.2 Synoptic View of Paragraph Relations (Management)

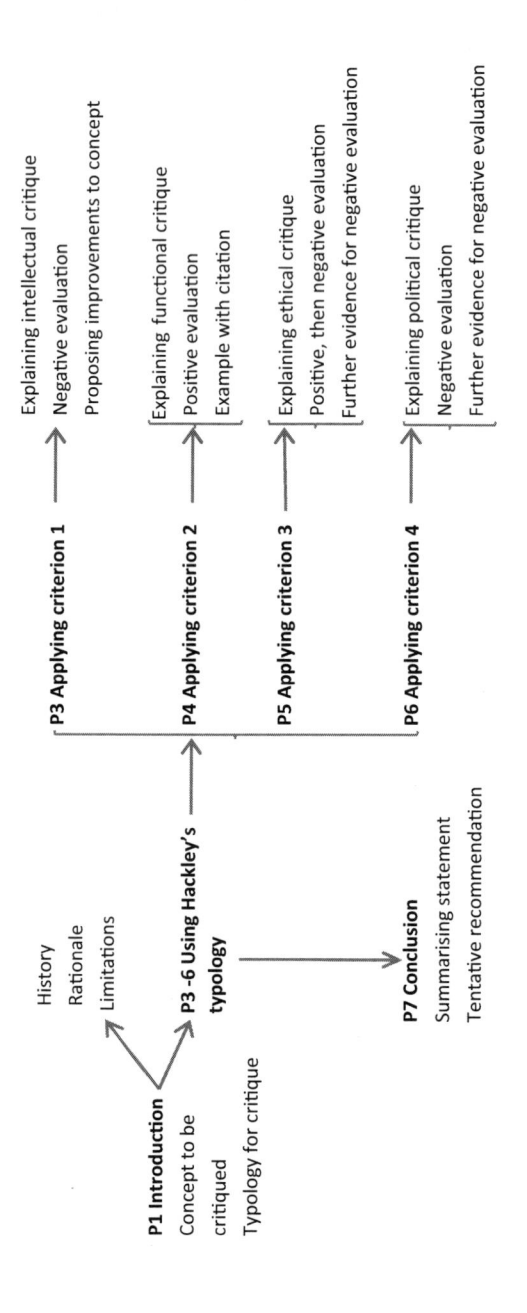

P1 Introduction
Concept to be critiqued
Typology for critique

P3-6 Using Hackley's typology

P3 Applying criterion 1
- Explaining intellectual critique
- Negative evaluation
- Proposing improvements to concept

P4 Applying criterion 2
- Explaining functional critique
- Positive evaluation
- Example with citation

P5 Applying criterion 3
- Explaining ethical critique
- Positive, then negative evaluation
- Further evidence for negative evaluation

P6 Applying criterion 4
- Explaining political critique
- Negative evaluation
- Further evidence for negative evaluation

History
Rationale
Limitations

P7 Conclusion
Summarising statement
Tentative recommendation

Appendix 7.3 Contents of Applied Linguistics Writing Guide

WRITING ON THE MA IN APPLIED LINGUISTICS

1. INTRODUCTION	2
2. MOVES IN MA ASSIGNMENTS	2
2.1. MOVE ANALYSIS -THREE EXAMPLES (high scoring assignments)	2
2.2. MOVE ANALYSIS - commentary	7
3. INTRODUCTIONS	8
3.1. INTRODUCTIONS in high scoring assignments	8
3.2. INTRODUCTIONS in low scoring assignments	11
4. DISCUSSING LITERATURE	13
4.1. DISCUSSION SECTIONS in high scoring assignments	13
4.2. DISCUSSION SECTIONS in low scoring assignments	16
5. CONCLUSIONS	18
5.1. CONCLUSIONS in high scoring assignments	18
5.2. CONCLUSIONS in low scoring assignments	20
6. CITATIONS IN INTRODUCTIONS	21
6.1. CITATIONS in high scoring assignments	22
6.2. CITATIONS in low scoring assignments	24
7. CITATIONS IN DISCUSSION SECTIONS	25
7.1. CITATIONS/DISCUSSION SECTIONS in high scoring assignments	25
7.2. CITATIONS/DISCUSSION SECTIONS in low scoring assignments	28
8. PRESENTING AND DISCUSSING FINDINGS FROM EMPIRICAL STUDIES in high scoring dissertations	30
8.1. Guided analysis	30
8.2. Independent analysis	40
8.3. Final reflection	43

Appendix 7.4 Example of Learning Instance in Pharmacy Workshop

S1:	There is also a question of how much information should go into each of the method sections.
S2:	We keep getting different advice on this one.
S1:	Yeah one says describe the whole experiment, while xxx said I don't want too much information.
S3:	It's really confusing. And they mark you down if you don't get it right, but it's just up to their taste.
S1:	Let's ask xxx. [calls lecturer, asks question]. And we keep getting confusing messages. In these examples, those who've written a lot about the experiment have lower grades.
L:	As you can see in Example 5, there is a lot of information on the experiment. I wouldn't say that this is not directly relevant. If you were to add this amount of information in a short report that would certainly take off some marks. But this is a very long report so you can afford to dwell a little bit on the origin of the experiment. But you all noticed the point, there is quite a lot of detail here [Example 5] that is not directly linked to the formulation.
S2:	So it's a bit up to us then?
	Yes, in the long report you have some leeway.
S4:	And how about writing about the disease?
L:	Better keep that short. The report is on the formulation, the disease is really background.
S1, S2, S4:	Yeah, ok, ok.

Appendix 7.5 Changes Made to an Introduction After Group Discussion on References

Title: Describe what is meant by a content-based approach to language teaching and learning and discuss the rationale for such an approach.

Introduction

In recent years bilingual education across Europe has become much more commonplace. For many, this may suggest a radical shift in educational policy and provision, but in fact content-based approaches to language learning and teaching have been thriving in various pockets of the world for some time. Notably, the Canadian education system has embraced immersion programmes for English-speaking Canadians since the mid-1960s, but a broad taxonomy would include Hispanic students in the U.S., immigrant students in many European and North American countries, secondary school students in Nigeria and other nations in Africa, among many others **(Mohan, 1986).** Take-up of bilingual approaches across Europe has been more recent, but current recognition among governments as well as the EU **(Grosser, 1999)** that bi- or multilingualism benefits both the individual and society now means these approaches have a more tenable foothold in education systems. This increasing prominence is mirrored by the rise in interest among applied linguists, many of whom advocate a bilingual approach **(e.g. Wode, 1999; Coffey, 2005).** In this essay I seek first to give a holistic account of what an integrated content and language approach to language teaching and learning actually is. This shall entail a discussion of the theoretical foundations and core principles involved in such practice. This understanding will enable the construction of a conceptual framework of optimum conditions which we will apply to help us navigate the possible arguments for and against a content-based approach being introduced in a context I am personally familiar with. In addition to this framework, I shall draw on some case studies in order to help broaden the discussion by relating the experiences of other institutions. Lastly, I shall conclude by setting forth my own position as regards my context and make tentative suggestions for further research.

(The changes made by the student group are marked in bold print).

References

Abasi, A. and Graves, B. (2008) Academic literacy and plagiarism: Conversations with international graduate students and disciplinary professors. *Journal of English for Academic Purposes* 7 (4), 221–233.

Abbott, R. (2013) Crossing thresholds in academic reading. *Innovations in Education and Teaching International* 50 (2), 191–201.

Ädel, A. and Reppen, R. (eds) (2008) *Corpora and Discourse: The Challenges of Different Settings*. Amsterdam: John Benjamins.

Allen, R.R. and Brown, K.L. (eds) (1976) *Developing Communication Competence in Children*. Skokie, IL: National Textbook Co.

Anderson, R.C. (1984) Role of the reader's schema in comprehension, learning and memory. In R.B. Ruddell, M. Rapp Ruddell and H. Singer (eds) *Theoretical Models and Processes of Reading 4th edition* (pp. 469–482) Newark: International Reading Association.

Angelil-Carter, S. (1997) Second language acquisition of spoken and written English: Acquiring the skeptron. *TESOL Quarterly* 31 (2), 263–287.

Andrews, R. (1995) *Teaching and Learning Argument*. London: Cassell.

Andrews, R. (2010) *Argumentation in Higher Education. Improving Practice through Theory and Research*. New York, Oxford: Routledge.

Ansell, M. (2008) The privatisation of English for Academic Purposes teaching in British Universities. *Liaison Magazine*. Higher Education Academy's Subject Area for Languages, Linguistics and Area Studies.

Archer, A. (2012) Changing academic landscapes: Principles and practices of teaching writing in the Writing Centre at UCT. In C. Thaiss, G. Bräuer, P. Carlino, L. Ganobcsik Williams and A. Sinha (eds) *Writing Programs Worldwide: Profiles of Academic Writing in Many Places* (pp. 353–364). Fort Collins, Colorado: The WAC Clearinghouse and Parlor Press.

Arkoudis, S. (2012) Standards in international education. Paper delivered at Australian International Education Conference (AIEC). http://www.aiec.idp.com/pdf/2012_Arkoudis_Fri_1115_212.pdf (accessed October 2013).

Arkoudis, S. and Starfield, S. (2007) *In-Course English Language Development and Support*. Canberra: Australian Education International.

Arkoudis, S., Watty, K., Baik, C., Yu, X., Borland, H., Chang, S., Lang, I., Lang, J. and Pearce, A. (2012) Finding common ground: Enhancing interaction between domestic and international students in higher education. *Teaching in Higher Education* 18 (3), 222–235.

Artemeva, N. (2008) Approaches to learning genres: A bibliographical essay. In N. Artemeva and A. Freedman (eds) *Rhetorical Genre Studies and Beyond* (pp. 9–11). University of Manitoba Winnipeg: Inksted Publications.

Artemeva, N. and Freedman, A. (2008) (eds) *Rhetorical Genre Studies and Beyond*. University of Manitoba Winnipeg: Inksted Publications.
Ascención Delaney, Y. (2008) Investigating the reading-to-write construct. *Journal of English for Academic Purposes* 7 (3), 140–150.
Askehave, I. and Swales, J. (2001) Genre identification and communicative purpose: A problem and a possible solution. *Applied Linguistics* 22 (2), 195–212.
Atai, M.R. and Mosayeb, F.M. (2014) Exploring the practices and cognitions of Iranian ELT instructors and subject teachers in teaching EAP reading comprehension. *English for Specific Purposes* 33 (1), 27–38.
Atkinson, D. (1997) A critical approach to critical thinking in TESOL. *TESOL Quarterly* 31 (1), 71–94.
Atkinson, D. and Ramanathan, V. (1995) Cultures of writing: An ethnographic comparison of L1 and L2 university writing/language programs. *TESOL Quarterly* 29 (3), 539–568.
Bakhtin, M. (1981) Discourse in the novel. In M. Holquist (ed.) *The Dialogic Imagination: Four Essays by M. Bakhtin* (pp. 259–422). Austin, Texas: University of Texas Press.
Bakhtin, M. (1986) *Speech Genres and Other Late Essays*. Austin: University of Texas Press.
Ballard, B. and Clanchy, J. (1991) Assessment by misconception: Cultural influences and intellectual traditions. In L. Hamp-Lyons (ed.) *Assessing Second Language Writing in Academic Contexts*. Norwood, NJ: Ablex.
Bawarshi, A.S. and Reiff, M.J. (2010) *Genre: An Introduction to History, Theory, Research, and Pedagogy*. West Lafayette, Indiana: Parlor Press and the WAC Clearinghouse.
Bathia, V.K. (1993) *Analysing Genre: Language Use in Professional Settings*. London: Longman.
Bathia, V.K. (2004) *Worlds of Written Discourse*. London: Continuum.
Bazerman, C. (1981) What written knowledge does: Three examples of academic discourse. *Philosophy of the Social Sciences* 11 (3), 361–388.
Beaufort, A. (2007) *College Writing and Beyond: A New Framework for University Writing Instruction*. Logan, Utah: Utah University Press.
Belcher, D. (1994) The apprenticeship approach to advanced academic literacy: graduate students and their mentors. *English for Specific Purposes* 13 (1), 23–34.
Benesch, S. (1993) ESL, ideology, and the politics of pragmatism. *TESOL Quarterly* 27 (4), 705–716.
Benesch, S. (2001) *Critical English for Academic Purposes*. Mahwah, NJ: Lawrence Erlbaum.
Bereiter, C. and Scardamalia, M. (1987) *The Psychology of Written Composition*. Hillsdale, NJ: Lawrence Erlbaum.
Berg, B. (2009) *Qualitative Research Methods for the Social Sciences*. Boston: Allyn & Bacon.
Berkenkotter, C. and Huckin, T. (1995) *Genre Knowledge in Disciplinary Communication: Cognition/Culture/Power*. Hillsdale, NJ: Lawrence Erlbaum.
Berman, R. and Cheng, L. (2001) English academic language skills: Perceived difficulties by undergraduate and graduate students, and their academic achievement. *Educational Linguistics* 4 (1), 25–40.
Bhatia, V.K. (1993) *Analyzing Genre: Language Use in Professional Settings*. London: Longman.
Bhatia, V.K. (2004) *Worlds of Written Discourse*. London: Continuum.
Biber, D. (1988) *Variation across Speech and Writing*. Cambridge: Cambridge University Press.
Biber, D. (2006) *University Language: A Corpus-Based Study of Spoken and Written Registers*. Amsterdam: John Benjamins.
Biber, D., Connor, U. and Upton, T. (eds) (2007) *Discourse on the Move*. Amsterdam: John Benjamins.

Bitchener, J. and Basturkmen, H. (2006) Perceptions of the difficulties of postgraduate L2 thesis students writing the discussion section. *Journal of English for Academic Purposes* 5 (1), 4–18.

Black, P. and Wiliam, D. (1998) Assessment and classroom learning. *Assessment in Education* 5 (1), 7–74.

Black, P., Harrison, C., Lee, C., Marshall, B. and Wiliam, D. (2003) *Assessment for Learning*. Maidenhead: Open University Press.

Block, E. (1992) See how they read: Comprehension monitoring of L1 and L2 readers. *TESOL Quarterly* 26 (2), 319–341.

Bloor, M. and Bloor, T. (1986) Languages for specific purposes: Practice and theory. *CLCS Occasional Papers 19*. Dublin: Trinity College, Centre for Language and Communication Studies.

Bourdieu, P. and Passeron, J.C. (1990) *Reproduction in Education, Society and Culture*. Newbury Park: Sage.

Boughey, C. (2002) 'Naming students' problems: An analysis of language-related discourses at a South African university. *Teaching in Higher Education* 7 (3), 295–307.

Brown, L. and Jones, J. (2013) Encounters with racism and the international student experience. *Studies in Higher Education* 38 (8), 1004–1019.

Bruner, J. (1978) The role of dialogue in language acquisition. In A. Sinclair, R. Jarvellla, and W. Levelt (eds) *The Child's Conception of Language*. New York: Springer.

Bunton, D. (2005) The structure of PhD conclusion chapters. *Journal of English for Academic Purposes* 4 (3), 207–224.

Byram, M. (1997) *Teaching and Assessing Intercultural Communicative Competence*. Clevedon: Multilingual Matters.

Canagarajah, A.S. (2007) Lingua Franca English, multilingual communities and language acquisition. *Modern Language Journal* 95 (3), 923–939.

Carless, D. (2006) Differing perceptions in the feedback process. *Studies in Higher Education* 31 (2), 219–233.

Carrell, P.L. (1984) Evidence for a formal schema in second language comprehension. *Language Learning* 34 (2), 87–122.

Carroll, J. (2005) 'Lightening the load': Teaching in English, learning in English. In J. Carroll and J. Ryan (eds) *Teaching International Students: Improving Learning for All* (pp. 35–42). Oxford, New York: Routledge.

Carson, J.G. (2001) A task analysis of reading and writing in academic contexts. In D. Belcher and A. Hirvela (eds) *Linking Literacies. Perspectives on L2 Reading-Writing Connections* (pp. 4–83). Ann Arbor: University of Michigan Press.

Chang, P. and Schleppegrell, M. (2011) Taking an effective authorial stance in academic writing: Making the linguistic resources explicit for L2 writers in the social sciences. *Journal of English for Academic Purposes* 10 (3), 140–151.

Charles, M. (2006) The construction of stance in reporting clauses: A cross-disciplinary study of theses. *Applied Linguistics* 27(3), 492–518.

Charles, M. (2007) Reconciling top-down and bottom-up approaches to graduate writing: Using a corpus to teach rhetorical functions. *Journal of English for Academic Purposes* 6 (4), 289–302.

Charles, M., Pecorari, D. and Hunston, S. (eds) (2009) *Academic Writing. At the Interface of Corpus and Discourse*. London, New York: Continuum.

Charney, D.H. and Carlson, R.A. (1995) Learning to write in a genre: What student writers take from model texts. *Research in the Teaching of English* 29 (1), 88–125.

Cheng, A. (2006) Understanding learners and learning in ESP genre-based writing instruction. *English for Specific Purposes* 25 (1), 76–89.
Chomsky, N. (1965) *Aspects of the Theory of Syntax*. Cambridge, MA: MIT Press.
Chowdry, H., Crawford, C., Dearden, L., Goodman, A. and Vignoles, A. (2010) Widening participation in higher education: Analysis using linked administrative data. IFS Working Paper W10/04. London: Institute for Fiscal Studies.
Clark, R. and Ivanic, R. (1997) *The Politics of Writing*. London: Routledge.
Clark, I. and Russell, D. (2014) US first-year composition and writing in the disciplines. In C. Leung and B. Street (eds) *The Routledge Companion to English Studies* (pp. 375–391). London, New York: Routledge.
Coffin, C. and Donohue, J. (2012) Academic Literacies and systemic functional linguistics: How do they relate? *Journal of English for Specific Purposes* 11 (1), 64–75.
Coffin, C. and Hewings, A. (2004) IELTS as preparation for tertiary writing: Distinctive interpersonal and textual strategies. In L. Ravelli and R. Ellis (eds) *Analysing Academic Writing* (pp. 153–171). London: Continuum.
Cohen, A. (1994) English for academic purposes in Brazil: The use of summary tasks. In C. Hill and K. Parry (eds) *From Testing to Assessment: English as an International Language* (pp. 174–204). London: Longman.
Cohen, A. and Upton, T. (2007) 'I want to go back to the text'. Response strategies on the reading subtest of the new TOEFL. *Language Testing* 24 (2), 209–250.
Cooper, L. (2014) 'Does my experience count?' The role of experiential knowledge in the research writing of postgraduate adult learners. In L. Thesen and L. Cooper (eds) *Risk in Academic Writing: Postgraduate Students, their Teachers and the Making of Knowledge* (pp. 27–47). Bristol: Multilingual Matters.
Cope, B. and Kalantzis, M. (eds) (1993) *The Powers of Literacy: A Genre Approach to Teaching Writing*. Bristol, PA: Falmer Press.
Cumming, A., Kantor, R., Baba, K., Erdosy, U., Eouanzoui, K., and James, M. (2005) Differences in written discourse in independent and integrated prototype tasks for next generation TOEFL. *Assessing Writing* 10 (1), 5–43.
Dann, C. (2008) From where I sit – A sad loss of literacy down under. *Times Higher Education*. See: http://www.timeshighereducation.co.uk/comment/from-where-i-sit/from-where-i-sit-a-sad-loss-of-literacy-down-under/403511.article (accessed 16 December 2014).
Deardorff, D. (2006) Identification and assessment of intercultural competence as a student outcome of internationalisation. *Journal of Studies in International Education* 10 (3), 241–266.
Devereux, L. and Wilson, K. (2008) Scaffolding literacies across the Bachelor of Education program: An argument for a course-wide approach. *Asia-Pacific Journal of Teacher Education* 36 (2), 121–134.
Devitt, A. (2009) Teaching critical genre awareness. In C. Bazerman, A. Bonini, and D. Figueiredo (eds) *Genre in a Changing World* (pp. 342–355). Fort Collins, CO: The WAC Clearinghouse and Parlor Press.
Dobson, B. and Feak, C. (2001) A cognitive modeling approach to teaching critique writing to nonnative speakers. In D. Belcher and A. Hirvela (eds) *Linking Literacies. Perspectives on L2 Reading–Writing Connections* (pp. 186–199). Ann Arbor: University of Michigan Press.
Dooey, P. (2010) Students' perspectives of an EAP pathway program. *Journal of English for Academic Purposes* 9 (3), 184–197.

Dörnyei, Z. (2007) *Research Methods in Applied Linguistics*. Oxford: Oxford University Press.
Dovey, T. (2010) Facilitating writing from sources: A focus on both process and product. *Journal of English for Academic Purposes* 9 (1), 45–60.
Dreyer, C. and Nel, C. (2003) Teaching reading strategies and reading comprehension within a technology-enhanced learning environment. *System* 31 (3), 349–365.
Drury, H. (2004) Teaching academic writing on screen: A search for best practice. In L. Ravelli and R. Ellis (eds) *Analysing Academic Writing* (pp. 233–253). London: Continuum.
Dudley-Evans, T. (2001) Team-teaching in EAP: Changes and adaptations in the Birmingham approach. In J. Flowerdew and M. Peacock (eds) *Research Perspectives on English for Academic Purposes* (pp. 225–238). Cambridge: Cambridge University Press.
Dudley-Evans, T. (2002) The teaching of the academic essay: Is a genre approach possible? In A.M. Johns (ed.) *Genre in the Classroom: Multiple Perspectives* (pp. 225–235). Mahwah, NJ: Lawrence Erlbaum.
Dudley-Evans, T. and St John, M.J. (1998) *Developments in English for Specific Purposes: A Multidisciplinary Approach*. Cambridge: Cambridge University Press.
Duff, P. (2007) Second language socialisation as sociocultural theory: Insights and issues. *Language Teaching* 40 (4), 309–319.
Duff, P. (2010) Language socialisation into academic discourse communities. *Annual Review of Applied Linguistics* 30, 169–192.
Dunning, T. (1994) *Statistical Identification of Language*. New Mexico State University. Technical Report MCCS, 94–273.
Durkin, K. and Main, A. (2002) Discipline-based study skills support for first-year undergraduate students. *Active Learning in Higher Education*, 3 (1), 24–39.
Elbow, P. (1973) *Writing without Teachers*. London: Oxford University Press.
Ellis, R. (2004) Supporting genre-based literacy pedagogy with technology–the implications for the framing and classification of the pedagogy. In L. Ravelli and R. Ellis (eds) *Analysing Academic Writing* (pp. 210–232). London: Continuum.
Etherington, S. (2008) Academic writing and the disciplines. In P. Friedrich (ed.) *Teaching Academic Writing* (pp. 26–58). London, New York: Continuum.
Evans, S. and Green, C. (2007) Why EAP is necessary: A survey of Hong Kong tertiary students. *Journal of English for Academic Purposes* 6 (1), 3–17.
Evans, S. and Morrison, B. (2011) The first term at university: Implications for EAP. *English Language Teaching Journal* 65 (4), 387–397.
Fairclough, N. (1995) *Critical Discourse Analysis*. Harlow: Longman.
Ferris, D. (2008) Feedback: issues and options. In P. Friedrich (ed.) *Teaching Academic Writing* (pp. 93–124). London, New York: Continuum.
Ferris, D. and Hedgcock, J. S. (2005) *Teaching ESL Composition: Purpose, Process, and Practice*. New Jersey: Routledge.
Flower, L. and Hayes, J. (1981) A cognitive process theory of writing. *College Composition and Communication* 32 (4), 365–387.
Flowerdew, J. (2002) Genre in the classroom: A linguistic approach. In A.M. Johns (ed.) *Genre in the Classroom: Multiple Perspectives* (pp. 91–104). Mahwah, NJ: Lawrence Erlbaum.
Flowerdew, J. (2011) Reconciling contrasting approaches to genre analysis: The whole can equal more than the sum of the parts. In D. Belcher, A.M. Johns and B. Paltridge (eds) *New Directions in Research for English for Specific Purposes* (pp. 119–144). Ann Arbor, MI: University of Michigan Press.

Flowerdew, J. (2013) *Discourse in English Language Education*. London, New York: Routledge.
Flowerdew, J. and Forest, R. (2009) Schematic structure and lexico-grammatical realisation in corpus-based genre analysis: The case of research in the PhD literature review. In M. Charles, D. Pecorari and S. Hunston (eds) *Academic Writing. At the Interface of Corpus and Discourse* (pp. 15–36). London, New York: Continuum.
Flowerdew, L. (1998) Corpus linguistic techniques applied to textlinguistics. *System* 26 (4), 541–552.
Flowerdew, L. (2002) Corpus-based analysis in EAP. In J. Flowerdew (ed.) *Academic Discourse* (pp. 95–114). Harlow: Pearson Education.
Flowerdew, L. (2008) *Corpus-based Analyses of the Problem-Solution Pattern*. Amsterdam: John Benjamins.
Flowerdew, L. (2012) *Corpora and Language Education*. London: Palgrave Macmillan.
Flowerdew, J. and Peacock, M. (2001) Issues in EAP: A preliminary perspective. In J. Flowerdew and M. Peacock (eds) *Research Perspectives on English for Academic Purposes* (pp. 8–24). Cambridge: Cambridge University Press.
Foster, S. and Deane, M. (2011) Enhancing students' legal writing. In M. Deane and P. O'Neill (eds) *Writing in the Disciplines* (pp. 88–102). London: Palgrave Macmillan.
Fotovatian, S. (2012) Three constructs of institutional identity among international students in Australia. *Teaching in Higher Education* 17 (5), 577–588.
Freedman, A. (1993) Show and Tell? The role of explicit teaching in the learning of new genres. *Research in the Teaching of English* 27 (3), 222–251.
Freedman, A. (1994) 'Do as I say': The relationship between teaching and learning new genres. In A. Freedman and P. Medway (eds) *Genre and the New Rhetoric* (pp. 191–210). London: Taylor & Francis.
Gardner, S. (2012) Genres and registers of student report writing: an SFL perspective on texts and practices. *Journal of English for Specific Purposes* 11 (1), 52–63.
Gee, J.P. (1990) *Social Linguistics and Literacies: Ideology in Discourses*. London: Falmer.
Gibbons, P. (2009) *English Learners, Academic Literacy, and Thinking*. Portsmouth, NH: Heinemann.
Grabe, W. (1991) Current developments in second language reading research. *TESOL Quaterly* 25 (3), 375–406.
Grabe, W. (2001) Reading–writing relations: theoretical perspectives and instructional practices. In D. Belcher and A. Hirvela (eds) *Linking Literacies. Perspectives on L2 Reading–Writing Connections* (pp. 15–47). Ann Arbor: University of Michigan Press.
Grabe, W. and Kaplan, R. (1996) *Theory and Practice of Writing*. London: Longman.
Granger, S. (1998) *Learner English on Computer*. London: Longman.
Green, A. (2007) *IELTS Washback in Context: Preparation for Academic Writing in Higher Education*. Cambridge: Cambridge University Press.
Guo, S. and Chase, M. (2011) Internationalisation of higher education: Integrating international students into Canadian academic environment. *Teaching in Higher Education* 16 (3), 305–318.
Halliday, M.A.K. (1975) *Learning How to Mean—Explorations in the Development of Language*. London: Edward Arnold.
Halliday, M.A.K. (1978) *Language as Social Semiotic: The Social Interpretation of Language and Meaning*. London: Edward Arnold.
Halliday, M.A.K. (1993) *Language in a Changing World*. Canberra: Applied Linguistics Association of Australia.
Halliday, M.A.K. (1994) *An Introduction to Functional Grammar* (2nd edn). London: Edward Arnold.

Halliday, M.A.K., McIntosh, A. and Strevens, P. (1964) *The Linguistic Sciences and Language Teaching*. London: Longman.

Hammond, J. and Macken-Horarik, M. (1999) Critical literacy: Challenges and questions for ESL classrooms. *TESOL Quarterly* 33 (3), 528–544.

Hamp-Lyons, L. (2011) English for academic purposes: 2011 and beyond. *Journal of English for Academic Purposes* 10 (1), 2–4.

Harris, A. and Ashton, J. (2011) Embedding and integrating language and academic skills: An innovative approach. *Journal of Academic Language and Learning* 5 (2), A-73–A-87.

Harwood, N. (2005) 'Nowhere has anyone attempted … In this article I aim to do just that': A corpus-based study of self-promotional I and we in academic writing across four disciplines. *Journal of Pragmatics* 37 (8), 1207–1231.

Hasan, R. (1996) Literacy, everyday talk and society. In R. Hasan and G. Williams (eds) *Literacy in Society* (pp. 377–424). London: Longman.

Hawkins, M. (2005) Becoming a student: Identity work and academic literacies in early schooling. *TESOL Quarterly* 39 (1), 59–82.

HEFCE (Higher Education Funding Council for England) (2013) International Research on the Effectiveness of Widening Participation. Report to HEFCE and OFFA by CFE and Edge Hill University. https://www.hefce.ac.uk/pubs/rereports/year/2013/wpeffectiveness/ (accessed April 2014).

HEFCE (Higher Education Funding Council for England) (2014) Differences in Degree Outcomes. http://www.hefce.ac.uk/whatwedo/wp/ourresearch/degree/ (accessed April 2014).

Hennebry, M., Lo, Y. and Macaro, E. (2012) Differing perspectives of non-native speaker students' linguistic experiences on higher degree courses. *Oxford Review of Education* 38 (2), 209–230.

Henry, A. and Roseberry, R.L. (1998) An evaluation of a genre-based approach to the teaching of EAP/ESP writing. *TESOL Quarterly* 32 (1), 147–156.

Herrington, A. and Moran, C. (eds) (2005) *Genre Across the Curriculum*. Utah State University Press: Utah.

Hinds, J. (1990) Inductive, deductive, quasi-inductive: Expository writing in Japanese, Korean, Chinese, and Thai. In U. Connor & A. M. Johns (eds) *Coherence in Writing: Research and Pedagogical Perspectives* (pp. 89–109). Alexandria, VA: Teachers of English to Speakers of Other Languages.

Hirvela, A. (2001) Incorporating reading into EAP writing courses. In J. Flowerdew and M. Peacock (eds) *Research Perspectives on English for Academic Purposes* (pp. 330–346). Cambridge: Cambridge University Press.

Hirvela, A. (2004) *Connecting Reading and Writing in Second Language Writing Instruction*. Ann Arbor, MI: University of Michigan Press.

Hirvela, A. and Du, Q. (2013) 'Why am I paraphrasing?': Undergraduate ESL writers' engagement with source-based academic writing and reading. *Journal of English for Academic Purposes* 12 (2), 87–98.

Holmes, P. (2006) Problematising communication competence in the pluricultural classroom: Chinese students in a New Zealand university. *Language and Communication* 6 (1), 18–34.

Hopkins, A. and Dudley-Evans, T. (1988) A genre-based investigation of the discussion sections in articles and dissertations. *English for Specific Purposes* 7 (2), 113–121.

Horner, B. (2014) Writing in the disciplines/writing across the curriculum. In C. Leung and B. Street (eds) *The Routledge Companion to English Studies* (pp. 405–418). London, New York: Routledge.

Horner, B. and Lu, M.Z. (2012) (Re)Writing English: Putting English in translation. In C. Leung and B. Street (eds) *English. A Changing Medium for Education* (pp. 59–78). Bristol: Multilingual Matters.
Hounsell, D. (1987) Towards an anatomy of academic discourse: Meaning and context in the undergraduate essay. In R. Saljo (ed.) *The Written World: Studies in Literate Thought and Action* (pp. 161–177). Berlin: Springer-Verlag.
Humphrey, S., Martin, J.R., Dreyfus, S., and Mahboob, A. (2010) The 3x3: Setting up a linguistic toolkit for teaching academic writing. In A. Mahboob and N. Knight (eds) *Appliable Linguistics: Reclaiming the Place of Language in Linguistics* (pp. 185–199). London: Continuum.
Hunma, A. and Sibomana, E. (2014) Academic writing and research at an Afropolitan university: An international student perspective. In L. Thesen and L. Cooper (eds) *Risk in Academic Writing: Postgraduate Students, their Teachers and the Making of Knowledge* (pp. 100–128). Bristol: Multilingual Matters.
Hunston, S. and Thompson, G. (eds) (2000) *Evaluation in text: Authorial Stance and the Construction of Discourse*. Oxford: Oxford University Press.
Hüttner, J. (2008) The genre(s) of student writing: developing writing models. *International Journal of Applied Linguistics* 18 (4), 146–165.
Hyland, K. (1998) *Hedging in Scientific Research Articles*. Amsterdam: John Benjamins.
Hyland, K. (2002a) *Teaching and Researching Writing*. Harlow: Pearson Education.
Hyland, K. (2002b) Specificity revisited: How far should we go now? *English for Specific Purposes* 21 (4), 385–395.
Hyland, K. (2003) Genre-based pedagogies: A social response to process. *Journal of Second Language Writing* 12 (1), 17–29.
Hyland, K. (2004) *Genre and Second Language Writing*. Ann Arbor: University of Michigan Press.
Hyland, K. (2005) *Metadiscourse: Exploring Interaction in Writing*. London: Continuum.
Hyland, K. (2008a) Genre and academic writing in the disciplines. *Language Teaching* 41 (4), 543–562.
Hyland, K. (2008b) As can be seen: Lexical bundles and disciplinary variation. *English for Specific Purposes* 27 (1), 4–21.
Hyland, K. (2009) *Academic Discourse. English in a Global Context*. London: Continuum.
Hyland, K. and Hamp-Lyons, L. (2002) EAP: Issues and directions. *Journal of English for Academic Purposes* 1, 1–12.
Hyland, K. (2011) Academic discourse. In K. Hyland and B. Paltridge (eds) *The Bloomsbury Companion to Discourse Analysis* (pp. 171–184). London: Bloomsbury.
Hyland, K. and Milton, J. (1997) Qualification and certainty in L1 and L2 students' writing. *Journal of Second Language Writing* 6 (2), 183–205.
Hymes, D. (1966) *Language in Culture and Society*. New York, London: Harper and Row.
Hymes, D. (1972) On communicative competence. In J.B. Pride and J. Holmes (eds) *Sociolinguistics* (pp. 269–293). London: Penguin.
Hymes, D. (1977) *Foundations in Socio-Linguistics: An Ethnographic Approach*. London: Tavistock Publications.
Hyon, S. (1996) Genre in three traditions: Implications for ESL. *TESOL Quarterly* 30 (4), 693–722.
Hyon, S. (2001) Long-term effects of genre-based instruction: A follow-up study of an EAP reading course. *English for Specific Purposes* 20 (4), 417–438.
Hyon, S. (2002) Genre and ESL reading: A classroom study. In A.M. Johns (ed.) *Genre in the Classroom: Multiple Perspectives* (pp. 121–141). Mahwah, NJ: Lawrence Erlbaum.

Iannelli, C. and Huang, J. (2013) Trends in participation and attainment of Chinese students in UK higher education. *Studies in Higher Education* 39 (5), 805–822.
Ivanič, R. (1998) *Writing and Identity: The Discoursal Construction of Identity in Academic Writing*. Amsterdam: John Benjamins.
Ivanič, R. (2004). Discourses of writing and learning to write. *Language and Education*, 18 (3), 220–245.
Ivanič, R. and Camps, D. (2001) I am how I sound: Voice as self-representation in L2 writing. *Journal of second language writing* 10 (1), 3–33.
Ivanic, R. and Lea, M.R. (2006) New contexts, new challenges: The teaching of writing in UK higher education. In L. Ganobcsik-Williams (ed.) *Teaching Academic Writing in UK Higher Education: Theories, Practice and Models* (pp. 6–15). London: Palgrave Macmillan.
Jacobs, C. (2005) On being an insider on the outside: New spaces for integrating academic literacies. *Teaching in Higher Education* 10 (4), 475–487.
Jenkins, J. (2014) *English as a Lingua Franca in the International University. The Politics of Academic English Language Policy*. London, New York: Routledge.
Jenkins, J. and Wingate, U. (in preparation) Internationalisation and English language policies and practices in UK universities.
Jones, J. (2004) Learning to write in the disciplines: The application of systemic functional linguistic theory to the teaching and research of student writing. In L. Ravelli and R. Ellis (eds) *Analysing Academic Writing* (pp. 233–253.) London, New York: Continuum.
Johns, A.M. (1997) *Text, Role and Context: Developing Academic Literacies*. Cambridge: Cambridge University Press.
Johns, A.M. (2002) (ed.) *Genre in the Classroom: Multiple Perspectives*. Mahwah, NJ: Lawrence Erlbaum.
Johns, A.M. (2006) Crossing the boundaries of genre studies: Commentaries by experts. *Journal of Second Language Writing* 15, 234–249.
Johns, A.M. (2008) Genre awareness for the novice academic student: An ongoing quest. *Language Teaching* 41 (2), 237–252.
Johns, A.M. (2011) The future of genre in L2 writing: Fundamental, but contested, instructional decisions. *Journal of Second Language Writing* 20 (1), 56–68.
Johns, T. (1994) From printout to handout: Grammar and vocabulary learning in the context of data-driven learning. In T. Odlin (ed.) *Approaches to Pedagogic Grammar* (pp. 293–313). Cambridge: Cambridge University Press.
Johns, T. (1997) Contexts: The background, development and trialling of a concordance-based CALL program. In A. Wichmann, S. Fligelstone, T. McEnery and G. Knowles (eds) *Teaching and Language Corpora* (pp. 100–115). Harlow: Addison Wesley Longman.
Jolliffe, D.A. and Harl, A. (2008) Studying the 'reading transition' from high school to college: What are our students reading and why? *College English* 70 (6), 599–617.
Kachru, B.B. (1985) Standards, codification and sociolinguistic realism: The English language in the outer circle. In R. Quirk and H.G. Widdowson (eds) *English in the World: Teaching and Learning the Language and Literatures*. Cambridge: Cambridge University Press.
Kaplan, R.B. (1972) *The Anatomy of Rhetoric: Prolegomena to a Functional Theory of Rhetoric*. Philadelphia: Center for Curriculum Development.
Kapp, R. and Bangeni, B. (2009) Positioning (in) the discipline: Undergraduate students' negotiations of disciplinary discourses. *Teaching in Higher Education* 14 (6), 587–596.
Kim, H.Y. (2011) International students' difficulties: Graduate classes as a community of practices. *Teaching in Higher Education* 16 (3), 281–292.

Kress, G. (2003) *Literacy in the Media Age*. London: Routledge.
Kress, G. (2007) Thinking about meaning and learning in a world of instability and multiplicity. *Pedagogies. An International Journal* 1 (1), 19–34.
Kress, G. and van Leeuwen (2001) *Multimodal Discourse: The Modes and Media of Contemporary Communication*. London: Edward Arnold.
Kwan, B.S.C. (2008) The nexus of reading, writing and researching in the doctoral undertaking of humanities and social sciences: Implications for literature reviewing. *English for Specific Purposes* 27 (1), 42–56.
Kwan, B.S. (2009) Reading in preparation for writing a PhD thesis: Case studies of experiences. *Journal of English for Academic Purposes* 8 (3), 180–191.
Langer, J.A. and Applebee, A.N. (1987) *How Writing Shapes Thinking: Writing and Learning in the Secondary School: A Study of Teaching and Learning*. Urbana, IL: National Council of Teachers of English.
Lantolf, J.P. and Thorne, S.L. (2007) Sociocultural theory and second language learning. In B. van Patten and J. Williams (eds) *Theories in Second Language Acquisition* (pp. 201–224). Mahwah, NJ: Lawrence Erlbaum.
Lave, J. and Wenger, E. (1991) *Situated Learning: Legitimate Peripheral Participation*. Cambridge: Cambridge University Press.
Lazar, G. and Ellis, E. (2012) Genre as implicit methodology in a collaborative writing initiative. *International Journal of English Studies* 2 (1), 155–168.
Lea, M. (2004) Academic literacies: A pedagogy for course design. *Studies in Higher Education* 29 (6), 739–756.
Lea, M. and Street, B. (1998) Student writing in higher education: An Academic Literacies approach. *Studies in Higher Education* 23 (2), 157–172.
Lea, M. and Street, B. (2006) The 'academic literacies' model: Theory and applications. *Theory into Practice* 45 (4), 368–377.
Leedham, M. (2014) *Chinese Students' Writing in English*. London, New York: Routledge.
Leki, I. (2001) Developing meaningful literacy courses. In D. Belcher and A. Hirvela (eds) Linking Literacies. *Perspectives on L2 Reading–Writing Connections* (pp. 201–206). Ann Arbor: University of Michigan Press.
Leki, I. (2006) Negotiating socioacademic relations: English learners' reception by and reaction to college faculty. *Journal of English for Academic Purposes* 5(2), 136–152.
Leki, I. and Carson, J.G. (1994) Students' perceptions of EAP writing instruction and writing needs across the disciplines. *TESOL Quarterly* 28 (1), 81–101.
Leung, C. (2005) Convivial communication: Recontextualising communicative competence. *International Journal of Applied Linguistics* 15 (2), 119–144.
Li, G., Chen, W. and Duanmu, J.L. (2010) Determinants of international students' academic performance. A comparison between Chinese and other international students. *Journal of Studies in International Education* 14 (4), 389–405.
Lillis, T. and Turner, J. (2001) Student writing in higher education: Contemporary confusion, traditional concerns. *Teaching in Higher Education* 6 (1), 57–68.
Lillis, T.M. (1999) Whose 'common sense'? Essayist literacy and the institutional practice of mystery. In: C. Jones, J. Turner and B. Street (eds) *Student Writing in the University* (pp. 126–147). Amsterdam: John Benjamins.
Lillis, T.M. (2001) *Student Writing: Access, Regulation, Desire*. London: Routledge.
Lillis, T.M. (2003) Student writing as 'Academic Literacies': Drawing on Bakhtin to move from critique to design. *Language and Education* 1 (2), 192–207.
Lillis, T.M. (2006) Moving towards an 'Academic Literacies' pedagogy: Dialogues of participation. In: L. Ganobcsik-Williams (ed.) *Teaching Academic Writing in UK*

Higher Education: Theories, Practice and Models (pp. 30–45). London: Palgrave Macmillan.

Lillis, T.M. and Scott, M. (2007) Defining Academic Literacies research: Issues of epistemology, ideology and strategy. *Journal of Applied Linguistics* 4 (1), 5–32.

MacMillan, M. (2014) Student connections with academic texts: A phenomenographic study of reading. *Teaching in Higher Education* 19 (8), 943–954.

Mahboob, A., Dreyfus, S., Humphrey, S. and Martin, J.R. (2010) Appliable linguistics and English language teaching: The scaffolding literacy in adult and tertiary environments (SLATE) project. In A. Mahboob and N.K. Knight (eds) *Appliable Linguistics* (pp. 25–43). London: Continuum.

Mann, S. (2000) The student's experience of reading. *Higher Education* 39, 297–317.

Marshall, J.D. (1987) The effects of writing on students' understanding of literary text. *Research in the Teaching of English* 21 (1), 31–63.

Marshall, S. (2010) Re-becoming ESL: Multilingual university students and a deficit identity. *Language and Education* 24 (1), 41–56.

Martin, J.R. (1984) Language, register and genre. In F. Christie (ed.) *Children Writing* (pp. 2–29). Geelong, Australia: Deakin University Press.

Martin, J.R. (1992) *English Text: System and Structure*. Amsterdam: John Benjamins.

Martin, J.R. (1999) Mentoring semogenesis: 'genre-based' literacy pedagogy. In F. Christie (ed.) *Pedagogy and the Shaping of Consciousness: Linguistic and Social Processes* (pp. 123–155). London: Cassell.

Martin, J.R. and Rose, D. (2008) *Genre Relations: Mapping Culture*. London, Oakville: Equinox.

Martin, J.R. and Rothery, J. (1980) *Writing Project: Report No. 1. Working Papers in Linguistics*. Linguistics Department, University of Sydney.

Martin, J.R. and Rothery, J. (1981) *Writing Project: Report No. 2. Working Papers in Linguistics*. Linguistics Department, University of Sydney.

Martin, J.R. and White, P.R. (2005) *The Language of Evaluation: Appraisal in English*. London: Palgrave.

Mauranen, A. (2008) Hybrid voices: English as the lingua franca of academics. In K. Flottum (ed.) *Language and Discipline Perspectives on Academic Discourse* (pp. 14–25). Newcastle: Cambridge Scholars Publishing.

McCarthy, L. (1987) A stranger in strange lands: A college student writing across the curriculum. *Research in the Teaching of English* 21 (3), 233–265.

McCulloch, S. (2013) Investigating the reading-to-write processes and source use of L2 postgraduate students in real-life academic tasks: An exploratory study. *Journal of English for Academic Purposes* 12 (2), 136–147.

McGinley, W. (1992) The role of reading and writing while composing from sources. *Reading Research Quarterly* 27 (3), 227–248.

McLeod, S.H. (1989) Writing across the curriculum: The second stage, and beyond. *College Composition and Communication* 40 (3), 337–343.

Middlesex University (2013) Academic writing and language. http://www.intra.mdx.ac.uk/students-teaching/learner-development (accessed November 2013).

Miller, C. (1984) Genre as Social Action. *Quarterly Journal of Speech* 70, 151–167.

Milton, J. and Hyland, K. (1999) Assertions in students' academic essays: A comparison of English NS and NNS student writers. In R. Berry, B. Asker and K. Hyland (eds) *Language Analysis, Description and Pedagogy* (pp. 147–161). Hong Kong: Language Centre, HKUST.

Mitchell, S. and Evison, A. (2006) Exploiting the potential of writing for educational change at Queen Mary, University of London. In L. Ganobcsik-Williams (ed.) *Teaching Academic Writing in UK Higher Education: Theories, Practice and Models* (pp. 68–84). London: Palgrave Macmillan.

Mitchell, S. and Riddle, M. (2000) *Improving the Quality of Argument in Higher Education. Final Report*. School of Lifelong Learning and Education: Middlesex University.

Mohan, B. and Lo, W.A.Y. (1985) Academic writing and Chinese students: Transfer and development factors. *TESOL Quarterly* 19 (3), 515–534.

Montgomery, C. (2008) Global futures, global communities? The role of culture, language and communication in an international university. In H. Haberland, J. Mortensen, A. Fabricius, B. Preisler, K. Risager and S. Kjaerbeck (eds) *Higher Education in the Global Village* (pp. 17–34). Roskilde, Denmark: University of Roskilde.

Monroe, J. (2003) *Local Knowledges, Local Practices: Cultures of Writing at Cornell*. Pittsburgh: University of Pittsburgh Press.

Morgan, B. (2009) Fostering transformative practitioners for critical EAP: Possibilities and challenges. *Journal of English for Academic Purposes* 8, 86–99.

Morita, N. (2004) Negotiating participation and identity in second language academic communities. *TESOL Quarterly* 38 (4), 573–603.

Morita, N. (2009) Language, culture, gender, and academic socialization. *Language and Education* 23 (5), 443–460.

Morley, J. (2008) Writing support in British higher education: An institutional case study. In P. Friedrich (ed.) *Teaching Academic Writing* (pp. 125–146). London: Continuum.

Morrison, J., Merrick, B., Higgs, S. and Le Métais, J. (2005) Researching the performance of international students in the UK. *Studies in Higher Education* 30 (3), 327–337.

Motta-Roth, D. (2009) The role of context in academic text production and writing pedagogy. In C. Bazerman, A. Bonini, and D. Figueiredo (eds) *Genre in a Changing World* (pp. 317–336). Fort Collins, CO: The WAC Clearinghouse and Parlor Press.

Mutch, A. (2003) Exploring the practice of feedback to students. *Active Learning in Higher Education* 4 (2), 24–38.

Nergis, A. (2013) Exploring the factors that affect reading comprehension of EAP learners. *Journal of English for Academic Purposes* 12 (1), 1–9.

Nesi, H. and Gardner, S. (2012) *Genres across Disciplines. Student Writing in Higher Education*. Cambridge: Cambridge University Press.

Newman, M. (2007) 'Appalling' writing skills drive tutors to seek help. *Times Higher Education* 16 March 2007.

Newell, G. (1984) Learning from writing in two content areas: A case study/protocol analysis. *Research in the Teaching of English* 18 (3), 265–287.

Nicol, D. (2010) From monologue to dialogue: improving written feedback processes in mass higher education. *Assessment and Evaluation in Higher Education* 35 (5), 501–517.

North, S. (2005) Different values, different skills? A comparison of essay writing by students from arts and science backgrounds. *Studies in Higher Education* 30 (5), 517–533.

Norton, B. (2000) *Identity and Language Learning: Gender, Ethnicity and Educational Change*. Harlow: Longman/Pearson Education.

Nystrand, M. (1986) *The Structure of Written Communication: Studies in Reciprocity between Writers and Readers*. Orlando, Florida: Academic Press.

Ochs, E. (1986) Introduction. In B. Schieffelin and E. Ochs (eds) *Language Socialization across Cultures* (pp. 1–13). New York: Cambridge University Press.

Ochs, E. and Schieffelin, B. (1994) Language acquisition and socialisation: Three developmental stories and their implications. In B.G. Blount (ed.) *Language, Culture and Society* (pp. 470–512). Illinois: Waveland Press.

Ochsner, R. and Fowler, J. (2004) Playing devil's advocate: Evaluating the literature of the WAC/WID movement. *Review of Educational Research* 74 (2), 117–140.

OECD (Organisation for Economic Co-operation and Development) (2013), *Education at a Glance 2013: OECD Indicators*, OECD Publishing. http://dx.doi.org/10.1787/eag-2013-en (accessed April 2014).

O'Maley, J. and Chamot, A. (1990) *Learning Strategies in Second Language Acquisition*. Cambridge: Cambridge University Press.

Oshima, A. and Hogue, A. (2006) *Writing Academic English 4th Edition*. Harlow: Pearson Education.

Owen, M. (2002) 'Sometimes you feel you're in niche time!' The personal tutor system, a case study. *Active Learning in Higher Education* 3 (1), 7–23.

Paré, A. (2014) Rhetorical genre theory and academic literacy. *Journal of Academic Language and Learning* 8 (1), A 83–A 94.

Paxton, M. (2007) Tensions between textbook pedagogies and the literacy practices of the disciplinary community: A study of writing in first year economics. *Journal of English for Academic Purposes* 6 (2), 91–188.

Paxton, M. (2011) How do we play the genre game in preparing students at the advanced undergraduate level for research writing? *Teaching in Higher Education* 16 (1), 53–64.

Paxton, M. (2014) Genre: a pigeonhole or a pigeon? Case studies of the dilemmas posed by the writing of academic research proposals. In L. Thesen and L. Cooper (eds) *Risk in Academic Writing: Postgraduate Students, their Teachers and the Making of Knowledge* (pp. 148–165). Bristol: Multilingual Matters.

Peck MacDonald, S. (1987) Problem definition in academic writing. *College English*, 49, 315–331.

Pennycook, A. (1997) Vulgar pragmatism, critical pragmatism, and EAP. *English for Specific Purposes* 15 (2), 85–103.

Percy, A. and Skillen, J. (2000) A systemic approach to working with academic staff: Addressing the confusion at the source. In K. Channock (ed.) *Sources of Confusion: Proceedings of the 2000 Language and Academic Skills Conference*. University of Wollongong.

Phan, L.H. (2009) Strategic, passionate, but academic: Am I allowed in my writing? *Journal of English for Academic Purposes* 8 (2), 134–146.

Phakiti, A. and Li, L. (2011) General academic difficulties and reading and writing difficulties among Asian ESL postgraduate students in TESOL at an Australian university. *RELC Journal* 42 (3), 227–264.

Plakans, L. (2009) The role of reading strategies in integrated L2 writing tasks. *Journal of English for Academic Purposes* 8 (4), 252–266.

Plakans, L. and Gebril, A. (2012) A close investigation into source use in integrated second language writing tasks. *Assessing Writing* 17 (1), 18–34.

Preece, S. and Martin, P. (2010) Imagining higher education as a multilingual space. *Language and Education* 24 (1), 3–8.

Pritchard, R.M. and Nasr, A. (2004) Improving reading performance among Egyptian engineering students: Principles and practice. *English for Specific Purposes* 23 (4), 425–445.

Purser, E. (2011) Developing academic literacy in context: Trends in Australia. In M. Deane and P. O'Neill (eds) *Writing in the Disciplines* (pp. 30–43). London: Palgrave Macmillan.

Purser, E., Skillen, J., Deane, M., Donohue, J. and Peake, K. (2008) Developing academic literacy in context. *Zeitschrift Schreiben*. See: www.zeitschrift-schreiben.eu/cgi-bin/joolma/index.php?option=com_wrapper&Itemid=26 (accessed 16 December 2014).

Quality Assurance Agency for Higher Education (QAA) Subject benchmark statements http://www.qaa.ac.uk/AssuringStandardsAndQuality/subject-guidance/Pages/Honours-degree-benchmark-statements.aspx (accessed May 2014).

Racelis, J.V. and Matsuda, P.K. (2013) Integrating process and genre into the second language writing classroom: research into practice. *Language Teaching* 46 (3), 382–393.

Ravelli, L.J. (2004) Signalling the organization of written texts: Hyper-themes in management and history essays. In L.J. Ravelli and R. Ellis (eds) *Analysing Academic Writing* (pp. 104–130). London: Continuum.

Rose, D. and Martin, J.R. (2012) *Learning to Write, Reading to Learn: Genre, Knowledge and Pedagogy in the Sydney School*. London: Equinox.

Rose, D., Lui-Chivizhe, L., McKnight, A., and Smith, A. (2003) Scaffolding academic reading and writing at the Koori Center. *The Australian Journal of Indigenous Education* 32 (1), 41–49.

Rose, D., Rose, M., Farrington, S. and Page, S. (2008) Scaffolding academic literacy with indigenous Health Sciences students: An evaluative study. *Journal of English for Academic Purposes* 7 (3), 165–179.

Römer, U. (2006) Pedagogical applications of corpora: Some reflections on the current scope and a wish list for future developments. *Zeitschrift Anglistik und Amerikanistik* 54 (2), 121–134.

Rothery, J. (1996) Making changes: Developing and educational linguistics. In R. Hasan and G. Williams (eds) *Literacy in Society* (pp. 86–123). London: Longman.

Russell, D., Lea, M., Parker, J., Street, B. and Donahue, T. (2009) Exploring notions of genre in 'academic literacies' and 'writing in the disciplines': Approaches across countries and contexts. In C. Bazerman, C. Bonini, and D. Figueiredo (eds) *Genre in a Changing World* (pp. 395–423). Fort Collins, Colorado: The WAC Clearinghouse.

Ryan, J. (2013) Transformative international education: Collaborative approaches to supporting international students. In J. Wrigglesworth (ed.) *Proceedings of the 2011 BALEAP Conference* (pp. 13–23). Reading: Garnet.

Ryan, J. and Viete, R. (2009) Respectful interactions: Learning with international students in the English-speaking academy. *Teaching in Higher Education* 14 (3), 303–314.

Sadler, D.R. (2010) Beyond feedback: Developing student capability in complex appraisal. *Assessment and Evaluation in Higher Education* 35 (5), 535–550.

Schraw, G. and Bruning, R. (1996) Readers' implicit models of reading. *Reading Research Quarterly* 31 (3), 290–305.

Schleppegrell, M. (2004) Technical writing in a second language: The role of grammatical metaphor. In L.J. Ravelli and R. Ellis (eds) *Analysing Academic Writing* (pp. 172–189). London: Continuum.

Scollon, R. (1991) Eight legs and one elbow: Stance and structure in Chinese English composition. Paper presented at International Reading Association, Second North American Conference on Adult and Adolescent Literacy, Banff.

Scott, M. and Tribble, C. (2006) *Textual Patterns: Keyword and Corpus Analysis in Language Education*. Amsterdam: John Benjamins.

Sengupta, S. (1999) Rhetorical consciousness raising in the L2 reading classroom. *Journal of Second Language Writing* 8 (3), 291–319.
Sengupta, S. (2002) Developing academic reading at tertiary level: A longitudinal study tracing conceptual change. *The Reading Matrix*, 2 (1), 1–37.
Shephard, J. (2006) Students today can't write, spell or count!' *Times Higher Education*. See: http://www.timeshighereducation.co.uk/news/students-today-cant-write-spell-or-count/201255.article (accessed 16 December 2014).
Simpson, J. and Cooke, M. (2010) Movement and loss: Progression in tertiary education for migrant students. *Language and Education* 24 (1), 57–73.
Sinclair, J.M. (1991) *Corpus, Concordance, Collocation*. Oxford: Oxford University Press.
Skillen, J. (2006) Teaching academic writing from the 'centre' in Australian universities. In L. Ganobcsik-Williams (ed.) (2006) *Teaching Academic Writing in UK Higher Education: Theories, Practice and Models* (pp. 140–153). London: Palgrave Macmillan.
Soudien, C. (2007) The 'A' factor: Coming to terms with the question of legacy in South African education. *International Journal of Educational Development* 27 (2), 182–193.
Spack, R. (1988) Initiating students into the academic discourse community: How far should we go? *TESOL Quarterly* 22, 29–51.
Spack, R. (1997) The acquisition of academic literacy in a second language: A longitudinal case study. *Written Communication* 14 (3), 3–62.
Spencer-Oatey, H. and Xiong, Z. (2006) Chinese students' psychological and sociocultural adjustments to Britain: An empirical study. *Language, Culture and Curriculum* 19 (1), 37–53.
Stroud, C., and Kerfoot, C. (2013) Towards rethinking multilingualism and language policy for academic literacies. *Linguistics and Education* 24 (4), 396–405.
Stubbs, M. (2009) The search for units of meaning: Sinclair on empirical semantics. *Applied Linguistics* 35 (2), 1–23.
Swales, J.M (1981) Aspects of article introduction. *Aston Research Reports, No. 1*. Birmingham: University of Aston.
Swales, J.M. (1985) *Episodes in ESP*. Oxford: Pergamon Press.
Swales, J. M. (1990) *Genre analysis: English in Academic and Research Settings*. Cambridge: Cambridge University Press.
Swales, J.M. (1998) *Other Floors, Other Voices: A Textography of a Small University Building*. Mahwah, NJ: Lawrence Erlbaum.
Swales, J.M. (2001) EAP-related linguistic research: An intellectual history. In J. Flowerdew and M. Peacock (eds) *Research Perspectives on English for Academic Purposes* (pp. 42–54). Cambridge: Cambridge University Press.
Swales, J.M. (2002) Integrated and fragmented worlds: EAP materials and corpus linguistics. In J. Flowerdew (ed.) *Academic Discourse* (pp. 150–164). Harlow: Pearson Education.
Swales, J.M. (2009) Afterword. In M. Charles, D. Pecorari and S. Hunston (eds) *Academic Writing. At the Interface of Corpus and Discourse* (pp. 291–294). London, New York: Continuum.
Swales, J.M. and Feak, C. (2012) *Academic Writing for Graduate Students 3rd Edition*. Michigan: University of Michigan Press.
Swales, J.M. and Lindemann, S. (2002) Teaching the literature review to international graduate students. In A.M. Johns (ed.) *Genre in the Classroom: Multiple Perspectives* (pp. 105–119). Mahwah, NJ: Lawrence Erlbaum.
Talmy, S. (2011) The interview as collaborative achievement: Interaction, identity, and ideology in a speech event. *Applied Linguistics* 32 (1), 25–42.

Tarone, E., Dwyer, S. Gillette, S. and Icke, V. (1981) On the use of the passive in two astrophysics journal papers. *English for Specific Purposes* 1 (2), 123–140.
Tardy, C.M. (2006) Researching first and second language genre learning: A comparative review and a look ahead. *Journal of Second Language Writing* 15 (2), 79–101.
TEQSA (Tertiary Education Quality Standards Agency) (2011) http://www.teqsa.gov.au/ (accessed September 2014).
Terraschke, A. and Wahid, R. (2011) The impact of EAP study on the academic experiences of international postgraduate students in Australia. *Journal of English for Academic Purposes* 10 (3), 173–182.
Thesen, L. (2014) Risk as productive: working with dilemmas in the writing of research. In L. Thesen and L. Cooper (eds) *Risk in Academic Writing: Postgraduate Students, their Teachers and the Making of Knowledge* (pp. 1–24). Bristol: Multilingual Matters.
Thesen, L. and Cooper, L. (eds) (2014) *Risk in Academic Writing: Postgraduate Students, their Teachers and the Making of Knowledge*. Bristol: Multilingual Matters.
Thesen, L. and van Pletzen, E. (2006) Introduction: The politics of place in academic literacy work. In L. Thesen and E. van Pletzen (eds) *Academic Literacy and the Languages of Change* (pp. 1–29). London, New York: Continuum.
Thies, L. (2012) Increasing student participation and success: Collaborating to embed academic literacies in the curriculum. *Journal of Academic Language and Learning* 6 (1), A-15–A-31.
Thomas, P. (2013) Transformation, dialogue and collaboration: Developing studio-based concept writing in Art and Design through embedded interventions. *Journal of Academic Writing* 3 (1), 42–66.
Thompson, D.K. (1993) Arguing for experimental 'facts' in science: A study of research article results sections in biochemistry. *Written Communication* 10 (1), 106–128.
Thompson, C., Morton, J. and Storch, N. (2013) Where from, who, why and how? A study of the use of sources by first year L2 university students. *Journal of English for Academic Purposes* 12 (2), 99– 109.
Thompson, P. and Tribble, C. (2001) Looking at citations: Using corpora in English for academic purposes. *Language Learning and Technology* 5 (2), 91–105.
Threadgold, T., Absalom, D. and Golebiowski, Z. (1997) Tertiary literacy conference summary: What will count as tertiary literacy in the year 2000? *Policy and Practice of Tertiary Literacy*, Vol. 1. Proceedings of the First National Conference on Tertiary Literacy 1996. Melbourne: Victoria University of Technology.
Tierney, R.J., Soter, A., O'Flahavan, J. and McGinley W. (1989) The effects of reading and writing upon thinking critically. *Reading Research Quarterly* 24 (2), 134–169.
Tran, L.T. (2009) Making visible 'hidden' intentions and potential choices: International students in international communication. *Language and Intercultural Communication* 9 (4), 271–284.
Tribble, C. (1996) *Writing*. Oxford: Oxford University Press.
Tribble, C. (2002) Corpora and corpus analysis: New windows on academic writing. In J. Flowerdew (ed.) *Academic Discourse* (pp. 131–149). Harlow: Pearson Education.
Tribble, C. (2009) Writing academic English: A review of current published resources. *English Language Teaching Journal* 63 (4), 400–417.
Tribble, C. (2011) Revisiting apprentice texts: Using lexical bundles to investigate expert and apprentice performances in academic writing. In F. Meunier, S. De Cock, G. Gilquin and M. Paquot (eds) *A Taste for Corpora. In Honour of Sylviane Granger* (pp. 85–108). Amsterdam: John Benjamins.

Tribble, C. and Wingate, U. (2013) From text to corpus: A genre-based approach to academic literacy instruction. *System* 41 (2), 307–321.
Turner, J. (2004) Language as academic purpose. *Journal of English for Academic Purposes* 3 (2), 95–109.
Turner, J. (2011) *Language in the Academy. Cultural Reflexivity and Intercultural Dynamics*. Bristol, Buffalo, Toronto: Multilingual Matters.
UK Council for International Students Affairs (UKCISA) (2014) http://www.ukcisa.org.uk (accessed 15 June 2014).
UK Universities (2013) http://www.universitiesuk.ac.uk/aboutus/members/Pages/default.aspx (accessed December 2013).
University of Cambridge (2014) Transkills Project, http://skills.caret.cam.ac.uk/transkills/ (accessed February 2014).
University of Cape Town (UCT) (2013) Language Development Group, http://www.ldg.uct.ac.za/collaboration/ (accessed 30 October 2013).
University of Bedfordshire (2014) Study support website, http://www.beds.ac.uk/studentlife/student-support/academic/studysupport (accessed April 2014).
University of Durham (2014) English Language Centre, https://www.dur.ac.uk/englishlanguage.centre/englishlanguage.courses/currentstudents/in-sessional/academicwritingunit/ (accessed April 2014).
von Glaserfeld, E. (1987) Learning as constructive activity. In C. Janvier (ed.) *Problems of Representation in the Teaching and Learning of Mathematics* (pp. 3–17). Hillslade, NJ: Lawrence Erlbaum.
van Pletzen, E. (2006) A body of reading: making 'visible' the reading experiences of first-year medical students. In L. Thesen, and E. van Pletzen (eds) *Academic Literacy and the Languages of Change* (pp. 104–129). London, New York: Continuum.
Vygotsky, L. (1978) *Mind in Society: The Development of Higher Psychological Processes*. London: Harvard University Press.
Walker, M. (2009) An investigation into written comments on assignments: Do students find them usable? *Assessment and Evaluation in Higher Education* 34 (1), 67–78.
Weaver, M. (2006) Do students value feedback? Student perceptions of tutors' written responses. *Assessment & Evaluation in Higher Education* 31 (3), 379–394.
Wette, R. (2010) Evaluating student learning in a university-level EAP unit on writing using sources. *Journal of Second Language Writing* 19 (3), 158–177.
Widdowson, H.G. (2000) On the limitations of linguistics applied. *Applied Linguistics* 21 (1), 3–25.
Wineburg, S.S. (1991) On the reading of historical texts: Notes on the breach between school and academy. *American Educational Research Journal* 28 (3), 495–519.
Wingate, U. (2010) The impact of formative feedback on the development of academic writing. *Assessment and Evaluation in Higher Education* 35 (5), 519–533.
Wingate, U. (2011) A comparison of 'additional' and 'embedded' approaches to teaching writing in the disciplines. In M. Deane and P. O'Neill (eds) *Writing in the Disciplines* (pp. 65–87). London: Palgrave Macmillan.
Wingate, U. (2012a) Using Academic literacies and genre-based models for academic writing instruction: A 'literacy' journey. *Journal of English for Academic Purposes* 11 (1), 26–37.
Wingate, U. (2012b) 'Argument!' Helping students understand what essay writing is about. *Journal of English for Academic Purposes* 11 (2), 145–154.
Wingate, U., Andon, N. and Cogo, A. (2011) Embedding academic writing instruction into subject teaching: A case study. *Active Learning in Higher Education* 12 (1), 1–13.

Wingate, U. and Tribble, C. (2012) The best of both worlds? Towards an English for Academic Purposes/Academic Literacies writing pedagogy. *Studies in Higher Education* 37 (4), 481–495.

Wray, D. and Lewis, M. (1997) *Extending Literacy: Children Reading and Writing Non-fiction*. London: Routledge.

Wu, S.Y. and Rubin, D. (2000) Evaluating the impact of collectivism and individualism on argumentative writing by Chinese and North American college students. *Research in the Teaching of English* 35 (2), 148–178.

Yakovchuk, N. and Ingle, J. (2013) Working with departments to develop students' writing: Two examples of collaborations on medical degrees at Queen Mary, University of London. In J. Wrigglesworth (ed.) *Proceedings of the 2011 BALEAP Conference* (pp. 65–83). Reading: Garnet.

Young, A. and Fulwiler, T. (1986) *Writing across the Disciplines: Research into Practice*. Upper Montclair, NJ: Boynton/Cook.

Index

Note: n refers to the notes and page numbers in italics refer to locations within a table or figure.

1994 Group universities *46*, 164

academic discourse communities 8, 14n2, 102–103, 125, 128–129. *See also* discipline-specific approaches
Academic Literacies model
  contributions to English for Academic Purposes 35
  criticisms of English for Academic Purposes 12, 49
  criticisms of genre approaches 21, 32–34
  features of 50
  as part of inclusive model *128*, 131, 140
  research on 22
academic literacy
  definition 6, 15
  implementation of inclusive model 150–163
  inclusive models 126–149
  pedagogy 3
  theoretical underpinnings 6–9, 12–13
  trivialisation of 40–41, 58–59
  types of development *60*
  university support for 9–11
Australia. *See also* Sydney School
  Academic Language and Learning (ALL) 63–65
  English for Academic Purposes in 38
  higher education participation rates 3
  integration of literacy instruction in 56–57, 59, 63–65, 130, 155
  international students in 5, 113
  primary schools 28, 31
  quality of student writing in 1
  reading-to-write instruction in 97–101
  student surveys in 45
  Writing Project 28
Australian Association for Academic Language and Learning 64
Australian Systemic Functional Linguistics (SFL). *See* Sydney School 70–72, 149n2
  contributions to English for Academic Purposes 35
  themes 137–138

Bank of English 73
Brazil 71
Brunei 68

Cambridge University *46*, 48
Canada 4, 26, 105
CARS (Creating a Research Space) model 30
China 4–5, 38. *See also* Confucian Heritage Cultures (CHC); Hong Kong; international students
Chomsky Noam 17
Cobuild English Dictionary and Grammar 73
cognitive process model 19
Collins Birmingham University International Database. *See* Bank of English
communicative competence 6–11, 17, 103, 154, 161–162
community-of-practice (CoP) model 6–7, 9, 102–103, 110–113
Composition Studies 12, 40
concordances 76

Confucian Heritage Cultures (CHC)
  106–109, 111–112. *See also* culture;
  international students
corpus linguistics 72–77
Coventry University 78
creative writing 19
creativity approach. *See* process
  approaches
Critical Discourse Analysis (CDA) 22–23
Critical EAP. *See also* English for
  Academic Purposes
  criticisms of English for Academic
    Purposes 15, 49, 50–51
  criticisms of genre approaches 32–34
  as part of inclusive model *128*, 131, 140
  and socio-political approach 23
critical thinking 19, 106–109, 122, 159–161
culture. *See also* social and cultural capital
  and critical thinking 106–109, 156–161.
    See also Confucian Heritage Cultures
    (CHC); international students;
    sociocultural theory
  intercultural competence 5, 9–11, 19
  and literacy conventions 9–11, 31–32,
    51–55, 81–83, 106–109, 111–113
  and socio-political approach 22–23
  and Sydney School 28

data-driven learning (DDL) 73–76
discipline-specific approaches 56–69,
  56–77
  Applied Linguistics 35, 59, 61, 103, 114,
    134, 139, 141, 169
  Business/Management 4, 30, 61, 68,
    104, *135*, *139*, 141–142, 168
  collaboration 56–59, 64, 127, 152
  Education 113
  epistemology 2, 6–7
  Health Science 97, 112
  History 138, 141–142
  Humanities 87
  integration 56, 129–130
  Law 4, 30, 104
  Life Sciences 87
  Medicine 83
  Pharmacy 136, 138–139, 141–142, 170
  Physical Sciences 87
  Social Science 4, 87
  Writing in the Disciplines 12

discourse analysis 74–75, 136–137
diversity
  ethnic 52–54
  increases in 2–5
  linguistic 5, 52–54
  socio-economic 3–4, 12, 19, 31, 49
Durham University *46*, 48

English as an Academic Lingua Franca 49,
  51–52
English for Academic Purposes. *See also*
  Critical EAP
  and corpus linguistics 75–77
  versus English for Specific Purposes 25,
    31–33
  as generic instruction 38–40, 43–45
  and integration *60*
  needs analysis in 51
  and skills approaches 21
  'transformational' critiques of 49–55
English for General Academic Purposes
  (EGAP) 40
English for Occupational Purposes
  (EOP) 38
English for Specific Academic Purposes
  (ESAP) 40
English for Specific Purposes 24–25,
  29–34, 70, *128*, 131

Further and Higher Education Act 1992
  (UK) 55n1

genre approaches. *See also* Australian
  Systemic Functional Linguistics
  (SFL); English for Specific Purposes;
  Rhetorical Genre Studies (RGS);
  Sydney School
  criticisms of 79, 99–101
  features of 6, 20–34
  linguistic 25
  move analysis 133–136, *134*, *135*,
    166–167
  as part of inclusive model *128*, 131
  pedagogy 67–77
  qualitative analysis 132–133
  and reading-to-write instruction
    85–87, 99–100
  sociological 25
  studies of 68

Hallidayan linguistic theory 24, 28–29
Harvard University 26
Higher Education Funding Council for England (HEFCE) 3–4
Higher Education Standards Framework (Australia) 63–64
'home' students
   availability of academic literacy instruction 38
   English language proficiency of 33, 38, 42–43, 115–118
   studies of 114–124
Hong Kong 85, 104
Hyland model. *See* genre approaches

IELTS (International English Language Testing System) 10, 17, 39
International Association of Applied Linguistics 35
international students
   availability of academic literacy instruction 38, 41–43, 48, 151
   from Brazil 4
   from China 4–5, 53, 103–104, 106–109, 111–112
   and English as an Academic Lingua Franca 51–52
   English language proficiency of 5, 10, 18, 38–39, 41–43, 64–65
   increases in number 3–5
   from India 103
   literature on 103–104
   from Malawi 112
   from Malaysia 103
   from Nigeria 52
   from sub-Saharan Africa 4, 108–109
   from Vietnam 107, 111–112
   from Zambia 112–113
Ireland 4, 116
Ivanič model. *See* process approaches

Journal of English for Academic Purposes 12, 35, 84
Journal of Second Language Writing 12

Kachruvian circles 4, 14n1

Lancaster University *46*, 48
language socialisation theory 6–8, 9, 102–103, 110–113
Lea and Street model. *See* skills approaches
lexical bundles 76
lexico-grammatical analysis 138–140

Martin, Jim 28–29, 30
Measuring the Academic Skills of University Students (MASUS) 98
Middlesex University 67
Million+ Group universities *46*, 164
mismatches 104–106
monolingualism 51–55
Multilingualism 52–54
Multilingualism model 49

New Rhetoric 25, 35. *See also* Rhetorical Genre Studies (RGS)
New Zealand 4, 38, 95
non-traditional students 11, 49, 65–66, 101, 104, 151, 162

Office for Fair Access (OFFA) 3–4
Organisation for Economic Co-operation and Development (OECD) 4–5
Oxford University 47

plagiarism 9, 105, 114
prescriptivism 71–72, 140
process approaches 16–20, *16*, 99–100

racism 5, 107, 111–112
reading skills
   academic journals on 83–84
   and academic literacy pedagogy 78–101
   epistemologies 81–83
   evaluation 89
   gisting 85
   interventions 95–101
   mining 89–90
   needs analysis 78
   note-taking *92*
   operations 88–89
   paraphrasing *92*, 95–96
   process of reading 80–81
   reader engagement 75–76

reading-to-write 13, 78–101
  and second-language acquisition 81
  strategies 80–81, 89–92, *92*
  types of reading 93–95
Rhetorical Genre Studies (RGS) 22, 24–27, 68, 71, *128*, 131, 140
Royal Literary Fund 47
Russell Group universities *46*, 114, 125n1, 165

scaffolding 31, 71–72, 97–101, 140, 143–144, 157
second-language acquisition 40, 80–81, 85, 88–91, 95–96
SFL. *See* Sydney School
Sinclair, John 73
Singapore 38
situated learning theory 6
skills approaches 16, 17–18, 96. *See also* writing skills
social and cultural capital 14n1, 19, 82
social constructivist theory 142
social practices approaches 21–22, 23
sociocultural theory 7, 21–22, 102–103
socio-political approaches 22–23
South Africa
  1998 Higher Education Act 65
  criticisms of literacy instruction in 12
  integration of literacy instruction in 56–57, 59, 65–67
  international students in 3–4, 4, 53–54, 108–109, 112–113
  linguistic diversity in 53–54, 65–67
  National Student Financial Aid 65
  secondary schools in 82–83
Swales 29–30, 69, 71, 100
Sydney School 24–25, 27–34, 65, 70–72, 98, 101, *128*, 131, 143

Teesside University 47
textbooks 69–70
textual modelling 68–70
TOEFL (Test of English as a Foreign Language) 10, 18, 39
Tribble, Chris 149n1

UK Council for International Student Affairs 4
United Kingdom
  Academic Literacies model in 12
  analysis of university websites 37–49
  criticisms of literacy instruction in 12
  English for Specific Purposes in 32
  higher education participation rates 3–4
  integration of literacy instruction in 67
  international students in 52–53, 151
  non-traditional students in 11
  process approaches in 19
  quality of student writing in 1
  student surveys in 45
  writing instructors in 41, 56–57
United States
  criticisms of literacy instruction in 12
  diversity of students in 3–4
  English for Specific Purposes in 32
  first-year composition in 12, 17, 18, 20, 26, 37–38, 41, 78
  process approaches in 19
  Rhetorical Genre Studies (RGS) in 26
University of Bedfordshire 43, *44*
University of Birmingham 42
University of Cape Town 66, 83–84, 154
University of Creative Arts Canterbury 47, 48
University of Kent 47
University of Leeds 47
University of Northampton 47
University of Southampton 47
University of Staffordshire 47
University of Sydney 97–100
University of the Western Cape 53–54, 65–67
University of Wollongong 63–64

Writing Across the Curriculum (WAC) 27, 44, 57
Writing in the Disciplines (WID) 12, 27, 44, 57
writing instruction
  assessment and feedback 158–159
  availability to non-native speakers 2, 5, 41–43, 129
  cost of 39–41
  differences between models 3
  dominant approach 37–49
  e-learning 156–157
  embedding into study programmes 11–12

writing instruction *(Continued)*
   extracurricular 1, 150
   lectures 155–156
   needs analysis 141
   personal tutoring 157
   in primary schools 28, 31
   writing centres 38, 42–43,
     66–67
writing instructors
   in disciplines vs. writing 9–10, 37,
     57–59
   as facilitators 19
   limitations of 130
   vs. literacy experts 153–155
   and reading skills 79
   responsibilities of 43–45
   and sociocultural issues 7, 106–109,
     110–113
   training 45
writing skills. *See also* skills approaches
   argumentation 2, *60*, 83, 104, 106–109,
     115–129 *passim*, 149, 159–161, 163n4
   as assessment tool 15
   grammar 1, 17–18, 19, 128
   note-taking 88–89
   revision 20
   rhetoric 17
   in secondary schools 31
   sources and referencing 2, 15, 114,
     120–121, 160, 170–171
   spelling 1, 17–18
   time management 119–120